STRATEGIC PLANNING IN EDUCATION

STRATEGIC PLANNING IN EDUCATION

Rethinking, Restructuring, Revitalizing

ROGER KAUFMAN

Professor and Director
Center for Needs Assessment and Planning
Florida State University

JERRY HERMAN

Professor and Area Head Administration, and Leadership
School of Education
University of Alabama

TECHNOMIC
PUBLISHING CO., INC.
LANCASTER · BASEL

Strategic Planning in Education
a **TECHNOMIC**®publication

Published in the Western Hemisphere by
Technomic Publishing Company, Inc.
851 New Holland Avenue
Box 3535
Lancaster, Pennsylvania 17604 U.S.A.

Distributed in the Rest of the World by
Technomic Publishing AG

Printed in the United States of America
10 9 8 7 6 5 4 3 2

Main entry under title:
   Strategic Planning in Education: Rethinking, Restructuring, Revitalizing

A Technomic Publishing Company book
Bibliography: p. 317
Includes index p. 323

Library of Congress Card No. 90-71737
ISBN No. 87762-770-3

To Jan and Janice
Our wives and two of the world's foremost strategists.

Contents

Preface

"Strategic planning" is in danger of becoming just an educational fad. It is much too valuable an advance to suffer such a fate. Some educators have borrowed a page from the industrialists' book and embraced it—often without a clear idea of what it is, what it should deliver, and how it differs from other types of planning. Done correctly, strategic planning considers and selects possible new futures for education and identifies the "whats", "whys", and "hows" for getting there.

While it is vital for our children's futures as well as our own that sensible, valid, and useful strategic planning be accomplished, there is a lot of confusion among educators and planners. People often call just about anything "strategic planning". As a consequence, models and approaches used are likewise muddled. Some approaches think it is intuitive planning, while others want to focus on splinters such as individual programs and projects. While most approaches have something to offer, almost all of them are incomplete.

After working together for a number of years on many educational applications, the two of us decided to combine our different experiences into an integrated approach for educational strategic planning. Strategic planning, if done correctly, isn't very different for varying contexts: people are people, and organizations are organizations. The key differences in strategic planning lie in the mission objective: where the organization is heading, and who are its basic clients and beneficiaries. Our approach encourages (even implores) that the primary client and beneficiary of any educational enterprise be seen as the society and community to which our outputs go. This approach intends to improve learner accomplishments and contributions both in school and in later life.

This humanistic approach cares enough about people and education to be results-oriented. It empowers the educational partners—learners, educators, citizens—to define a vision and develop a strategic plan to achieve educational success with long-range payoffs.

We could not have done this book without help. Our thanks go to many of our students and clients who helped shape and educate us. LaVerne

Johnson toiled through numerous revisions of this on the word processor and Melissa Van Dyke and Dennis Bowers worked on the graphics.

Special thanks are due to several professionals who reviewed developing versions of this work and helped to make it better than it would have been otherwise: Agustin Campos, Department Head of Education at Universidad Feminina-UNIFE in Lima, Peru; Kevin Hardy, management consultant from Canberra, Australia; Alicia Rojas of San Jose State University, Phil Grisé of the Center for Needs Assessment and Planning (CNAP) and abundant gratitude to Kathi Watters also at CNAP at Florida State University who made major editorial and communications contributions.

And finally to the educators around the world, our appreciation for forming a partnership to plan and think strategically for our mutual benefit. Our intention is to help you help your partners to define and achieve a very successful world. On purpose.

ROGER KAUFMAN   JERRY HERMAN
Tallahassee, FL   Tuscaloosa, AL

January, 1991

Introduction

What This Book Does

This is a book—primarily a guide—for educational executives, board members, and planners who want to help create a better future for their students, communities, teachers, and themselves. It provides a proven, practical, and understandable framework for strategic planning, along with the steps and stages to do it. This book fills in the details of both *what* has to be done (and why), and demonstrates *how* to get each step of strategic planning accomplished. It applies to strategic planning in education from nursery school through college.

Strategic planning—defining and creating a better future—is unusually timely now. Most people involved in education—teachers, administrators, board members, learners, parents, employers, and community constituents—realize that education must be changed radically [28,100]. Our society, students, communities, and values, have changed spectacularly in recent years, but our educational systems are still the ones which were designed for students and communities of decades ago. The Nelson Family and the well-scrubbed characters of *Father Knows Best* not only aren't anything like what we now see, they probably never did exist.

Simply tinkering with the system will not suffice. Dramatic changes are in order, including *rethinking* what education should deliver, *restructuring* the educational enterprise to deliver the required results, and *revitalizing* the students and the system to make an extraordinary change in and for society.

Because of this, three basic planning themes run through the book: (1) RETHINKING, (2) RESTRUCTURING, and (3) REVITALIZING of educational agencies. As you read, these three themes should serve as templates for you to use, and the book itself will be divided into these three sections.

Rethinking (Chapters 1-7)

Educational realities and purposes have changed and enlarged dramatically. This will continue. Challenges are part of our lives—we have seen them in the past as we reacted to Sputnik, and in the current world as we encounter increasing overseas domination of our markets. No longer do we encounter exclusively middle-class learners with a homogeneous cultural background, but students with a rich array of cultures, values, problems, languages, and expectations.

Peter Drucker reminds us that doing the right things are more important than doing things right. This book provides frameworks and methods for rethinking education from goals and missions to curriculum and delivery. But rethinking alone is not enough—we must be responsive to societal realities, able to identify opportunities, and willing to develop a better tomorrow with our educational and societal partners.

Restructuring (Chapters 8–11)

As noted in the Prologue, simply doing more efficiently what we are already doing will not help us adjust to our new realities. Adding a course or two here, a new staffing pattern there, or inviting parents to the schools, are usually quick-fix patches on a very thin fabric. In addition to modifying and improving what we do and how we do it, we also must question current objectives and be ready to change them in order to deliver on our promises to society.

This book provides the methods and techniques for restructuring education—from planning based upon societal requirements and payoffs, through enriching content, to providing the best methods for delivering learning opportunities. It will not go into the many reasons for restructuring, since those are aptly dealt with in many other places. The role of this book is not to find fault, but rather to provide guidance and tools on how to set things right—at every educational level. We can make contributions to both educational effectiveness and societal improvement at the core. Planning is more than patchwork efforts or superficial reactions to crises. It is accomplished by the partners who can and will be affected by what is used, done, and delivered—they become stewards of the quality of our results.

Revitalizing (Chapter 12)

Not everything in education is wrong or useless. In fact, much which is currently done should be continued by design, not by default. By energizing valid, thoughtful, and responsible rethinking and restructuring of education, we will bring new vitality and responsiveness to our curriculum, learners, and citizens. Unlike a dose of vitamins here, or a workout there, this approach integrates the useful old with the robust new to provide educational methods and payoffs which will guide us successfully into future generations. Successful planning has to be positive, built with the insights and contributions of all educational partners, and must result in solid, understandable, and valid changes. These are not one-shot quick-fixes, but systemic improvements and additions to our educational system. The alternative to revitalization will be a continual disaffected community who will look elsewhere for their educational services.

This book emphasizes *practical advice* on strategic planning. It is written by a planner-professor (with executive experience in both the public and private sectors and consulted worldwide on needs assessment and strategic planning) and a superintendent-professor-consultant (who has led school districts; taught others how to be successful executives; and also has consulted with educators, school boards, and the private sector on strategic planning and management).

From the outset, a process for educational strategic planning is provided. That framework is utilized with subsequent parts highlighted as each building block is provided and detailed on the way toward constructing a holistic approach. Numerous examples are provided from actual educational settings, along with supporting guidelines, definitions of terms, and exercises.

What Strategic Planning Is and Contributes

Strategic planning is a dynamic, active process. It scans current realities and opportunities in order to yield useful strategies and tactics for arriving at a better tomorrow. It is not a linear, lock-step process derived or implemented in an authoritarian manner. Nor is it intuitive or built on hunches and raw feelings. It involves the educational partners in defining and supporting the purposes and missions, and it provides blueprints for results-oriented progress.

We develop a specific strategic planning model and approach which has four major areas: SCOPING, DATA COLLECTING, PLANNING, and IMPLEMENTATION AND EVALUATION. To provide such a focus, we begin each chapter with these four elements presented in boxes while highlighting the one which is featured. SCOPING includes Chapters 1–3. DATA COLLECT-

ING encompasses Chapters 4–7. PLANNING includes Chapters 8–11, and IMPLEMENTATION AND EVALUATION is covered in Chapter 12.

When we view strategic planning in full, we note that *Rethinking* involves the tools and results from SCOPING and DATA COLLECTING. *Restructuring* includes completion of PLANNING and the resulting blueprint for action. *Revitalizing* puts all of the scoping, data collecting, and planning to work, actually bringing about useful educational results (IMPLEMENTATION). The Chapters are thus organized like this:

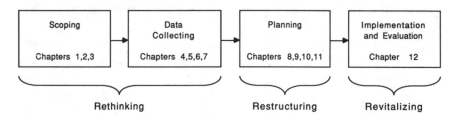

Strategic thinking—a fortunate by-product—is often more important than any plan. It is a way of viewing our educational world and constantly acting to deliberately improve the future. Strategic thinking is a dynamic, changing, and changeable way of planning and doing.

Once you have embarked on strategic planning, you should realize that:

- Current visions and objectives might change.
- The control (and blame) of education moves from a few central administrators and board members to be shared by the educational partners: educators, citizens, and learners who are the clients and beneficiaries of the system.
- Strategic planning leads to strategic thinking and becomes a way of life—dynamic, changing, and changeable. Strategic thinking is more important than any plan itself.
- It intends to deliberately create a better future, not simply attempt to react to situational crises and problems.
- Strategic planning best takes place in an atmosphere of mutual trust and common destinations.
- It pays, not costs.

The Prologue (page xxi) attempts to capture the sense of the importance of strategic thinking in education.

What It Costs to Plan or Not Plan Strategically

Education is one generation's investment in the next. It is an expensive enterprise and, thus, should become an investment, not simply a cost. Many states support education as its highest budget area, and most cities allocate funds with somewhat of a sigh and a stubborn hope that productive citizens will come out on the other end of our schooling pipeline. We try harder all the time, but often are frustrated with the seeming intractability of it all. Various groups offer solutions, but none seem to stem the tide of growing ignorance and disappointing results. We have implemented "excellence" programs and lengthened school days and years, added "tough" subjects and deleted others, increased credential requirements, and made teachers take tests; still these *solutions* (however well intended) don't seem, to make enough of our students more prepared for life and work. We can implement more quick-fix solutions, throw increasing dollars and people at the problem, or we can plan and think strategically—moving from reactive to proactive planning.

We can either be the proactive masters of change or the reactive victims. Strategic planning is the forward-looking option. It intends to create a better future. It encourages educational partners to join together to define and achieve better results and contributions. The results of our current educational planning and doing efforts are often seriously wanting; simply attempting to increase the efficiency of our current efforts seems to involve choosing to work harder without working smarter. Drifting into the future without setting a proper course is reactive and hopeful—it means relying on luck to turn things around. Just as Naisbitt reminded us in the early 80's that things were rapidly changing [83] he now assumes that they will continue to transform dramatically in the future [84]. Simply wandering into tomorrow without (1) knowing the prevailing forces and trends, and (2) an active attempt at creating the reality we want, is to miss the opportunities of creating a better life. Strategic planning, as described here, can help us to move systematically toward defining and creating a better world.

Caring Enough to Be Precise

We will use some words and concepts in very specific ways. The most important thing for success in education is having the correct destination;

selecting the right target requires us to be very precise in identifying *where* to go, *why* to go there, and *how to know when we've arrived.*

The process of strategic planning and the specifications we derive should not be loose or lax. We should care enough about our educational partners—learners, educators, and citizens—to make certain we are headed in the right direction for the shared benefit of all. As we develop concepts and tools, please keep in mind that we are "nailing down" definitions, terms, and procedures, and that some of these will be somewhat different from the conventional wisdom which has landed us where we are now.

Prologue

Restructuring: A Case Which Could Have Happened
—Roger Kaufman

It was 1861, and the world was vibrant, alive, throbbing. On a warm clear June 4th day in St. Joseph, Missouri, the Board of Directors of the *Pony Express* called a strategic planning meeting. Although operating as the envy of the modern world for fourteen months, there were rumors of possible problems. Even potential competition!

The world was changing. People were moving Westward. Inventions were jumping up like popcorn from a hot griddle. Dreamers were painting seductive visions of trains, messages sent through wires, pictures which would move. Even one "fool" was talking of people flying like birds.

The directors met. They included a consultant from a prestigious university. The Chairman of the Board began with praise for their shared accomplishments. He reeled them off with a proud demeanor: mail from St. Joseph to San Francisco in ten days; jobs for people; linking cities formerly isolated; new speed records almost weekly; safety improving; laudatory newspaper articles; visitors from around the world. He noted that never before had such a miracle been wrought. But then his mood changed.

"Technology", he bellowed.

"We have to look at technology. There is talk, perhaps more than chatter, that cities will be linked by some contraption that a Sam Morse has been playing with called the 'telegraph'.

"Our task, before any of us leaves, is to recognize if there are threats to our operation, and if so, what do we do to overcome them. Strategy!"

He looked over to the professor, who slowly uncoiled from his slouch and explained to the group about "SWOTs": Strengths, Weaknesses, Opportunities, and Threats. But first, the academic noted, "We have to have a vision, and a broad declaration of our purposes and direction. We must have a mission statement."

They broke into small groups and brainstormed some ideas. Then they interacted as a creative group, and came up with a mission statement: "Excellence in Delivering the Mail". Satisfied with their work, they quit for a brief lunch.

After eating, they examined their SWOTs. *Strengths* were easy: letters between St. Joseph and the Coast in ten days, reliability, positive image, increasing customers. *Weaknesses?* Well, being composed of a pair of operating companies, there was some loss of efficiency in trying to serve two masters. Also, some of the express riders were not of the best background and breeding. *Opportunities* included the possibility of turning the Pony Express into a public utility and doing some research and development of their own (the professor suggested a research grant to try to breed a six-legged horse which could run faster than the conventional variety). One person suggested that they might get into a new business, or convert the current horse stops into a franchised chain of boarding houses. *Threats* were tough for them. After much soul-searching, they admitted that new competitors with wires and poles could possibly deliver messages in less time (if, of course, it wasn't just a flash-in-the-pan). Cautiously, one board member (futilely) remarked that the world was changing very, very rapidly and that perhaps they might want to consider going out of business while they still had a profit.

Now they turned to developing a strategic plan based on the SWOTs. The creativity blazed. Ideas flowed. "Faster horses." "More rest stops to increase energy and cut down on fatigue." "Stronger horses." "More riders." "Reduce the loads." "Increase schedules." "Streamline the harnesses and saddles." "Expand service to New York." "Get rid of the Unions." "Hire only riders with master's degrees." "More horse-tenders and aids to the riders." "Better whips." "Higher wages." "Increase productivity through longer hours." "Get a law passed that restricts any communication services to being provided by the Pony Express." "Everyone will attend a *quality* seminar." "Increase options: let clients select their rider, the routes, time of pickup and delivery. . . ." "Give penalty bonuses to customers for late delivery." "Get government subsidies."

They had all the ideas generated now, and based on their mission statement ("Excellence in Delivering the Mail") they picked the tactics. The Pony Express was to be RESTRUCTURED. This was to be serious business, to save themselves and make a better future for their company.

The "restructuring committee" set about its task with dispatch, for the positive energy generated had to be captured. Time was weighing heavily on their future. The restructuring plan was generated within two days. It included: (1) immediate adding of services to New York and Boston; (2) more riders and support staff; (3) mandatory attendance at a highly recognized quality seminar; (4) improved whips; (5) more frequent departures; (6) more options to clients; (7) incentive bonuses to workers for higher productivity; and (8) an improved image with the expanded services using the new slogan "Unlimited Pony Service (UPS)". An almost unanimous vote was given (one person dissented, saying that the restructuring plan failed to account for the changed realities of the world . . . that the idea of horses delivering the mail was as dead as, well as dead as high-buttoned shoes and celluloid collars).

On June 15th the restructuring plan was put into operation with vigor, energy, and hope. In October the Pony Express was closed due to the competition from the Pacific Telegraph Company, which had strung wires where horses once sweated and ran. While restructuring had been well-intentioned, it assumed that all that had to be done was to make the operation work better and harder. The board members had not considered new realities and opportunities, nor generated fresh goals, objectives, and missions.

More than 130 years later, school children in traditional settings, reading conventional books, interacting with one teacher for 30+ students, attending classes for only two-thirds of the year, still read of the romance of the Pony Express. A very few of them wonder if there are some lessons to be learned in that saga for them. Today.

MORALS

(1) You better look at the world that is becoming, not the one you wish to observe.

(2) Missions should be related to reality and results, not just to philosophy and ringing rhetoric.

(3) Working smarter is much better than working harder—the hide you save might be your own.

(4) Restructuring, or change, should be based upon the realities of the future, not just the facts of the past (most generals fight the last war, not the one at hand).

(5) No amount of good intentions can substitute for useful consequences.

(6) Create the future you want, not the one that already is.

(7) Don't ride a failing horse until it drops dead under you.

PART 1

Rethinking

Types of Strategic Educational Planning

Education at All Levels Has Many Common Factors

While it is usual to differentiate among levels of education—such as pre-school, elementary, middle (or junior high), high, and post-secondary—all have some things in common:

- societal stakeholders
- purpose
- learners
- faculty
- physical and financial resources
- administration and management

This book presents a strategic educational planning model and process which relates these common factors. They are all vital. Of course, the curriculum, content of courses, responsive methods for presenting material, and the level of instruction will vary significantly.

We emphasize a strategic planning process which zeros in on educational purpose, results, consequences, and payoffs: what should education deliver? to whom? and why? From this base you may sensibly decide what should be taught, managed, and evaluated, while knowing exactly why you should do it. Considerations of educational curriculum, materials, methods, and approaches—so much a part of the educational literature—become appropriate and useful only after sensibly selecting educational goals and directions. Strategic planning will identify, derive, and select shared visions and purposes so that curriculum and instructional planning may be rooted in common payoffs.

Deciding on Purpose Before Selecting Method

A PUBLIC TRUST

At each and every level, education has purpose. It is not a learning experience for its own sake. Educators and agencies are chartered by the pub-

3

lic to see that students will have the skills, knowledges, abilities, and values to be contributing citizens—not a casual undertaking.

Responsive and responsible education places the individual and his or her future into a perspective which includes knowledge, understanding, mutual respect, positive self-esteem, competence, caring, confidence, work, and community.[1] The planning of education and its curriculum centers importantly on the contextual realities which learners experience external to the classroom. While most of our action-oriented energies and resources will be invested in what goes on in classrooms, playgrounds, gyms, and at extracurricular events, the content and focus of these should be toward the development of future citizens.

Educational planning intends to create a better future for individuals, groups, organizations, and society. Planning identifies where to go, why to go there, and provides the basic criteria for determining if and when you have arrived. Poor planning will take you to unwanted and unintended destinations, possibly ones even worse than those currently being reached. Planning should ask and answer important questions about purpose. This chapter and the next one pose some of the more important questions, and then link those with possible responsive educational planning perspectives. As we will continuously see, responsive, responsible, and useful education is results-based and results-oriented. What education delivers is more important than how it does its job. First we must define the results to be delivered, and then select the best ways to get them accomplished.

Frames of Reference for Planning: Who Really Is the Client?

Planning can be targeted at several levels:

- the learner and educators
- the educational agency, program, or entire curriculum
- the society and community of which these are a part

Regardless of the selected frame of reference used in planning, our intentions should be responsive and responsible—to produce new and useful results while continuing to deliver those which are functional.

MIXED AUDIENCES, MIXED MESSAGES

Who is the educational client? Whose or what needs do we address? Do schools and programs exist to serve learners, teachers, administrators, scholars, unions, school board members, the press, employers, government, society? All of these? Who are the primary beneficiaries of the planning and its consequences? Is the basic client the society served by the educational system, or is it the system itself?

Listen to the discourse as educators get together to plan. It often starts out with "we are here for the children"; "we have to develop critical thought and inquiring minds" or "get good jobs for our graduates", and then swiftly turns to matters of administrator convenience—publication of research, discipline, keeping one lawsuit-proof, course development, testing, public relations, or teacher satisfaction. Who are the primary clients for educational planning and delivery? Let's see.

One way to clearly determine different varieties of planning is to identify who really benefits from the results. The possible beneficiaries include: society, the educational system, a nursery school program, an entire school, a university, professors, teachers, principals, parents, and students. Who is the primary client? Who really benefits? Everyone should.

THREE MAJOR CLIENT GROUPS

There are three basic orientations to planning (regardless of the "business" one seems to be in). They are dependent on the primary clients and beneficiaries of the plan itself. These three orientations are [52,55]:

(1) The individuals or small groups within the organization
(2) The organization itself
(3) The society which the organization (whether or not it formally recognizes the fact) serves

Of course, one may (and really should) choose to plan to include all three client groups. Let's take a closer look at each, in the sequence of the most usual (but not the most useful).

The Organization-as-Client

Most approaches to planning (especially those labelled "strategic") assume that the organization's survival is paramount and that any planning must deliver organizational continuation, well-being, and growth. While concern for the student, the taxpayer, the economy, or the environment is often expressed (and even meant), it is the organization which benefits from the plan. While this mode of planning might identify learner performance both in and out of school, the underlying primary focus and concern tends to be on making the system more successful, *not necessarily* on the benefits to the student, community, and/or taxpayers. Such topics of self-interest as organizational funding levels, personal liability,[2] salary levels, facilities acquisition or improvement, prestige, and additional territory often "drive" this type of planning focus.

This is not to say that the well-being of the organization or its employees is not extremely important. It usually is. Any educational organization must be chartered to perform as well as to have competent, well-equipped, properly supported, and concerned professionals. The critical, and often uncomfortable, primary issue is not just the organization's continuation but whether the organization should be the primary client and beneficiary. Some "restructuring" in schools today results from realizing the stark reality that simply "doing what we are now doing but better" will not suffice.

The Individual- or Small Group-as-Client

Organizations are composed of people (and, of course, of physical and financial resources). Often, an individual or small group becomes the primary focus and beneficiary of planning. Educational organizations might target students and their course-level (or test) performance, teachers, or programs. Individual-as-client planning foci could include the improvement of student mastery of the capitals of the world, sentence structure, or home electrical wiring properties; the ability to communicate with visual symbols; development of social and job skills; or the ability to pass a competency test. Such an individual competence focus can be very useful and productive. It is the basic rationale for programs in instructional improvement, instructional systems design, competency-based education, computer-assisted instruction, communication improvement programs, criterion-referenced assessment, and so on.

Another variety of individual-as-client focus is the individual (or small group). Objectives could include gaining resources for the biology department, getting a raise, or capturing a bigger budget. When the payoff is for individual position or power, we often call this approach "office politics".

The Society-as-Client

The much rarer approach to educational planning is one where the current and future good of society is the primary focus and interest. From this perspective, any educational part (such as a school, course, activity, or program) is a means to societal ends.

When using the society-as-primary-client planning mode, you bring center-stage current and future societal opportunities, requirements, and problems. This starting point includes:

(1) Defining current results and future requirements
(2) Identifying educational requirements for helping to bring about genuine societal good

This approach operates on the basis of that which is good for society is also good for the organization and its people.[3] Even though legislators, government senior executives, educational managers, and educational agency planners should be taking this approach, being human they tend to quickly slip into the organization-as-client mode.

Educators may be one of the very few groups which can have a singular interest in the stewardship of our planet. The public-trust mission is to help people be self-sufficient, self-reliant, and mutually contributing members of society—now and in the future [48]. Education and schools are clearly means—potentially potent—to societal ends.

Different World-Views and Their Relationship to Selecting a Planning Perspective—Outside-In Versus Inside-Out[4]

What perspective should educational planning partners select? What basic client should they plan for:

- learners?
- the school system?
- the vocational program?
- a content or subject area?
- teachers?
- society?

Whether one sees himself/herself as the center of the planning universe or as a potential contributor to a better world is key to which mode of strategic planning is selected. Let's look at two "world views".

INSIDE-OUT PLANNING

If one plans *for* the organization as the primary client, it is as if one were *looking from within the organization outside into the operational world where learners graduate, and where citizens live, play, and work.* This focus is on the good of the organization. It carries some assumptions which might make major change difficult, such as altering a major mission of the system or identifying opportunities and problems which currently do not exist. Inside-out planning usually projects the current educational mission(s), goals, purposes, and activities forward in time.

Inside-out planning is primarily reactive. It represents the personal orientation and worldview of those who feel more comfortable fixing something which is broken while assuming that it is worth fixing. Such people start work analyzing the problems and then seek methods for repairing the damage. The success of any reactive approach hinges on current objectives and purposes being valid and useful.

OUTSIDE-IN PLANNING

If one plans *for* society as the primary client and beneficiary, then an alternative perspective is gained. Planning in this way is as if one were *looking into the organization from outside—from the vantage point of society—back into the realm of organizational results and efforts*. Social good, now and in the future, becomes paramount. The role of the educational organization as only one of many means-to-ends (providers) becomes obvious. In this type of planning the client is all of society and, by logical extension, all of the other educational partners.

Outside-in planning is primarily proactive. It represents an orientation which constructively challenges the status-quo (without just critiquing or deriding it) and identifies possible new purposes and payoffs. This perspective is most comfortable to professionals who seek to effect positive change and growth, not just to do damage control or to increase the efficiency of current operations.

The differences between these two planning perspectives is how one views the world. In the *Inside-out* mode, the client (and beneficiary) is the organization; its survival and well-being will likely be paramount. The *Outside-in* mode sees the basic client (and beneficiary) as society, and anything which the organization can or should contribute is identified and considered in that light.

Figure 1.1 shows the two different "views". We suggest the *Outside-in* view as more realistic and practical. It clearly recognizes that education and educational agencies are means to societal ends, and reduces the likelihood that the primary client and beneficiary of education will be the organization itself or its people.

When choosing the Inside-out mode, there is a likely bias towards maintaining the status-quo rather than towards creating a fresh set of purposes and responses. The Outside-in approach encourages new visions and

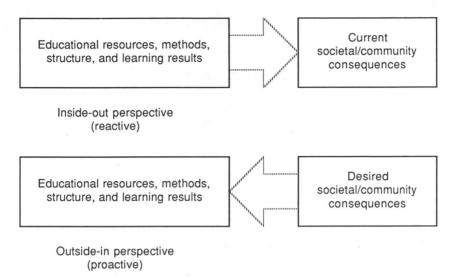

FIGURE 1.1 Inside-out and outside-in perspectives for educational strategic planning.

answers. Comparing the two approaches' products could identify the matches and mismatches between them—like the transcontinental railroad builders which started one team in the East and another in the West with an intent to meet halfway. Good intentions might not be the same as good results.

INTEGRATING BOTH APPROACHES

In reality both perspectives are important. Effective planning will integrate both by first using the (proactive) outside-in approach. Through identifying what kind of world (a shared "North Star") educational partners wish their children and grandchildren to live in, educational goals and objectives are derived for reaching that end. After setting the vision and mission, deriving the building-block objectives and related methods, the inside-out perspective may be used and a comparison of "What Is" may be made against "What Should Be" in order to determine what to keep and what to change. The rest of the book deals with the tools and methods for doing just this.

The Common Good

The degree to which organizational purposes are identical to societal purposes is the extent to which an educational agency is likely to be suc-

SOCIETY-AS-CLIENT

↓

ORGANIZATION AS CLIENT

↓

EDUCATOR/COURSE-AS-CLIENT

↓

LEARNER AS CLIENT

↓

SPECIFIC COURSE/LEARNING EXPERIENCE

FIGURE 1.2 A rational educational planning sequence.

cessful [41,42,48,52,63,87,88,103,116]. Common visions, purposes, and missions will provide a common set of results – a "North Star" – towards which all educational stakeholders may steer. When there are shared purposes and payoffs, a common good is created leading to a win-win situation and a cooperative environment.

Because organizations (including educational ones) are means to societal ends, and because they are judged by the extent to which they contribute to everyone's benefit, the rational approach for planning should be the society-as-client mode. In that regard, a rational planning sequence is shown in Figure 1.2. (While the major planning flow is from top-to-bottom, in operation the levels interact. The arrows actually also move in both directions.)

When an educational organization's mission contributes to the well-being of today's and tomorrow's society it is likely to be successful. In practice, there are different "fits" among society, school, curriculum, educator, and learner. Based on the degree of alignment there are different possibilities regarding optimism for the contributions and future of the educational agency, as shown in Figure 1.3. The upper segment of the figure shows how different aspects of an educational operation, when splintered and unrelated, will likely lead to an ineffective system. The middle section of Figure 1.3 shows overlap among the various aspects which (if they are moving together) can offer some hope for positive payoffs. The lower part of the figure shows an integration of the various facets which bodes well for educational success.

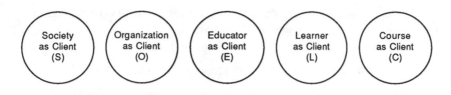

An educational agency headed for trouble.

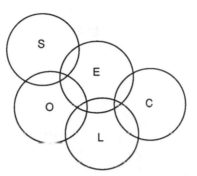

An educational agency which is going to be partially responsive and accepted.

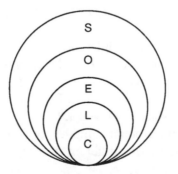

An educational agency which is being responsive and will likely be accepted.

FIGURE 1.3 Three varieties of operational purposes and the anticipated organizational success and acceptance predicated upon the degree of planning based on current and future societal good.

Prudent planning really operates in the direction opposite to most approaches, moving from the "top"—what type of system and world do we want to create—to the lowest level (Figure 1.4):

(1) Identify and select the consequences and payoffs desired.
(2) Identify the ends, or en-route results, which will deliver those.
(3) Select the best means (and if possible, considering wants in the decision) to get us there.
(4) Treat the educational organization as a provider, not as a client itself.

TYPES OF STRATEGIC PLANNING: MEGA, MACRO, MICRO

Strategic planning has been with us for some time. Bryson [10] identifies and describes more than fifteen useful, used, and available possibilities. While there are many different definitions and approaches, almost all tend to view strategic planning as a method for improving organizational payoffs and consequences in face of competition, obstacles, or adversity [13,85]. Most popular strategic planning approaches tend to: (a) take the inside-out, or organization-as-client orientation, (b) select the organization itself as the primary client and beneficiary, thus reacting to problems rather than also seeking new opportunities and purposes.

SELECTING THE RIGHT STRATEGIC PLANNING MODE

One may formulate several different strategic planning modes which differ in degree and purpose regarding what questions they pose, and who the primary clients and beneficiaries are. We suggest three types of strategic planning, each one homing in on different sets of primary clients and beneficiaries: Micro, Macro and Mega.

Table 1.1 provides three optional modes for strategic planning based on different planning targets—the different primary clients and beneficiaries of the plans:

- Mega level planning: society and community—our city, nation, and world
- Macro level planning: the educational organization itself—our school or educational system
- Micro level planning: an individual or small group, such as the administration, some teachers, a special-interest faction

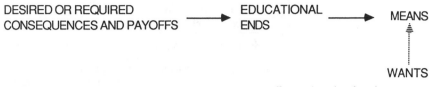

FIGURE 1.4 A "top-down" (from desired results and payoffs to educational ends to means and wants) planning sequence.

Strategic Planning Plus

Most strategic planning approaches are concerned with the Macro level—they assume that the primary beneficiary of that which gets planned and delivered is the educational organization. We strongly urge adding societal payoffs—Mega level concerns—to conventional strategic planning (Figure 1.5).

"Strategic planning plus" [55] adds consideration of current and future societal good to the usual strategic planning approaches.

MEGA INCLUDES MACRO AND MICRO, AND MACRO INCLUDES MICRO

It is important to realize that all three levels of planning are important. Mega results come from Macro contributions. Macro results come from Micro contributions.

The concepts of Mega, Macro, and Micro planning are developed in Chapter 3.

Table 1.1 Three levels and types of educational planning and results.

Levels of Planning	Description of Type of Results	Typical Examples
MICRO	Results which are building-blocks for larger result.	Test score, course passed, competence gained, etc.
MACRO	Results which can, or are delivered outside to society; quality of contribution.	Graduate, certificate of completion, liscensure, etc.
MEGA	The social impact and payoffs of results.	Individual self-sufficiency, self-reliance, collective social payoffs, etc.

$$+ \quad \begin{array}{l} \textbf{Micro Level Concerns} \\ \textbf{Macro Level Planning} \end{array}$$

$$\textbf{Strategic Planning Plus}$$

FIGURE 1.5 Strategic planning plus.

THE EDUCATIONAL PLANNING PARTNERS

From a holistic perspective, the basic planning question is "*Who are the clients?*" The partners (and thus the clients) for planning include three human groups and their actual or anticipated performance. The human partners include the learners, educators, and society/community. The fourth "partner"[5] consists of actual or required performance—what gets accomplished, and the individual *and* societal payoffs which should result [48].

The human partner groups are best comprised of people who are representative of the actual constituents. The perceptions of these partners

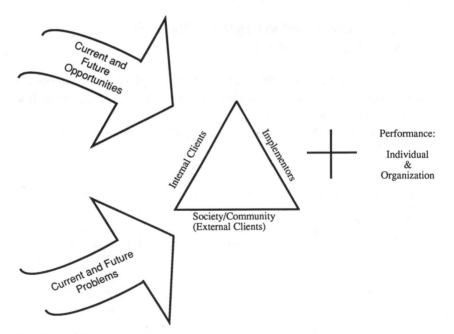

FIGURE 1.6 The partners (and clients) for planning include learners, educators, and society/community plus actual or required performance. Feeding into the partnership are considerations of current and future opportunities (including but not limited to educationally-related ones).

constitute "reality", and thus are called "soft" data due to the private nature of their source.[6] The actual performance relates to actual results; because the base is independently verifiable, it is termed "hard" data[7] [48].

An active, participatory partnership in planning is important — vital — in order to:

(1) Obtain both hard and soft data
(2) Capture reality
(3) Better assure that all of the clients, including their values, are properly considered and served
(4) Transfer ownership [23] from the planners to all of the educational clients

The educational planning partnership is shown in Figure 1.6.

BIASES, PERSPECTIVES, AND IDEOLOGIES

Many educators are involved in planning. They come from diverse backgrounds, frequently holding beliefs which have been unquestioned for some time. Strategic planning requires everyone to examine and re-examine these beliefs.

Because of these diverse clienteles [9] and to better communicate to this multiplicity, we now offer three possible types of planning from different perspectives and supply each of these viewpoints with alternative names to communicate the richness of their meaning. The alternative perspectives all relate to three major types of planning:

(1) One which takes as the primary client and beneficiary the individual or small group
(2) One which takes as the primary client the organization itself
(3) A still different one which has as its primary beneficiary society itself

Planning and Incentives

EDUCATION IS DIFFERENT FROM RUNNING A BUSINESS

Education isn't a profit-driven business, so some of the conventional business-oriented concepts don't fit. Strategic planning is most often employed in business to define markets and identify what products to sell;

to find out what to expand, what to contract, what to reject, and what to keep [1]. Education doesn't exactly operate in the free marketplace, but there are some sources of competition, including (but not limited to) private enterprise, ignorance, indifference, and competing agencies. Market expansion and modification in education may be viewed as what curriculum and services should be offered to whom, as well as when and where. It makes sense to modify and add to current models of strategic planning, as we will see next.

USING A MEGA APPROACH

Although we can identify three major strategic planning approaches, the challenge of getting the societally-oriented type (Mega planning) understood, appreciated, and used still faces us. Currently, most formal and informal incentives arise from looking out for ourselves and/or our organization. In addition, we tend to be an impatient lot—often in a hurry to get results and not willing to take the time or trouble to relate the three planning levels, or to wait for the higher-level consequences and payoffs.

"KILLING" ONE'S ORGANIZATION THROUGH SUCCESS

Attempting to put one's own system out of business through success (every learner will perform perfectly in school, on the job, and in life) is not irrational. But few people will either accept that way of thinking about educational planning or seriously consider reducing their job or their organization's allotment of power. Frequently we inappropriately judge ourselves and others on the basis of how much we get in the budget, how many people we supervise, how big we grow.

Should not every organization try to reduce the time, effort, resources, and personnel required to meet its objectives? Should not each person strive for perfect efficiency? Should not each organization attempt to be so successful that society can get along without them? Yet we all tend to assume that such an "idealistic" purpose is impossible; we attempt to capture as much money and territory as possible—we feather our own nests.

Further efforts towards Mega planning should be finding and using incentives for increasing societal accomplishments and contributions, not simply increasing one's own territory and position. Major value shifts might be required. We only have to address and reward the increased cost-utility of so doing [103].

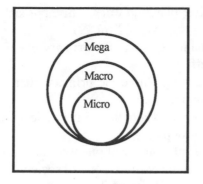

FIGURE 1.7 The nested relationship among Mega, Macro, and Micro planning.

Summary

Planning intends to create a useful, productive future. It is best based upon results which are both measurable and valuable. Different types of planning can be shown by noticing the domains addressed, and who is chosen, knowingly or unwittingly, as the primary beneficiary of planning results. Three levels of strategic planning were introduced, each related to the primary beneficiary addressed:

Mega level: society and community

Macro level: the organization itself

Micro level: an individual or small group within the organization

All of the Micro level results compose the Macro level ones. Further, Mega level results and consequences are the contributions of both Micro and Macro levels. No matter where we enter our educational system, we affect all of the other parts. A decision to work only at the Macro or Micro levels does not alter the reality that changes at any level will (or should) have consequences for all other levels. We prefer the Mega level as the primary planning focus, and suggest that society is the primary client.

Figure 1.7 displays the relationship among the levels of strategic planning and, thus, who are served as the basic clients/beneficiaries.

The choice to both think and plan strategically is vital. Much of our society's future well-being depends upon making this choice.

Glossary

Inside-Out Planning: planning as if one were looking from within the organization outside into the operational world where learners graduate, and where citizens live, play, and work. This approach is primarily reactive (also see "rolling-up," pages 276–279).

Macro Planning: planning where the primary client and beneficiary is the organization itself.

Mega Planning: planning where the primary client and beneficiary is the society and community.

Micro Planning: planning where the primary client and beneficiary is an individual (or small group).

Outside-In Planning: planning as if one were looking into the organization from outside—from the vantage point of society—back into the realm of organizational results and efforts. This perspective is primarily proactive (also see "rolling-down," pages 276–279).

Proactive: taking the initiative before the fact rather than waiting to react after the fact.

Strategic Planning Plus: Mega planning; the addition of concern for societal good to usual strategic planning frameworks and assumptions (thus the term "strategic planning *plus*").

Exercises

1. Why is it important to differentiate among planning's primary clients (society, organization, individuals)? What are the three levels of planning based on who is the primary client and beneficiary?

2. Who are the primary planning partners? What is a non-live partner?

3. What are the implications of using only: (a) Micro level planning? or (b) Macro level planning?

4. What are the advantages and disadvantages of using a proactive (outside-in) approach? A reactive (inside-out) approach?

5. Identify three examples of educational planning where omission of the Mega level was counterproductive.

Endnotes

1 As a major mission, education prepares people to be self-sufficient, mutually contributing, and self-reliant in today's and tomorrow's world. As a minimum, the individuals educated in this system should produce at least as much as they consume.

2 We have just seen the beginnings of liability and/or educational mal-

practice lawsuits. Defining and accomplishing justifiable measurable objectives should reduce one's exposure.

3 Planning at the society-as-client level is also often typified by serious environmentalists and futurists.

4 Another way to do strategic planning is to first define the ideal state—the vision—and then derive downward the essential elements for achieving it. This "rolling-down" concept is detailed on pages 276–279.

5 Of course this isn't a partner—only a major and equal level source of planning data and requirements. We refer to this "hard" data as a "partner" simply to emphasize its importance in strategic planning.

6 Examples of "soft" data might flow from attitude assessments about what the schools are doing and delivering, from opinionaires, or from judgments planning partners might make in a school board meeting or PTA session.

7 Data of this variety is independently verifiable, such as: dropout rates, arrests, parents on welfare, graduates, those getting into and staying in college, income rates, etc.

Scoping	Data Collecting	Planning	Implementation and Evaluation

Selecting Important Results

Education serves society. Learners don't stop at the front doors of the schools—they exit and take their places directly in society. How well the completers and/or leavers do—the result stemming from our educational contributions—is critical to educational planning, implementation, and accountability. Results are central for planning and doing. They are so central, that the most important single characteristic of successful planning is creating and maintaining a results-orientation. Ends—what education should deliver—provide the basic rational basis for selecting means—what we do and how we deliver learning opportunities. Following are some considerations which underlie strategic planning, and a model which is useful for relating means and ends.

A Results-Orientation

THREE TYPES OF RESULTS

In order to select and orchestrate appropriate resources and solutions, planning should be results-oriented. The ability to make sensible changes—to get more valuable payoffs—should be first based upon required results that are not currently delivered.

Two planning/doing options are worth considering. First, we might want to plan to modify current programs in order to improve the results they deliver (and thus assume that the current objectives are useful). Another option is to identify educational results which are not currently addressed, and to develop programs for delivering these new results. The first option seeks to improve on our current efforts, while the second proactively creates new purposes. Of course, both options have their place in any educational agency.

Regardless of whether we are proactively or reactively intending to increase our efficiency, there are three types of results. By differentiating among these types, we will be able to plan better where we are going and

21

why we are going there, and we will be able to justify our selections. If we want to change our results and create a better educational future, the conditions which characterize that world must be described. We have to identify what results we are getting now and define the results we want delivered. Strategic planning is most (but not exclusively) concerned with proactive planning (which improves on our current results while selecting new and useful ones at all three levels).

In Chapter 1 we noted that there are three client groups for strategic planning:

- society and community: Mega planning
- the educational organization itself: Macro planning
- individuals or small groups within the organization: Micro planning

For each of the three client foci of planning there is a specific type of result. To keep them sorted out, each has a distinct label.

Results at the Mega level are called "Outcomes", those at the Macro level are termed "Outputs", and those at the Micro level are called "Products". Table 2.1 shows the three types of results [47,48,49,55] along with a description of each and some typical examples.

Unfortunately, many educators do not recognize the relationships among the three levels of planning and results—they either fail to differentiate among them or they ignore their linkages. By so doing, they can inadvertently change a part of an educational system (e.g., add an interesting course, change the job description for some teachers) without contributing to the whole educational system. All three results types are related—sensible planning assures that they are. The three results are "nested"; Products contribute to Outputs, and Outputs contribute to Outcomes. If we choose to work only with Products or Outputs, we assume, with great risk, that the higher-order results will be satisfactory. A splintered focus on only a part of a system, such as a course (e.g., Spanish, nuclear biochemistry, geometry, welding, nutrition, hand-eye coordination, reading readiness), would be analogous to spending all of our time designing and developing a fender for a car then expecting the whole car to work effectively and efficiently. Curricula are composed of a number of learning opportunities, including individual courses and activities. Just as one course does not make an entire curriculum a success, its completion does not ensure a student's competence in a chosen field. Thus, all three levels of results merit our concern.

There is a model which relates the three types of results with the means and resources for their delivery. The model allows us to plan, to keep track of our progress, and to evaluate our payoffs and consequences.

A Planning Framework: The Organizational Elements Model (OEM)

The three types of results (Product, Output, and Outcome) are elements of a larger framework called the "Organizational Elements Model," or "OEM" [47,48,49,55]. It is shown in Figure 2.1. The OEM relates what organizations[1] use, do, deliver, and the consequences which result. The five Organizational Elements cluster in three domains:

- organizational efforts (that which organizations use and do)
- organizational results (those things they produce within their organization)
- societal consequences (the payoffs to and for society)

Each Organizational Element is related to the others in building-block fashion: organizational efforts (Inputs and Processes) contribute to organizational results (Products and Outputs), and these contribute to societal consequences and payoffs (Outcomes).

Strategic planning intends to improve our educational system and the world in which it operates. Graduates (Outputs) who cannot get and keep

Table 2.1 Three types of educational results and their associated level and scope of planning.

Type of Results	Description	Typical Examples	Level & Scope of Planning
PRODUCTS	Results which are building-blocks for larger result.	Test score, course passed, competence gained, etc.	MICRO
OUTPUTS	Results which can, or are, delivered outside to society; quality of contribution.	Graduate, certificate of completion, licensure, etc.	MACRO
OUTCOMES	The social impact and payoffs of results.	Individual self-sufficiency, self-reliance, collective social payoffs, etc.	MEGA

	INPUTS (raw materials)	PROCESSES (how-to-do-its)	PRODUCTS (en-route results)	OUTPUTS (the aggregated products of the educational system which are delivered or deliverable to society)	OUTCOMES (the effects of outputs in and for society and the community)
EXAMPLES	Ingredients, existing human and educational resources; existing needs, goals, objectives, policies, board regulations, laws, money, values, societal and community characteristics, quality of life.	Educational means, methods, procedures; "excellence programs;" voucher plans; in-service training; teaching; learning; mediating; managing.	Course completed; competency test passed; competency acquired; learner accomplishments; teacher accomplishments; the educational "building blocks."	Graduates; program completors; job placements; certified licensees; etc.	Self-sufficient, self-reliant, productive individual; socially competent and effective; contributing to self and to others; no addictive relationship to others or to substances; financial independence.
SCOPE	INTERNAL (Organization)				EXTERNAL (Societal)
CLUSTER	Organizational Efforts		Organizational Results		Societal Results/Impacts

FIGURE 2.1 The five Organizational Elements, including the scope and clusters of the elements.

jobs, and who do not become contributing citizens, are the failures of our system. Learners who pass courses in writing (Products) but cannot muster communication skills in life also indicate the break-down of an educational enterprise. In order to be successful, educational planners should ask and answer questions concerning "what is it we are concerned with?" and "what should we deliver?"

Shown in Table 2.2 are some basic questions[2] addressed by educational planning, which focus each of the Organizational Elements.

Each of these planning-related questions could be addressed individually without considering the others. However, it is not sensible to deal with any one independently. A results chain exists, whether formally recognized or ignored.

A Results Chain

The basic and fundamental starting place for educational planning begins with achievement of positive societal consequences: Outcomes. The rational results chain is shown in Figure 2.2.

Notice the arrows which connect the five Organizational Elements: Outcomes, Outputs, Products, Processes, and Inputs. If there is any misalignment or lack of "fit" between any of the elements, the system is at risk. Integration of the levels provides effective and efficient educational consequences—if we have first chosen the correct Outcomes.

Similar to a results chain for that which the educational agency does and delivers, there is likewise a similar "life" chain, shown in Figure 2.3,

Table 2.2 Basic planning questions related to each of the five Organizational Elements.

OUTCOMES:	"Are you concerned with the usefulness and contribution of what your organization delivers to external (outside-the-organization) clients who pay (directly or individually) for it?"
OUTPUTS:	"Are you concerned with the quality of what your organization delivers?"
PRODUCTS:	"Are you concerned with the effectiveness of the methods and procedures used by an individual or small group within your organization?"
PROCESSES:	"Are you concerned with the efficiency of the methods and procedures used by an individual or a small group within your organization?"
INPUTS:	"Are you concerned with the availability and/or quality of resources used by an individual or small group within your organization?"

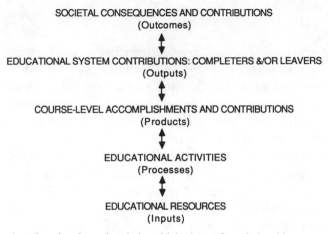

FIGURE 2.2 An educational results chain which shows the relationships among the Organizational Elements.

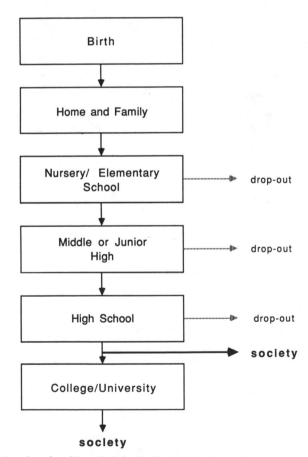

FIGURE 2.3 An educational "results" chain. Each block shows the primary educational vehicle and the usual progression.

formed by the incremental consequences of an individual's educational progression from birth through the completion of formal education (either completion of high school or higher education) before entering society. Learners start their education at birth with opportunities provided by parents and family. Then nursery and/or elementary school experiences take over, progressing to middle (or junior high) which then leads to high school. After high school (either by completion or drop out) the choice is either higher education (and delayed societal participation) or passage directly into society. It is possible to drop out at any point on this progression with early exit (shown as dotted pathways) which likely will have sizeable social costs for both the individual and society.

Choosing the Correct Objectives

Selecting where to go—educational purpose—should not be based on history, precedent, or fashion [61]. When choosing educational objectives, one may:

(a) Rely on "What Is"—the status-quo—and simply go where others are going or where they say to go.

(b) Select a new destination and create a new "What Should Be."

(c) Change what is not, or will not be, successful and keep that which is functional.

A useful process for identifying, defining, and justifying items (b) and (c) is called needs assessment [47,48,49,55].

Needs and Needs Assessment

WHERE ARE YOU GOING? WHY?

A part of planning (discussed extensively in Chapter 7) is the identification of needs—not wants. Not only do we have to set measurable destination-specifying expectations for ourselves, we should also be able to justify why we are heading there. Critical to accomplishing this is to differentiate ends and means.

As simple as this is, it is a wonder that the confusion is so widespread. Means are not ends, and wishes aren't results. Strategic planning in general, and needs assessment in particular, rely on the vital difference between "ends" and "means"; "needs", and "wants", and "wishes" all have very specific and different meanings.

Unfortunately, many educators assess "wants" or desired processes (e.g., computer-assisted instruction, school-based management, team-building) and/or resources (e.g., more teachers, higher pay) without first defining the gaps between current results and required ones. Choosing a solution (Input or Process) before knowing the gaps between current and required results is like prescribing a drug before knowing the illness.

One linguistic "trap" uses "need" as a verb to *prescribe* a solution, resource, method, or approach (e.g., we "need" to use computers, we "need" more teachers, we "need" to add to the budget, we "need" to restructure schools, we "need" to increase drug education, etc.). We are very used to using "need" as a verb and justifying it as something vitally important. Regardless of how much we want a solution or resource, they are not needs. They are but potential ways to meet needs. Leaping to select solutions, or resources, before identifying the needs (gaps in results) is to choose "quasi-needs"—which are frequently solutions in search of problems.

Don't get us wrong! Many of these solutions, or processes, are important and will be used in functional education. We just want to make certain the problem is identified before selecting the solution.

Simply (at least for planning purposes) "need"[3] is:

a gap between current and required results (or ends); a discrepancy[4] between "What Is" and "What Should Be".

Wants and wishes are usually related to means—ways to close the gaps or meet the needs (see Figure 1.4). Here are some basic terms we will be using throughout the book:

ENDS: Results, contributions, accomplishments.
MEANS: Methods, resources, processes, procedures, how-to-do-its.
WISHES (or WANTS): Preferred or valued means.
NEEDS: Gaps in ends, or results, between "What Is" and "What Should Be."[5]
QUASI-NEEDS: Gaps between "What Is" and "What Should Be" for Inputs and Processes. Quasi-needs relate to means, not ends. They are best considered after needs have been identified and selected.
NEEDS ASSESSMENT: Identifying needs, placing them in priority order, and selecting the ones most important for reduction or elimination.
PROBLEM: A need selected for reduction or elimination.
THE ORGANIZATIONAL ELEMENTS MODEL (OEM): Five elements which

describe that which organizations use (Inputs), do (Processes), deliver within themselves to internal clients (Products), deliver to external clients (Outputs) and the consequences and payoffs for the external clients and society (Outcomes). All of the Organizational Elements interrelate, contributing to each other and to an overall purpose.

Let's now turn to considerations for putting all of these concepts to work. First, building on the planning definition of need as a gap in results, let's take a look at an additional dimension of the Organizational Elements Model (OEM) for identifying needs, and relating the needs to methods (Processes) and resources (Inputs).

Identifying Needs and the Two-Tiered Organizational Elements Model

When limiting the use of the otherwise overworked word "need" to a gap in results (and thus gaps between "What Is" and "What Should Be"), a two-tiered OEM provides a holistic frame of reference for educational planning. The OEM is shown in Figure 2.4. A need, as used in planning, is a gap in results. There are three types of needs, one each for the three varieties of results: Outcomes, Outputs, and Products. The three varieties of needs are shown with regular arrows while the quasi-needs are shown with shaded arrows.

Using this two-tiered model, *one may plan to close the identified and selected gaps (needs) for any or all results levels: Products, Outputs, and Outcomes.* Choosing to respond to needs only at the Product or the Output level leaves one assuming or knowing that meeting those needs will provide for successful societal consequences.

RELATING THE OEM AND OUTSIDE-IN/INSIDE-OUT PLANNING

Figure 2.5 shows the relationship between the organizational elements model and inside-out and outside-in planning. Remember, the inside-out perspective is usually *reactive*. It primarily seeks to improve the current methods and operations, not questioning basic purposes and current missions. Outside-in planning offers the possibilities of creating new realities. It is *proactive*.

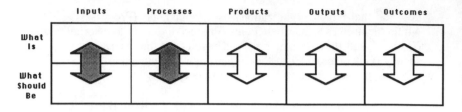

FIGURE 2.4 The two-tiered Organizational Elements model including the dimensions of "What Is" and "What Should Be".

A RESULTS CHAIN BASED ON NEEDS, FOR GAPS BETWEEN "WHAT IS" AND "WHAT SHOULD BE"

Needs, at least for the purposes of planning, are gaps in results. Because of this, then, there is a results chain which is based on the gaps and has the two dimensions: "What Is" and "What Should Be" (see Figure 2.6). If we want to plan an entire successful educational system—as we will see later is both an important and often-ignored venture—we can derive the results chain for the two dimensions of "What Is" and "What Should Be".

This two-dimensioned OEM serves as a planning guide to remind us that any educational system has both current and desired resources, activities, and results. It is often tempting to forget that these dimensions are continuing, important, and worthy of our planning attention.

Using the Organizational Elements Model (OEM) as a Planning Template

The OEM can be used as a planning template for:

(1) Assuring that all intended and essential elements are included in planning
(2) A reminder that all elements interact with each other
(3) A cue that gaps in Inputs and/or Processes (quasi-needs) are not addressed before the gaps in results (needs) are identified and selected

When actual planning starts, one enters the data collected in the OEM

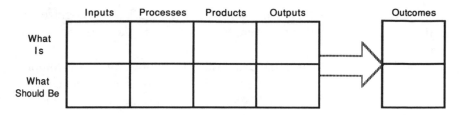

Inside-Out Perspective

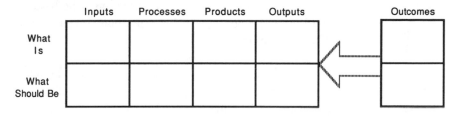

Outside-In Perspective

FIGURE 2.5 Two worldviews for strategic planning: Inside-out and outside-in. The latter is recommended.

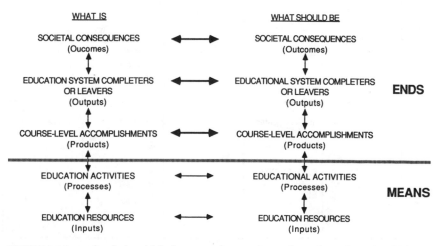

FIGURE 2.6 A results chain which shows needs: gaps in results and quasi-needs which are gaps in means.

framework, such as the incomplete one in Figure 2.7, and recognizes: (a) that all important cells are covered; and (b) where data may be missing or incomplete.

Note in Figure 2.7 that the data are: (a) hypothetical, (b) incomplete (there are no entries in "What Should Be" for Inputs and Products); and that (c) the entries for "What Should Be" for Processes are probably premature—they have been selected before the needs have been identified, documented, and selected.

Often, unfortunately, in planning, solutions have been selected before needs. This can result in an organization pursuing solutions which do not address the actual problems. Using the OEM as a template helps identify what is missing, what is incomplete, and what scope of planning is actually being used.

A first-time strategic planning effort will move through the OEM as shown in Figure 2.8. With experience, you might find a shift to the sequence shown in Figure 2.9 useful.

	Inputs	Processes	Products	Outputs	Outcomes
What Is	entering students have an average 934 SAT; average class size is 43; Etc.	93% of classes use only lectures; computers are used for drill and games; Etc.	average GPA is 2.27; Etc.	43% of enrollees never finish; 88% of non-completers were in sciences; Etc.	71% of graduates find jobs paying lower than national average; Etc.
What Should Be	———	use computer assisted Instruction***; use individualized methods***; Etc.	———	at least 97% graduate; Etc.	at least 95% of graduates find jobs; at least 50% should be at or above national average; Etc.

FIGURE 2.7 The OEM used as a "planning template". Items with a *** are Processes which are probably selected prematurely—before selecting to close the gaps in Products. Not all cells are filled out here.

Quasi-needs are gaps between "What Is" and "What Should Be" for Inputs and/or Processes. They are gaps, to be sure, but not gaps in results; they are not needs. Use of the OEM as a template alleviates the pitfall of examining gaps between "What Is" and "What Should Be" for Inputs and/or Processes.[6]

Planning, starting at any level, has direct or indirect impact on all other levels. When selecting any level, there are consequences at all other levels. Let's look at a couple of examples.

EXAMPLE 1: A NURSERY SCHOOL

A new nursery school law gets passed. The following is a sequence which resulted from the passing of a new state law concerning safety of nursery school children. Note how each element has impact on others:

ACTION OR CONSEQUENCES	BASIC ORGANIZATIONAL ELEMENT	LEADS TO
Lobbying	Process	Product
Passed Bill	Product	Input
Law becomes school policy	Input	Processes
Procedures established for handling children while at school	Processes	Products
Changed classroom lay-outs	Product	Inputs
Changed playground con-duct	Product	Inputs
Fewer reported accidents	Product	Inputs
Completers of Nursery programs in good psych-ological and mental health	Output	Outcome
No deaths or serious injuries	Outcome	Inputs
Learners enter regular elementary programs healthy	Input	Processes

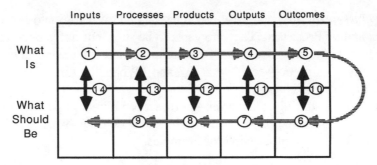

FIGURE 2.8 A first timer's strategic planning sequence (moving from 1 through 14).

EXAMPLE 2: MEDICAL SCHOOL RESEARCH

A research break-through on AIDS at the Medical College.

ACTION OR CONSEQUENCES	BASIC ORGANIZATIONAL ELEMENT	LEADS TO
New technique for treating AIDS	Product	Input
New technique is taught in medical school classes and medical workshops	Process	Input
New technique is used	Process	Product
45% decrease in critical AIDS symptoms in drug users	Product	Output
61% Symptom-free discharges	Output	Outcome
Death rate reduction of 43%	Outcome	Input
Findings available for further research	Input	Processes
Research methods sought	Process	etc.

Putting the OEM to Work

The OEM is dynamic. It provides a framework for relating critical dimensions for strategic planning:

- ends and means
- needs and solutions

• organizational efforts, organizational results, and societal and community payoffs

The two examples shown above relate the dynamic nature of the OEM — planning and related activities moving from element to element, and sometimes back and forth among the elements. The OEM is not linear, lock-stepped, or single-dimensioned. A change in one part of any educational system causes, directly or indirectly, change in all other parts. In our first example, a law on nursery schools was a Product of the legislature, which then became an Input to the nursery schools themselves. This Input spawned Process which yielded Products . . . and these Products led to Outputs and Outcomes. The sum of all of the nursery school elements became Inputs to the regular school system.

The OEM is a useful template, or framework, for strategic planning and strategic thinking. With it, you and your planning partners are able to relate what you wish to accomplish with the best means and resources for getting visions turned to realities.

Summary

There are three varieties of results: (1) *Products* are the building-block results collected to make up (2) organizational results, called *Outputs*, which can or will be delivered to society, and (3) *Outcomes*, which are the consequences and payoffs for these results in and for society. The three types of results are "nested" with Products making up Outputs, and Outcomes encompassing them all.

Each of the three results featured by the OEM relate to different levels, or scopes, of planning. Planning at the Mega level focuses on results called *Outcomes*. Results at the Macro level are labeled *Outputs*, and those at the Micro level are *Products*.

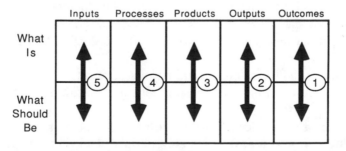

FIGURE 2.9 A possible strategic planning sequence for experienced planning groups.

For planning purposes, a *"need"* is the gap between current and desired/required results. *"Means"* are the possible resources and/or methods for closing those gaps. A *needs assessment* is a tool for identifying and prioritizing needs so that important and useful objectives can be identified.

A framework, called the *Organizational Elements Model* (OEM) is provided which relates organizational efforts, organizational results, and societal consequences. It may be used as a planning template, or frame of reference, for identifying "What Is" and "What Should Be".

A summary of possible questions to be asked and answered, each clustered by their *primary* Organizational element and classified by the type of strategic planning primarily addressed, are provided in Table 2.3. Change at any level will have consequences for all other levels.

Glossary

Ends: results, consequences, payoffs.

Means: ways and resources, solutions, how-to-do-its, processes.

Need: a gap between current and required results (or ends); a discrepancy between "What Is" and "What Should Be".

Needs Assessment: identifying, prioritizing, and selecting the most important needs for reduction or elimination. There are three types of results (Products, Outputs, and Outcomes) and because a need is a gap in results, there may be three varieties of needs assessments.

Organizational Elements Model (OEM): five elements which identify dimensions of what organizations use, do, produce, deliver, and the consequences of those results for society. The OEM has three domains: organizational efforts (what organizations use and do), organizational results (things produced within the organization) and societal consequences. The five elements: Inputs (resources/ingredients, laws, rules, regulations, personnel, funds, etc.), Processes (how-to-do-its, methods, means, processes, solutions, procedures), Products, Outputs, and Outcomes.

Outcomes: the social impact and payoffs of results for society.

Outputs: results which can, or are, delivered outside an organization to society.

Problem: a need selected for reduction or elimination.

Products: results (ends) which are building blocks for a larger result.

Quasi-Needs: gaps between "What Is" and "What Should Be" for Inputs

Table 2.3 Important strategic planning questions clustered by Organizational Element and each one's primary level.

Question	Planning Level		
	MEGA	MACRO	MICRO
Outcome- (Mega) related:			
1. Do you want to purposely improve our society, including measurable improvement of people's self-sufficiency, self-reliance, quality of life, and shared mutual commitment to these?	X		
2. Are you interested in both social and economic trends as well as opportunities for the future which might not exist now or be readily apparent now?	X		
3. Are you willing to add to or delete from the current objectives of educational systems?	X		
4. Do you want to change the future and stop only reacting to the past?	X		
Output- (Macro) related:			
5. Do you want to improve the current educational system's abilities to achieve its current purposes now and in the future?		X	
6. Do you want to improve the completion and graduation rates of the educational system?		X	
Product- (Micro) related:			
7. Do you want to improve student mastery at the course and testing levels?			X
Process-related:			
8. Do you want to help learners to be more successful in their daily learning efforts?			X*
9. Do you want to improve the efficiency of teaching and educational activities?			X*
10. Do you want to coordinate and integrate all of the services available to citizens in helping to improve learner success in and outside of schools?			X*
Input-related:			
11. Do you want to improve the accountability for current educational resources?			X*
12. Do you want to get additional resources?			X*

*These really relate to "quasi-needs" because they are not necessarily based on results-referenced gaps.

and Processes. Quasi-needs relate to means, not ends. They are best considered after needs have been identified and selected.

Results Chain: the linked results which any organization, whether it realizes it or not, produces: Outcomes are delivered through Outputs, and Outputs are delivered from Products, and those are delivered through Inputs and Processes.

Exercises

1. List the five organizational elements and provide an example of each for your educational agency.

2. What are the basic elements in a results chain? Identify the three types of results, the two types of means and show a results chain for your educational agency.

3. What are the differences among: ends, means, wishes, solutions, resources, methods? Give examples of each for your educational agency.

4. Define a "need" and give an example for your organization of a need at each of the three levels of results (Products, Outputs, and Outcomes).

5. Why is it important to use "need" as a noun, not as a verb? Give three examples of specific instances where "need" used as a verb has resulted in solutions/methods being selected which resulted in poor or incorrect results.

6. Give two levels for using the Organizational Elements Model (OEM). Why is it useful to do needs assessment and planning based on the two levels?

7. What is a quasi-need? How does it differ from a need? Give examples from your agency. Why might the term *training needs assessment* be deceptive?

8. Identify the three levels, or scopes of planning and the variety of results which characterize each.

Endnotes

1 While this discussion could apply equally to all organizations—business, education, military, and government—the differences among them come from the unique needs they address, and the missions they choose. We use "organization" here to mean educational ones.

2 Based, in part, on Reference [50]. Used with permission.

3 For the sake of planning.

4 A discrepancy is not necessarily a deficiency. One may have too much of something as well as too little.

5 Needs may be identified at the level of any or all of the three varieties of results: Products, Outputs, Outcomes.

6 Planners and developers employing a reactive, or inside-out, perspective will often start with an analysis of "quasi-needs" without first identifying and selecting needs. Such an approach may employ a so-called "training needs assessment" or a questionnaire asking for judgments of "what is 'needed' [sic]".

CHAPTER 3	Scoping	→	Data Collecting	→	Planning	→	Implementation and Evaluation

A Strategic Planning Approach for Education

Strategic planning is *usually* seen as inside-out-referenced planning in the face of obstacles or competition. The sources of competition in education include other universities and colleges, employer-supplied courses, proprietary schools, unconvinced legislators, indifferent government planners, increased pressure for financial conservatism, and the changing values of our society relative to family, work, home, and drugs. Another type of "obstacle" we face is obsolescence, which could come from not having planned on the basis of future opportunities. Strategic planning is long-range planning with a vision.

Following is an educational — from nursery school through higher education — strategic planning process which is both outside-in and inside-out compatible. We will describe the elements, how they relate, and then give some details on each step. We say "some" because each of the elements, other than Step I, are detailed in later chapters.

The Essential Elements of Educational Strategic Planning

Following is the basic strategic planning model and process used throughout this book. It may be applied to any and all:

- educational systems, public and private
- any educational level, from nursery/preschool to higher education

The suggested framework, shown in Figure 3.1, has four major clusters:

- scoping
- data collecting
- planning
- implementation and evaluation

Let's now work our way through the basic functions of this framework. Special emphasis is given in this chapter to selection of the strategic plan-

41

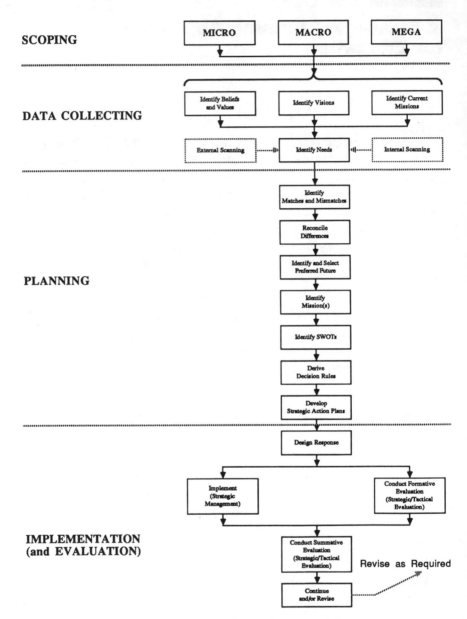

FIGURE 3.1 A strategic planning framework.

ning type. The rest of the process is developed in subsequent chapters. Each of the four clusters of strategic planning relate to the basic themes of strategic planning:

(1) Rethinking: scoping and data collecting
(2) Restructuring: planning
(3) Revitalizing: implementation and evaluation

SCOPING

I. Select the Type and Scope of Strategic Planning from Three Alternatives

First we determine what will be the "size"—or scope—of our planning: Mega, Macro, or Micro. The decision to choose one of the three strategic planning scopes, based on who the primary client is and who benefits. Mega, Macro, or Micro provide the alternative options. It is the decision to choose one of them which marks the beginning of strategic planning.

Review the material in Table 2.1, Figure 2.1, the questions from Table 2.2, and the results chain shown in Figure 2.2. (By your recalling these, we won't have to go through it again here.) These materials are useful in choosing the scope of strategic planning: Mega, Macro, or Micro. It is at this phase of strategic planning that the planning partners should take the opportunity to rethink underlying philosophies, perspectives, and biases.

Here is a review concerning the three levels, or scopes of planning.

Mega Level Planning

This, the most basic, yet rarest, choice for strategic planning, identifies existing needs and future opportunities, while also striving to accomplish the intentions of Micro and Macro planning. This outside-in, society-as-primary client and beneficiary approach intends to create a successful future for individuals, organizations, and society. Use of this mode extends current organizational goals and objectives into the future and seeks functional new organizational purposes to derive new or modified responses.

Societally-oriented—Mega—strategic planning is holistic, not only dealing with "What Is" and "What Should Be" but also adding the dimension and formal consideration of "What Could Be". The time-frame usually employed can be several years into the future.

Mega level strategic planning assumes:

- The unit of improvement is society as well as the educational system, including all of its parts.
- While the future does rest, in part, on factors beyond our direct control, some things can and often should be changed. We can and should shape the future, not just react to it.
- People care about the future and wish to purposely design, develop, implement, and evaluate an educational system which not only is efficient in reaching its current goals and objectives but will also identify new missions which contribute to society (and eliminate useless missions and methods).
- The primary client and beneficiary is and should be society, now and in the future.

Two examples of the Mega level choice are (a) planning a vocational education system and its curriculum based upon future needs, values, goals, opportunities, quality of life, and visions rather than on just future projections for jobs; and (b) developing an entire university intended to improve a nation's mental and economic resources (as in the case of Australia's Bond University [110]) rather than simply recruiting students to fill available slots.

Because of its commitment to societal payoffs for learners and citizens, a society-as-client perspective seems especially important for a contributing education system.

Macro Level Planning

This planning method identifies ways to better reach existing overarching (not just course-level purposes) organizational missions and accepted current societal objectives. Macro strategic planning addresses the improvement of current organizational efficiency. It is an inside-out approach, choosing as its primary client the organization itself. When concerned with external clients (Outcomes), this variety of planning seeks to determine the extent to which the client is satisfied with the organization. The concern is not *primarily* to help that client and society, but to use the feedback to make the organization more successful.[1] The time frame in which it operates is usually a year or more into the future.

Macro Strategic Planning *assumes:*

- The goals of the educational system and its operational units are known, valid, and useful.

- The unit of improvement is the educational system as well as all of its parts.
- The accomplishment of these goals and objectives will be suitable to allow learners to be self-sufficient and self-reliant in today's and tomorrow's worlds.
- The primary beneficiary of the planning is the organization.
- The future is basically determined by others (such as legislators, business executives, advisory groups, nature) and we can only attempt to forecast and respond to the trends.

An example might be assessment of the placements of university completers to see if they obtained jobs for which they trained. Such an inquiry, however, does not seek to determine the extent to which the completers are (a) self-sufficient, (b) self-reliant, (c) successful individuals and citizens, and (d) thriving in the future.

In a Macro planning approach, the emphasis is upon "did they get a job based on our organization's contributions?" not additionally on "did we help this individual be a successful, functioning, contributing parent, friend, and citizen?"

Micro Level Planning

A subset of the Macro level planning (organization-as-client). Micro level planning takes the individual educator and/or the individual learner's performance at the course-level as the primary client. Its operational time frame is usually short-term, frequently in units of weeks or months in the future, but not years. Some might, correctly, call this "tactical planning".

Micro level, individual-oriented planning may have two optional foci: (a) concern for the teacher (or professor), individual administrator, or small affinity group (such as the Philosophy Department, or second grade teachers) and/or (b) concern for the student as he or she attempts to perform at a course, activity, or test level.

Option (a) is frequently concerned with payoffs for individual educators (or a small group) such as hours of work, leave policy, safety, pay, power, status, or affiliation.

Option (b) primarily identifies ways to improve the implementation of what is currently in place and ongoing such as using team-building to improve cooperation, developing a competency-based course or curriculum, selecting a standardized test, applying an instructional systems development approach, or using video-disk-based instruction. This

Product-level concern is based on reaching accepted current course-level or individual student performance in a course, test, or activity goals and objectives.

Micro level strategic planning *assumes:*

- The goals of the system and its operational units are known, valid, and useful.
- The unit of improvement is the individual and/or the course, activity, or specific intervention.
- The primary beneficiary is the individual (such as an administrator, teacher, or very small specialty group, such as reading experts), and/or student competence in a course or on a performance test.
- All such improvements, when taken together, will contribute to the measurable improvement of the impact and payoffs for the entire educational system.

Examples of Micro planning might include development of an improved university astronomy course of instruction to meet existing objectives, or the development of a university professor's skills in the design of instructional opportunities.

Figure 3.2 provides a summary of how each of the three strategic planning modes (a) relate to the OEM and (b) relate to each other.

All Three Frames of Reference Are Useful and Important

All modes—Mega, Macro, and Micro—should be included. Using only one or another, however, will be better than using none of them. The choice of each has underlying assumptions. The relationships—indeed a taxonomy—among the three types of strategic planning are shown in Figure 3.3.

Strategic Planning Modes and Associated Educational Questions

When making the choice of the scope to be used for planning, the questions posed in Table 2.2 should be considered. Upon using those questions, keep in mind the relationships between types of results and scopes of planning shown in Table 2.1.

One theme which runs through this chapter and book is that there are different levels of results, and that the size—unit of attention—of the planning frame of reference has profound implications for the success of any

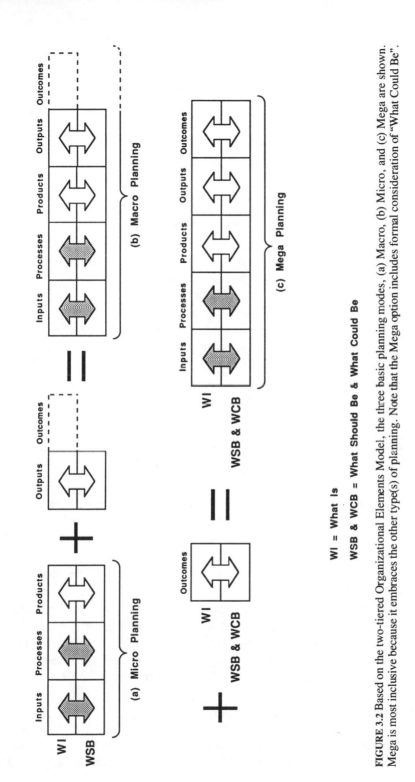

FIGURE 3.2 Based on the two-tiered Organizational Elements Model, the three basic planning modes, (a) Macro, (b) Micro, and (c) Mega are shown. Mega is most inclusive because it embraces the other type(s) of planning. Note that the Mega option includes formal consideration of "What Could Be".

FIGURE 3.3 A taxonomy of strategic planning.

effort. If one chooses too narrow a frame of reference, he/she might be stuck with a very well developed component not contributing to the whole (or as Peter Drucker reminds us, we are now getting better and better at doing that which should not be done at all!). If one selects a frame of reference which only extends the current organizational goals into the future, possible new objectives and payoffs might be overlooked. If one just gazes at the future without taking care of today, the whole adventure might be disastrous. Picking the most useful frame of reference is a serious responsibility for any educational planners entrusted with the future of their systems and citizens.

The Interactive Nature of the Three Types of Results and Three Types of Planning

The planner's life would be a lot easier if things related in a linear, lock-step fashion—if we could simply move from a Product to an Output to an Outcome, from Micro to Macro to Mega. Sorry, that's just not the way it works.

In Chapter 2 we noted in two hypothetical examples that the results at any one level had consequences for the other levels. There are interactions both within and between levels—among Micro, Macro, and Mega layers. For example, that which a student learns in reading is applicable to understanding mathematics, and concepts mastered in history could be important in philosophy. So don't think that the levels are linear—one leads directly to the next higher—it just isn't that way.

Which Planning Level Should Be Selected?

Conventional approaches to planning (and the planning literature) often focus on the here-and-now or on a simple look to meeting current and impending crises and problems [75]. The immediate is an important consideration, and must not be minimized or ignored. But there are other considerations which are equally (if not more) important, considerations that involve changing the future to benefit society and all in it. We frankly urge you to choose MEGA PLANNING. With that option, both the reactive and proactive concerns will be addressed.

When you and your strategic planning group make the choice of level, please keep in mind that each level of results has impact upon all others. When we formally recognize that fact and want to help control it to our advantage, we elect the Mega option. Regardless of which scope you select—Mega, Macro, or Micro—the functions to be accomplished (following) are basically the same.

DATA COLLECTING

After choosing a scope, one then moves to *data collecting* which involves several steps, including the identification of:

- beliefs and values
- visions
- current missions (which will vary with the scope for strategic planning selected)
- needs

II. Identify Beliefs and Values

Beliefs, values, and wishes all affect the ways partners address planning. These should be formally identified and shared in order to make public what are ordinarily private points of view. Consensus should be reached. The beliefs of each individual are often strongly held, but unchallenged. The success of the entire process of strategic planning might hinge on the planning partners' ability to consider new philosophies, or to reconsider basic beliefs about people, society, and education (including what it should accomplish, how much it should take on, and what should be rewarded).

Most beliefs come from very early learning, and thus are quite resistant to change. Be patient, helpful, and understanding. Lead others to question their own beliefs so that constructive change might be possible.

Chapter 4 deals with this in detail.

III. Identify Visions

Strategic planning is long-range planning to achieve a vision. Here, the planning partners identify and define: "What Is", "What Should Be", and "What Could Be". Based on this, agreement is also reached concerning alternate and preferred futures. Trend analysis and projection, which include taking a 10–20 year leap into the future, are useful resources for this step.

All planning partners could imagine the type of world they would like their children to live in, the type of organization they would like to work in, and the vision they would like to be partners in creating. Visions relate to contributions, not to procedures, resources, or methods. The development of complete scenarios which express each planning partner's vision is usually helpful.

This is the subject of Chapter 5.

IV. Identify Current Missions

While doing steps II–IV, the current educational mission is obtained. If necessary, it should be rewritten into performance/results terms, including measurable statements of: where are you going, and how will you know when you have arrived? As part of determining current mission(s), formal consideration of existing laws, rules, regulations, and policies should be included – not that they will be adhered to blindly, but they would serve as a logical step toward identifying what currently guides the educational system and its parts.

In addition, a determination should be made of the operational missions for each part of the system. Doing a conflict (match/mismatch) analysis of missions – relating the different parts of the organization and each one's contribution to the overall purposes – should also be completed at this step.

Most education systems have mission statements which are directional and inspirational, but which usually do not have enough specificity for strategic planning. It is common, when performing this step, to add measurable criteria to these mission statements, thus converting them to mission objectives. Chapter 6 provides the details on how to do this.

V. Identify Needs

Using the definition of a "need" as a gap in results, and employing available sources of needs information (including both "hard" and "soft" data) both the internal educational organization as well as the external society and communities are scanned. Futures and future opportunities are identified and documented. Evaluation data is used to determine "What Is". The Organizational Elements (OEM) Model—described in Chapter 2—is a useful "template" for doing a needs assessment.[2] (Figures 2.6 through 2.9 provide some guidance on using the OEM in this manner.) There are likely to be some initial disagreements among planning partners relative to deriving and selecting the needs. Needs identification and assessment usually requires that any disagreements be surfaced, considered, and resolved. This activity is similar to the first two steps in the subsequent PLANNING phase—Identify Matches/Mismatches and Reconcile Differences—but differ only in that those subsequent steps deal with matches and mismatches among (a) beliefs and values, (b) visions, (c) current missions, and (d) identified needs.

Some of the rationale for needs assessment was covered in Chapter 2, and the details of doing one are the topic of Chapter 7.

PLANNING

Data alone are not useful. You can't run a successful school system exclusively with it. Data has to be used to determine where to go—to develop a strategic plan. The steps include:

- identifying the agreements among visions, beliefs, and current mission
- reconciling differences
- selecting the preferred future
- identifying missions
- identifying strengths, weaknesses, opportunities, and threats
- deriving decision rules
- developing strategic action plans

VI. Identify Matches and Mismatches: Integrating Visions, Beliefs, Needs, and Current Missions

This step includes taking the results from the SCOPING (and DATA COLLECTING) phases: identifying visions, beliefs, needs, and current mission and finding things in common and identifying differences. Because so much of the planning partners' experiences are important to them, a challenge of this step is the integration of actual performance data with partner perceptions (called "hard" and "soft" data respectively).

Obtaining educational partner active participation is essential (not just here, but in all steps as well). This is a topic of Chapter 8. This step may be combined with step VII (Reconciling Differences).

VII. Reconcile Differences

Finding common ground, based on reality, is the major product of this step. Using previous data and information in negotiating what is right, not just what is acceptable, requires patience and often the collection of more data. At this step, the planning partners frequently have to go back and revisit data which came from the statement of beliefs, visions, and needs as compared with the existing mission. This step frequently requires great patience and skill in group dynamics and shared problem solving. Concern and caring for people's deep-seated values and biases is important here. The relationship between ends and means should be emphasized again. You might also suggest that people having trouble giving up deeply felt but unrealistic positions (usually related to means, not ends) examine (a) the payoffs that they are getting now from their position, and (b) the more functional payoffs they could obtain from a change. (See References [29,30] for a very practical model for decisions and change.) Often, steps VI and VII are combined. Reconciling differences is a topic of Chapter 8.

VIII. Identify and Select Preferred Future

Based upon the reconciled beliefs, visions, identified needs, and existing missions, the planning partners select their preferred future—the organizational (and societal) world in which they would like to live, or see exist. This is a commitment to a future, and it discourages a drift in the same directions as the organization is now heading. This is covered in Chapter 8, and builds on Chapter 5 as well.

IX. Identify Missions

From the foregoing steps and their products, this function delivers a written mission statement based upon visions, beliefs, and needs. This often requires some changes to the existing mission statement (as identified in step IV). The skills of preparing measurable performance indicators, and writing mission statements—in terms of results at the appropriate (and selected) level—are key. This is a topic of Chapter 8.

X. Identify SWOTs: Strengths, Weaknesses, Opportunities, and Threats

The definition of educational Strengths, Weaknesses, Opportunities, and Threats is made, and the required information is obtained and analyzed. As in all steps, agreement of the planning partners is essential.

Useful here are the tools of both internal and external scanning. It is important to assure that scanning includes both internal and external opportunities, as well as threats. At this step you have to be very careful not to slip into a reactive mode. Chapter 9 covers this step.

XI. Derive Decision Rules

Decision rules, or policies, are necessary so that all partners in the education arena have the same "marching orders", visions, and intentions. These decision rules provide strategic goals and objectives with measurable criteria (performance requirements). Part of this step includes prioritizing needs (on the basis of the question: What do you give and what do you get?). This is the topic of Chapter 10.

XII. Develop Strategic Action Plans

This is the last step in the "Planning" cluster. The needs, visions, beliefs, and missions are integrated. Based on the SWOTS and the decision rules, the product of this step is answering the key questions:

What?
How?
Who?
When?
Why?
Where?

At this step is also the identification of Outcomes, Outputs, and Products. Operational, or in-process, milestones for implementation are set, along with the consideration of alternative approaches (methods-means analysis). Chapter 11 deals with this.

IMPLEMENTATION AND EVALUATION

The strategic plan has now been developed and agreed upon by the educational partners. It now has to be implemented and evaluated.

XIII. Put the Strategic Plan to Work

This is not planning, but involves actually putting the plan into action and getting the required results. As part of this phase, the following activities are included:

- designing the response—implementing that which has been planned ("strategic management")
- conducting formative evaluation ("strategic/tactical" evaluation)
- conducting summative evaluation ("strategic/tactical" evaluation)

Based upon the evaluation, decisions are made about continuing and revising as required. Of course, strategic planning, implementation, and evaluation is a continuing process. Chapter 12 provides the highlights of doing this so that the proper details and tools can be selected from extensive literature on the topic.

This strategic planning framework will allow you to consider three optional levels (or scopes) for planning, and to systematically move from collecting relevant data to actually developing a plan, and then move the plan to implementation and evaluation. The chapters which follow provide the details of actually doing and using strategic planning.[3]

Strategic Thinking

Strategic planners tend to agree on at least one concept: the actual plan itself is subordinate to the process of strategic thinking [10]. Strategic thinking is characterized by a switch from dealing with one's organization as a splintered conglomerate of disassociated parts (and employees) standing alone and competing for resources, to viewing and dealing with one's organization as a united holistic (system) integrating each part in relationship to the whole based on agreed-upon, mutually rewarding visions and payoffs. It is a simultaneous switch from reactive, authoritarian means and process-oriented, budget-driven tactics to a future-oriented, proactive, holistic frame of reference where means are selected on the basis of mutually rewarding ends. Strategic thinking relates organizational means and products to societally useful ends on an ongoing and proactive basis. The shift will normally be from considering just parts and splinters (e.g., course content, activities, methods of teaching, "classroom of the next century") to conceiving integrated wholes—a total curriculum target to help students be self-sufficient in the future. This shift in thinking and interacting with the educational world is the essence of strategic thinking.

STRATEGIC PLANNING IS NOT SIMPLY INTUITIVE, IT IS RATIONAL

Some strategic planning approaches [20] state that strategic planning is intuitive—knowable without the conscious use of reasoning.[4] People, values, education, individual differences, subject matter content, organizations, and society are far too complex to be thus dismissed. If educational change were obvious and easy, the schools would already be approaching perfection. The approach we offer is rational, not just dependent upon people's intuition or instincts. It is results-based, and does not rely merely on hunches or raw feelings. While perceptions, values, and beliefs are formally considered, they are integrated and tempered with "hard" cmpirical data and actual performance.

When embarking upon educational strategic planning, there are some features and factors which could be useful once you get into it. Not everyone will immediately understand the basic nature of the process. To assist you and others in understanding some of the subtle dimensions of planning strategically, additional considerations are provided in the Epilogue.

Summary

Planning intends to create a useful, productive future. Strategic planning resolves to make certain that the correct missions, goals, values, and needs are identified and used in selecting strategies and tactics.

There are some important differences and relationships among Mega, Macro, and Micro (strategic) planning. Chapter 2 posed basic questions which any planning effort can pose, and related to each of these are optional types of planning and whether they are Mega, Macro, or Micro planning focused. This chapter identified a generic process for strategic planning in education.

Strategic planning may be seen as having four major clusters:

- scoping
- data collecting
- planning
- implementation and evaluation

A framework for educational strategic planning is suggested and includes thirteen steps: I. Select the type of strategic planning from among three alternatives; II. Identify beliefs and values; III. Identify visions; IV. Identify current missions; V. Identify needs; VI. Identify matches and mismatches: integrating visions, beliefs, needs, and current missions; VII. Reconcile differences; VIII. Identify and select preferred future; IX. Identify missions; X. Identify SWOTs: Strengths, Weaknesses, Opportunities, and Threats; XI. Derive decision rules; XII. Develop strategic action plans; XIII. Put the strategic plan to work.

Thinking strategically will usually follow from strategic planning—this process is likely to be more important for the educational partners than any one strategic plan. Educators and their partners can choose to both think and plan strategically. Much of our society's future well-being depends upon this choice being made.

Glossary

Macro Planning: planning which identifies ways and means to better reach existing overarching (not just course-level purposes) organizational missions and accepted social objectives (validated or assumed).

Mega Planning: planning which includes all of the organizational elements, and the planning dimensions of (a) What Is, (b) What Should Be, and (c) What Could Be. By its proactive perspective, it takes an outside-in, society-as-client perspective and views society as the basic client of education.

Micro Planning: planning which takes the individual educator and/or the individual's performance learner as the primary client.

Strategic Planning: proactive planning which identifies problems and opportunities for organizations. The suggested framework has four major clusters: Scoping, Data Collecting, Planning, and Implementation. The suggested approach includes Mega, Macro, and Micro frames of reference. Thirteen steps are provided.

Strategic Thinking: the way in which people in the organization view and respond to day-to-day opportunities and situations. A way of organizational life and response.

SWOTs: Strengths, Weaknesses, Opportunities, and Threats.

Exercises

1. What are the implications of using all of the steps of the strategic planning processes provided in this book? What happens if you skip or miss a step?

2. What are the implications of basing strategic planning on intuition?

3. Differentiate between the uses and implications of doing strategic planning at the Micro, Macro, and Mega levels.

4. Using the 13 steps of strategic planning, identify the major considerations for planning for your educational agency.

5. Why is it often necessary to convert existing mission statements to a mission objective? How might they differ?

6. Why might strategic planning be considered threatening to some in your educational agency?

7. Respond to a possible allegation that using the Mega level of strategic planning is not "practical". Why would someone offer that as an objection? What is "practical"?

8. What are the differences between proactive and reactive planning? What are the implications for each perspective?

9. What are the differences and relationships between planning and evaluation?

10. Why might strategic thinking be more important than any strategic plan?

Endnotes

1 This distinction between Mega planning and Macro planning might help respond to Windham's [114] stinging critique of classical Macro planning.

2 Also helpful are the nine steps of doing a needs assessment provided in Reference [47].

3 Although the model (Figure 3.1) might appear to be linear, each step actually depends upon and interacts with all others. Responsive strategic planning considers the complexities of learners, staff members, educators, communities, and society all working in unison. This relationship is not a linear, lock-step progression.

4 Webster's *New World Dictionary*.

Identifying Beliefs

Among the first tasks that should be undertaken during the strategic planning process, after selecting the Mega, Macro, or Micro planning scope, is the identification of beliefs. Beliefs are explored from various viewpoints – that is, what the stakeholders (those persons involved in the strategic planning process and representing critical constituencies in the community) believe about the Mega (world) environment, the Macro (organizational) environment, and the Micro (individual or sub-group) environment. The beliefs should be formally identified, placed in writing and shared, thereby making the public and all persons associated with the organization aware of the foundation upon which the remainder of the strategic plan is based. By formally stating and examining beliefs with other planning partners, the opportunity to change from original, Macro or Micro orientation to a Mega direction exists *before* continuing the strategic planning process. If the guiding beliefs are not formally identified and a consensus developed – now or later – the organization will likely run aground at many points, like a rudderless ship, while taking the journey to the preferred destination (i.e., the vision of "What Should Be").

Beliefs can be related to social, political, economic, and aesthetic values.[1] A belief statement may also include a set of very specific beliefs about various stakeholders of an organization as well as how that organization should operate at the people level. This is easily illustrated by a listing of possible beliefs for a school district.

Beliefs—A Starter List

Below is a listing of beliefs already identified by a variety of practitioners. Add any statements you desire. Your final statement of beliefs should be placed in a comprehensive statement format. It is an important piece of information for use in creating the desired future vision for your school district.

INSTRUCTIONS: Read each statement once. Check whether or not you agree (A) or disagree (D) with each statement. Once you have individually completed this listing, assemble your stakeholders' group and work to reach consensus on each statement. If your group cannot reach consensus, try to change the wording in any statement in a way that promotes consensus.

BELIEFS ABOUT LEARNERS

A   D

☐ ☐ **1.** All learners can learn.

☐ ☐ **2.** They develop at different rates.

☐ ☐ **3.** They should have a safe and healthy environment.

☐ ☐ **4.** They must have social as well as intellectual experiences.

☐ ☐ **5.** Learners should feel good about the school they attend.

☐ ☐ **6.** They should feel their input is important.

☐ ☐ **7.** They have varying learning styles.

☐ ☐ **8.** They are capable of self-discipline.

☐ ☐ **9.** Learners should develop a strong self-image.

☐ ☐ **10.** They should develop the ability to think rationally.

☐ ☐ **11.** They should understand and respect cultural, religious, and ethnic differences.

☐ ☐ **12.** They should understand and utilize technology.

☐ ☐ **13.** They should participate in democracy.

☐ ☐ **14.** Other (please list).

BELIEFS ABOUT PARENTS OR GUARDIANS

A   D

☐ ☐ **1.** Parents and guardians are major stakeholders and they should have input to major decisions related to their child's education.

☐ ☐ **2.** They should be made aware of teacher expectations.

☐ ☐ **3.** They should actively support teachers' efforts.

☐ ☐ **4.** They should set high expectations for their children.

A   D

☐   ☐   **5.** They should experience positive contacts with school personnel.

☐   ☐   **6.** Parents have the responsibility to seek assistance if their child requires help.

☐   ☐   **7.** Parents should positively reinforce their child's efforts.

☐   ☐   **8.** They must establish education/learning as a high priority.

☐   ☐   **9.** Parents must take an active interest in their child's education.

☐   ☐   **10.** Parents should provide opportunities for their children to become self-disciplined.

☐   ☐   **11.** They should serve as role models.

☐   ☐   **12.** They should insist on a Mega vision and mission.

☐   ☐   **13.** Other (please list).

BELIEFS ABOUT EMPLOYEES

A   D

☐   ☐   **1.** Employees should be role models for students.

☐   ☐   **2.** They must be interested in the health and welfare of students.

☐   ☐   **3.** They should display initiative and operate with minimal supervision.

☐   ☐   **4.** Employees should possess a strong desire to be the best they can be.

☐   ☐   **5.** They should display a positive attitude towards students and their learning.

☐   ☐   **6.** Teachers should set high expectations for both student learning and student achievement.

☐   ☐   **7.** Teachers should utilize activities which promote students' ability to think.

☐   ☐   **8.** Employees should have input into decisions which affect them.

☐   ☐   **9.** Teachers should evaluate student performance in a fair, objective, and consistent manner.

A   D
☐   ☐   **10.** Teachers should make full use of instructional time.

☐   ☐   **11.** Teachers should work together in a cooperative manner.

☐   ☐   **12.** Employees carry out responsibilities more cooperatively and efficiently when they share ownership.

☐   ☐   **13.** Employees require recognition, encouragement and support for their efforts.

☐   ☐   **14.** They require opportunities for growth and development.

☐   ☐   **15.** They respond when job expectations are regularly monitored and evaluated.

☐   ☐   **16.** Teachers should address the needs, wants, unique characterstics, and expectations of "each student" in the class.

☐   ☐   **17.** Employees should provide regular and consistent feedback and communications to both students and parents (or guardians).

☐   ☐   **18.** Employees should have a Mega vision.

☐   ☐   **19.** They should be results-oriented.

☐   ☐   **20.** Other (please list).

BELIEFS ABOUT COMMUNITY MEMBERS

A   D
☐   ☐   **1.** The community should participate in the planning process of the school district.

☐   ☐   **2.** The community should communicate its expectations for the school district.

☐   ☐   **3.** The community must take an active interest in the welfare and education of all children.

☐   ☐   **4.** The community should join the school district in providing enriching education activities outside of the regular school day and school year.

☐   ☐   **5.** The community should serve as a resource for student learning.

☐   ☐   **6.** The community and the school district should work in harmony on issues of mutual concern.

A   D

☐   ☐   **7.** Community members can contribute valuable voluntary resources and services to the schools.

☐   ☐   **8.** Community members can be instrumental and supportive forces for positive change.

☐   ☐   **9.** Community members should recognize the school as a valuable community asset.

☐   ☐   **10.** The community members should share in the responsibility for successes and failures.

☐   ☐   **11.** They should insist on a Mega vision and mission.

☐   ☐   **12.** Other (please list).

BELIEFS ABOUT ADMINISTRATORS

A   D

☐   ☐   **1.** Administrators should cooperatively establish a Mega vision and should disseminate that vision to all stakeholder groups.

☐   ☐   **2.** They should be knowledgeable about child growth and development, curriculum construction and alignment, learning modes, supervision, and exemplary management theories and practices.

☐   ☐   **3.** They should know how to manage, monitor, and work with people.

☐   ☐   **4.** They should focus on student learning and mastery, and they should encourage close monitoring of student achievement and the supplying of feedback.

☐   ☐   **5.** Administrators should provide instructional support for teachers.

☐   ☐   **6.** They should practice effective supervision, including growth target identification, monitoring, conferencing, feedback, and evaluation.

☐   ☐   **7.** Administrators are responsible for developing and maintaining a safe, orderly, and healthy environment.

☐   ☐   **8.** Administrators should be role models for teachers and students.

A   D

☐   ☐   9. They should spend most of their time on matters related to instruction, student performance, and learners' success in and beyond school.

☐   ☐   10. They should establish high expectations for behavior and achievement for students, employees, and for themselves.

☐   ☐   11. Other (please list).

BELIEFS ABOUT GOVERNANCE

A   D

☐   ☐   1. The operation of the school district must be a shared responsibility of the community, the board of education, learners, and the employees of the district.

☐   ☐   2. Governance decisions should be based upon a balance between the academic and human needs, wants, and expectations and the requirements of the students.

☐   ☐   3. Governance decisions should be made on the basis of long-term planning to achieve the vision of "What Should Be".

☐   ☐   4. Governance decisions should be based upon the beliefs of the district and on the trending information garnered from internal and external scanning activities.

☐   ☐   5. Other (please list).

Alternative Additional Approaches

Beliefs may also be harvested by asking the planning partners to respond to a series of questions in each of the above categories of "I believe that (learners, etc.) _____."

Once all the beliefs have been identified, other approaches to focusing the magnitude or priorities of the beliefs include: (1) a five or seven point rating scale indicating the relative strength of each of the beliefs, (2) a listing of "What Is" and "What Should Be" for each belief, and (3) a selection of the top five (or ten) beliefs, and the five (or ten) least important beliefs. Abbreviated examples of each of these approaches will identify their uses.

AN EXAMPLE SCALE

BELIEFS ABOUT LEARNERS (Circle the number 1, 2, 3, 4 or 5, where 5 is the strongest belief and 1 is the weakest belief.)

All Learners

1	2	3	4	5	can learn
1	2	3	4	5	develop at different rates
1	2	3	4	5	should have a safe and healthy environment
1	2	3	4	5	must have social as well as intellectual experiences
1	2	3	4	5	should feel good about the school they attend
1	2	3	4	5	should feel that their input is important
1	2	3	4	5	have varying learning styles
1	2	3	4	5	are capable of self-discipline
1	2	3	4	5	should develop a strong self-image
1	2	3	4	5	should develop the ability to think rationally
1	2	3	4	5	should understand and respect cultural, religious and ethnic differences
1	2	3	4	5	should understand and utilize technology
1	2	3	4	5	should develop an understanding of democracy
1	2	3	4	5	Other (please list)

A seven point scale would accomplish the same purpose, but it allows the raters a wider array of rankings. Also, the seven point (or for that matter, the five point) scale could utilize words instead of numbers to anchor the ratings. For example, the scale could state (a) the most important, (b) next to the most important, (c) very important, (d) important, (e) somewhat important, (f) of little importance, and (g) of no importance. Of course, a scale could be devised using numbers or using words other than those listed.

Using these phrases the scale would resemble the five point scale. In either case, scaling assists the stakeholders in selecting the relative importance of each belief, and this is helpful as they continue strategic planning.

USING A "WHAT IS" AND "WHAT SHOULD BE" ANALYSIS

BELIEFS ABOUT PARENTS OR GUARDIANS (For each belief listed on the following pages, write a statement of the current state ("What Is") and a statement of the desired state ("What Should Be").

Parents and guardians are major stakeholders and they should have input into major decisions related to their child's education.

"What Is"

_____.

"What Should Be"

_____.

They should be made aware of teacher expectations.

"What Is"

_____.

"What Should Be"

_____.

They should actively support teachers' efforts.

"What Is"

_____.

"What Should Be"

_____.

They should set high expectations for their children.

"What Is"

_____.

"What Should Be"

_____.

They should experience positive contacts with school personnel.

"What Is"

_____.

"What Should Be"

_____.

Parents have the responsibility to seek assistance if their child requires help.

"What Is"

_____.

"What Should Be"

_____.

Parents should positively reinforce their child's efforts.

"What Is"

_____.

"What Should Be"

_____.

They must establish education/learning for future self-sufficiency as a high priority.

"What Is"

_____.

"What Should Be"

_____.

Parents must take an active interest in their child's education.

"What Is"

_____.

"What Should Be"

_____.

Parents should provide opportunities for their children to become self-disciplined.

"What Is"

_____.

"What Should Be"

_____.

Parents should serve as role models.

"What Is"

_____.

"What Should Be"

_____.

Other (please list).

"What Is"

_____.

"What Should Be"

_____.

A "What Is" and "What Should Be" analysis of beliefs assists the stake-holders in determining the discrepancy level that exists for each belief. In turn, this method of identifying the gaps assists in prioritizing actions to be taken. They can then decide the tactics they wish to utilize to close the "gap".

It is crucial that a stakeholders' group, which has identified numerous beliefs, find some method of determining which are the most important, which are the most crucial to the mission (to move toward the vision) of the district, and which require the most immediate action to implement. The final method of having stakeholders list the five (or ten) most and least important beliefs is a very useful method in establishing priorities or relative values. If, for example, there are one hundred original beliefs and the ten most and least important are identified, eighty beliefs remain. These eighty can then be put through the same decision process. The sixty, forty, and twenty remaining can also be prioritized, using the same methodology. Many "beliefs" are usually dropped or merged.

Many of the beliefs listed by the stakeholders will reflect the organization's culture. It is crucial that strategic planners understand the culture of the organization in order to take advantage of that culture, and in order to avoid traps as the strategic planning evolves.

The Organizational Culture[2]

WHAT IT IS

As do people, organizations have personalities—unique ways they do their "business" and ways in which the employees transact with each other and their outside worlds. Organizational culture is a composite of the values and beliefs of its people. Definitions could include:

- the way we do things
- what we stand for
- the symbols we use and honor
- our philosophy and approach
- the way we interact among ourselves and with our clients

All of these describe key characteristics of an organization's essence, be-ing, and existence.

HOW ORGANIZATIONAL CULTURE IS REVEALED

An organization often expresses its values and beliefs in existing vision statements (Chapter 5) and/or its mission statement (Chapter 6). Others use symbols [8] to express their culture (rituals, types of buildings, modes of dress, types or organizational charts, levels of formality, etc.). Organizations, in the final analysis, are what they do.

The values and beliefs which make up a successful organization's culture generally are shared by all members, are used to shape and fine-tune the organization, and are clearly stated [22]. Successful organizations' cultures are in harmony with the external world. The successful organizations deliberately intend to make a useful contribution to their external world society.

While each organization has its unique culture, organizations vary in the extent to which each culture is formalized and clearly understood. When doing strategic planning, the nature (both known and informal) of the organizational culture can be very important in (a) getting the process understood and accepted, and (b) knowing what tools and techniques are likely to be effective.

UNEARTHING AN ORGANIZATION'S CULTURE

In understanding an organization's culture, you may have to become a sleuth and observe some of the following indicators:

(1) Stated values and beliefs (read the charter of the organization; scan the organization's literature to see what the organization says about itself; read the minutes, policy statements, mission objectives, stated visions; study the architecture; discover the symbols used and shown to others)

(2) Look for the "heroes" which serve as current and past role models (former founders, board members, chief executive officers, extraordinary teachers, important citizens)

(3) Rituals (how new employees are "broken in"; patterns and frequency of meetings at the various levels of operation; who eats with whom, when, and where; how accomplishments are recognized; who gets the merit pay; who socializes with whom, when, and where; how school is started and ended)

(4) Communication patterns and channels (who talks and writes to whom, when, why, and how responded to; paper trails versus oral communication; gossip; spies; soothsayers; liars)

(5) Responses to good and bad news ("we did it", panic, denial, "make it right", head-on, dodging bullets, celebration, sharing the goodies, stealing the limelight)

The culture of any educational organization can be scanned and understood. What you find represents the personality dynamics of the operation. Realize that your observation represents "What Is". Recall that one function of strategic planning may be to derive a different "What Should Be".

TRUST AND MUTUALITY: THE CORE OF STRATEGIC THINKING AND PLANNING

An important reason for studying the organizational culture is to determine the readiness for strategic thinking and planning. In an atmosphere of trust, non-territoriality and mutual interest and support, strategic planning is most possible.

Often a missing component is a well-defined and common "North Star"—a shared destination which benefits all—a win-win situation (the caring about all of the educational partners and their self-sufficiency, self-reliance, mutual contributions, and quality of life offers a worthy shared mission). Very early in the strategic planning process, agreement on a shared beneficial reality and selection of strategic planning as a prime vehicle for defining and getting there are essential. The questions in Table 2.2 offer the basis for a dialogue on finding and committing to a set of organizational values for planning and accomplishment.

Once the organization's culture has been identified, the focus taken by the stakeholders' planning group makes a significant difference in the final strategic planning project. In other words, the planners who view their planning from the Mega view will likely differ from the planning group that view planning from the Macro view, and both the Mega and Macro view planners will probably differ in approach from the stakeholders' planning group which views planning from a Micro view. This difference can be amplified by presenting an example of each approach utilizing a university, a school district, and an individual school building as model organizations.

Mega View Strategic Planning: A University Organization Example

The university planning group has decided to start its planning with a Mega view, work through a Macro view, and end with a Micro view. The

Mega view is one that encompasses society as the primary client and beneficiary, the Macro encompasses the university as the entity, and the Micro view represents the various colleges within the university as the primary client. At this juncture, it is crucial that differences among the terms beliefs, values, and wishes be defined as they relate to the strategic planning process. Each relates to currently unexamined bases for making decisions:

BELIEFS are those perceptions based upon fact or that are projected as becoming factual at some point in the future. An example belief is that science can discover cures for all diseases.

VALUES are those perceptions concerning chosen alternatives, methods, or conditions which are relatively stable and held in high esteem by an individual or group. An example value is that all persons must operate in an ethical manner.

WISHES are those items that an individual or group desires to happen. They may or may not be based upon fact, and they may or may not be related to a bedrock value. They usually relate to means.

Now that definitions are in place, the university example of beliefs can be examined. The stakeholders' planning group at the university, utilizing a Mega (societal view) focus, reached consensus on the following beliefs:

- All persons can be provided with sufficient nutritious food and safe water.
- A cure, sooner or later, can be found for all diseases.
- All persons can obtain a basic literacy standard.
- A global understanding about mutual self-sufficiency, self-reliance, and shared inter-relations must be promoted if the United States is to remain influential in the world's scheme of things and world peace achieved.
- People are inherently good.
- While perfection probably can never be reached, we can get increasingly close.

The university stakeholders' planning group had not only reached consensus on the Mega level beliefs, but it also decided that the university has four basic functions to perform: (1) research, (2) service, (3) publication and communication of research findings, and (4) teaching. Once the social view had been decided upon, the planning group next determined the university's role in causing these beliefs to become fact. The university or organizational level is the Macro focus, while the colleges, depart-

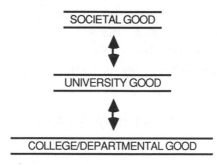

FIGURE 4.1 The Mega, Macro, and Micro foci for a university.

ments, and activities within the university, constitute the Micro focus. Figure 4.1 depicts the three planning levels for a university.

Often the discussion of beliefs prematurely raises a feasibility question: "How could we get that done?" Rather than discourage the planning partners, list the possible ways and means they generate, and let it be known that the list identifies "place holders" for later consideration and possible selection when tactics and strategies are picked (Chapter 11) and once all of the requirements have been established.

Looking Ahead: Could We Be Successful?

Now, a few examples of strategic goals for the Macro and Micro levels will illustrate some of the specific directions taken. These goal directions should be reviewed for usefulness and compatibility with needs, visions, and missions as well as (later in the planning process) supplemented by detailed action plans (as discussed in Chapter 11). Here are some tentative strategies the planners considered, and the ones to be utilized will be selected after each is analyzed for best fit.

MACRO UNIVERSITY STRATEGIC GOAL EXAMPLES

(1) The university will obtain $10,000,000 in grant money over the next five years to open and operate a research center to discover a cure for AIDS.

(2) The university will obligate itself to developing methods for higher corn and wheat yields.

(3) The university will cooperate with language arts teachers in inner city elementary schools for the purpose of finding ways to improve the literacy levels of children in those schools.

(4) The university will modify its freshman requirements in order to provide a more global view of society.

MICRO COLLEGE STRATEGIC GOAL EXAMPLES

(1) By the year 1999, the medical staff of the newly created center for AIDS research will have discovered means of reducing the negative effects of AIDS and, hopefully, will have found a cure.

(2) By 1995, the Agriculture School's scientists will have produced hybrids for corn and wheat that will increase the yield of each by a minimum of fifty percent without reductions in food value.[4]

(3) The staff of the School of Education will create new partnerships with a minimum of ten inner city elementary schools. Together with the schools' staffs, they will have developed techniques and tactics that will prove that the children's reading scores on a nationally validated normed test have improved by a minimum of ten percentile points. This improvement is to take place, at the latest, by 1994.

(4) The staff in social sciences will combine their talents to provide required courses in global understanding to all freshmen. They will provide foreign exchange opportunities for all students above the freshman level. A ten year follow-up study will prove that students who have gone through this more intensive global studies orientation have a superior understanding of global conditions when compared with a control group which has not been exposed to the global orientation, and at least 40 percent of them are making a global contribution.

Now, possible direction can be taken because a Mega planning focus has been described. It is time to turn to an example which utilizes a Macro planning focus. The Macro focus example will involve a public school district.

A MACRO STRATEGIC PLANNING VIEW: A LOCAL SCHOOL DISTRICT EXAMPLE

The local school district stakeholders included representatives of all parties who had an interest in its activities. A committee of thirty people was organized, and the membership had representatives from the student body, parents, teachers, administrators, non-teaching employees, general citizenry, local government, civic organizations, business, and industry. All identified organizations or interest groups were asked to nominate two persons who would represent them on this very important central district planning committee. This group worked diligently for a period of two months, and the members derived a list of beliefs. Some of these building block beliefs are listed below:

- Although the time necessary to do so may vary, all children can learn.
- A safe and healthy environment is necessary.
- Student achievement shall be the primary measure of success when assessing the effectiveness of the school district's programs.
- All persons in the organization must have high expectations of students, and they must hold high expectations for their own performance.
- Parental and community support is necessary if the school district is to prosper and fulfill its commitment to student learning.
- Adequate human, financial and material resources must somehow be delivered in order for the school district to meet its commitment to high quality student learning.
- A positive climate shall exist in the school district. This climate can be assessed by measuring the degree to which such factors as: (1) high expectations, (2) high results, (3) caring, (4) trusting, (5) recognition, and (6) opportunities for input are present.

Although the list of beliefs agreed upon by the school district's strategic planning committee is a very important inventory, it neglects or assumes the broader impact on society that would have been broached had the planning focus initially been Mega. That is, the district's planning committee would have focused on their societal beliefs and, then, moved to the role of the school district in attempting to cause these beliefs to turn into specific products. There is no statement in the Macro focus listing that the planners developed (although it might be implied) that they expect students to ultimately become productive members of a global society. Instead, the Macro focus led the planners to list beliefs that dealt specifically with the school district environment.

It can be assumed that once the school district level has reached consensus on its beliefs, the individual schools within the district would be free to develop their own *related* belief statements. A caveat exists, however. Even though the individual building levels could develop belief statements that may vary somewhat from those of the district, the building level beliefs could not be in conflict with those of the school district level.

To complete the Mega, Macro and Micro examples, the discussion will now focus on the Micro level of strategic planning. That is, the hypothetical example shall present the beliefs arrived at by the local school building level planners for an elementary school and by the planners for a nursery (preschool) school.

MICRO FOCUSED STRATEGIC PLANNING: A LOCAL ELEMENTARY SCHOOL BUILDING EXAMPLE

The planners at the local school building level, the principal and whomever she/he wishes to include in the strategic planning process, can approach planning from a Mega (societal), Macro (school district level), or Micro (school building level/curriculum/course) focus. The results of their planning will look significantly different, depending upon the focal view used. The example discussed assumes a Micro planning focus, and the beliefs arrived at demonstrate this rather myopic focus.

- Each student shall be taught in accordance with his/her individually planned educational program.
- Active parental involvement is a requirement.
- Cooperative learning by designing vertical teams is the preferred mode of delivery.
- Teachers and administrators shall be provided a site-based continuous staff development program designed to meet their specifically identified needs and characteristics.
- Support for the school's programs and efforts must be available from the board of education, the superintendent, and the central office staff.
- School climate must be positive and high.
- The principal must demonstrate strong instructional leadership.
- Time on task must be maximized.[3] That is, engaged time (the time students are actually engaged in learning, usually with a mastery level of 85% or greater) must be monitored and preserved.
- Student achievement must be expected, must be at a high level, must be carefully monitored, and must be used as a signal to modify instructional content or methods of instructional delivery.
- Social development is a key purpose of education.

Although there are a few beliefs overlapping with the Macro beliefs, the building-level beliefs are much more specific. They may or may not have an influence on what happens in other school buildings in the district. Certainly, the Micro approach utilized by the school building's planners does nothing to identify or purposely assist, in any systematic way, the achievement of beliefs which are societal in nature.

MICRO FOCUSED STRATEGIC PLANNING: APPLE PIE PRESCHOOL EXAMPLE

The owner of Apple Pie Preschool and the staff have assembled a planning group consisting of representative parents of the children they serve. The owner has also recruited a child psychologist and a kindergarten teacher for the local school district to serve as planning team members. The planning group is divided into two Micro-focused groups, one planning team for the one month to one year group, and one planning team for the two to five year olds (if the focus would have been on the entire nursery school, the planning focus would have been of the Macro type). The beliefs arrived at for each group demonstrate the lack of Macro (and Mega) focus. Obviously, the two Micro-focused beliefs should be combined into a set of beliefs for the entire Apple Pie Preschool. Then a holistic direction is provided for the strategic planning activities which would follow the statement of beliefs (using a rolling up approach).

The beliefs of the one month to one year planning group were:

- A nurturing environment is a necessity.
- The parent(s) of the children should be provided with information and training in nurturing these youngsters.
- A system of continuous (daily if necessary) communication between the teacher and the parent should be a reality.
- The health and safety requirements of the child while at the school should be guaranteed.

The beliefs of the one- to five-year-old group were:

- The children should be taught listening skills.
- They should be taught social skills (e.g., how to get along with other children).
- The children should be taught verbal skills.
- They should be encouraged to be creative. An example would be students making up stories, and the teachers writing the students' stories on large newsprint.

- The environment should be one that emphasizes happiness, health, safety, and success.
- Special attention should be provided for "children-at-risk".
- Parenting classes should be offered to all who place their children in the care of Apple Pie Preschool.

Notice that many of these "beliefs" deal with means (being taught) and not ends (mastery). Means are activities or methods, while ends are results.

Not only do differences exist because of the planning focus utilized, but differences exist in some significant ways between the strategic planning in private schools as compared to public schools. In each case, however, the planning focus can be of the Mega, Macro, or Micro type.

Let's explore some of the variables or concerns that must be addressed from a private school's view when compared to a public school's view. Further, let's also address some similarities as both types proceed with their strategic planning.

Similarities and Differences between Private and Public School Strategic Planning

A private school in the inner city, a private school for the affluent, and a private religious school may differ somewhat in beliefs, strategic goals, and action plans when viewing society, their total organization, and their individual unit. In other words, private schools, like public schools, will differ in the degree of their planning concerns and approaches. A public school in a wealthy suburb may more closely resemble a private school in a wealthy suburb than it will a public school in the inner city or in a rural area. For this purpose, however, a chart such as that shown in Figure 4.2 will display the major differences that should be accounted for when conducting strategic planning for a private or public school (obviously, these differences will be generalizations which may not hold true when applied to a specific situation).

The listing of possible differences in Figure 4.2 demonstrates a Macro focus. If a Mega focus were taken, the variations would be considerably reduced. On the other hand, differences would increase if a Micro focus were chosen. Regardless of the foci chosen, some overlap would probably appear even in the areas listed as differing between public and private

Variable or Item	Public	Private
• Choice of planning focus (mega,macro, or micro)	Same	Same
• Societal view	Differ	Differ
• Curriculum*	Same Differ	Differ Differ
• Funding	Differ	Differ
• Mega view (if used)	Same	Same
• Macro view	Differ	Differ
• Micro view	Differ	Differ
• Focus on student achievement	Same	Same
• Type of stakeholders	Differ	Differ
• Support systems	Differ	Differ
• Stakeholder involvement	Probably Differ	Probably Differ
• Community-at-large invlovement	Differ	Differ
• Role of principle, headmaster, or administrator	Probably Differ	Probably Differ
• Expectations of students after graduation	Probably Differ	Probably Differ

* In the area of curriculum, the private school might well opt for a traditional liberal arts curriculum and the public school might well offer a more comprehensive curriculum. On the other hand, both might offer identical or similar comprehensive curriculums.

FIGURE 4.2 Major possible differences for which the strategic planners must account when dealing with private or public schools.

schools. Let's examine a few illustrative examples to demonstrate overlap and demonstrate the changes that would probably result if the foci would shift from a Macro to a Mega focus or to a Micro focus.

In the area of curriculum, a Mega view would probably result in the study of world interdependency, cultural studies, and technological interchange. The Micro view might cause differences in the content of religious studies programs, the emphasis placed on certain topics in biological science, and in the manner in which the subjects are taught by individual teachers. On the other hand, the content of English courses, the method of teaching music, and the content of mathematics courses probably would be very similar, varying perhaps only in terms of the relevant examples used in teaching. If the Macro view was utilized, differences could appear between and among private schools which were strictly college preparatory, private schools which emphasized the teachings of a particular religious sect, and public schools which offered a comprehensive program. Even in the Macro-focused schools, however, common practices would appear in some of the basic skill subjects and in many of the teaching methods utilized.

In the variable area of the type of stakeholders, similarities and differences would again appear when comparing public and private schools and their planning structures. Representative students, parents, teachers, administrators, and support groups would probably be included in the stakeholders' groups of both the public and private schools' strategic planning committees. The differences that would exist, however, would probably be that the public school would have very broad representation from the community at large, the private college preparatory school would have a somewhat narrower representation, and the private school of a specific religious sect would probably have an even narrower representation on its stakeholder committee.

Now that the Macro, Mega, and Micro views which guide strategic planners have been reviewed, and the differences that must be kept in mind when conducting strategic planning for private and public schools have been explored, it is reasonable to turn to the uses of belief statements as the process of strategic planning proceeds. The belief statements arrived at by consensus of a stakeholders' strategic planning group become foundation documents upon which the entire finalized strategic plan rests. Sometimes consensus on beliefs must wait until visions and needs data have been collected to supply alternative points of view, and "hard" data consensus should be obtained at any point possible or revisited at each segment of the strategic planning process.

Uses of Belief Statements within the Process of Strategic Planning

Agreed-upon beliefs should be combined with other information. Data is collected by (a) scanning the external (outside the organization doing the planning) environment, (b) scanning the internal (within the organization) environment, along with (c) agreed-upon Critical Success

Factors (CSFs) — see Chapter 5 for further explanation — which absolutely must be in place to produce a high-quality school, school district, or university. These combined data create the building blocks which allow the strategic planners to develop their data base and vision of "What Is" and "What Should Be" at some future point in time. The belief statement is also a primary aid in developing a mission statement (as discussed in Chapter 6). This type of statement is a brief description of what the organization or institution sees as its reason for existence, or a statement of organizational purpose.

The vision of "What Should Be", coupled with the mission objective of the organization, allows the planners to have purposes and guidelines clearly in mind as they proceed with (1) the consideration of new missions, and (2) the development of the strategic plan related to those missions. The planners can go about developing strategic goals, objectives, and action programs which will cause achievement of the desired future vision. If the beliefs have not been identified as an initial step in the strategic planning process, the strategic plan may very well be doomed to failure because: (1) the culture of the organization has not been identified and considered in the planning, (2) new beliefs have not been considered, (3) the stakeholders do not have an agreed-upon set of beliefs from which programs, strategies, and outcomes can be identified and developed, and (4) there are no base-line values for possible reconsideration and revision if there are mismatches between values, needs, and mission. Like the spacecraft operators who have not identified which planet they are to find, the strategic plan will drift this way and that, hoping that the unknown destination will magically be reached.

If beliefs, to be effective, require (a) a basis in future reality and (b) a consensus among the stakeholders, how does one go about achieving consensus? Without consensus, the leader will not have followers, the organization will not be defined on an important element of its culture, and a clear vision will not exist to pull together all those who must support a school, school district, or university. There are a variety of consensus-building techniques available to strategic planners; a few of these helpful tools will be identified.

Consensus-Reaching Techniques

Three helpful consensus-reaching techniques are (1) the Delphi Technique, (2) the Fishbowl Technique, and (3) the Telstar Technique. In each case these formats are devised to cause consensus to be reached from viewpoints that may initially be disparate. In each case, the length of time it takes to attain consensus will vary from group to group, but eventually consensus will be reached. Consensus result reaching is a process that cannot be rushed; whatever time is required to reach consensus, it is time well spent. Unity of purpose and action is the result if the planners are patient. Remember that consensus is not necessarily identical to validity.

THE DELPHI TECHNIQUE

The Delphi Technique is one for reaching consensus without face-to-face meetings of the participants, where all participants are asked to perform an initial listing function. In the case of beliefs, each participant would be asked to write out her/his list of beliefs that should be included in a consensus listing to guide the school, school district, or university. An individual, who is assigned to that function by the planning team, will then collect and collate all the initial belief statements. These initial statements would then be forwarded to all participants with the request that they indicate with which belief statements they agree, and with which they disagree. The participants are also asked to suggest alterations to those statements with which they could agree if some wording changes were made [12,48].

The planner then assembles this second list of statements, clearly indicating the statements in their original and modified forms, and indicating how many participants agreed with each statement. The planner then redistributes this listing and requests each participant to modify what she/he must in order to arrive at agreement on the belief.

This process continues as many times as necessary to arrive at a consensus of beliefs. In other words, unanimous beliefs, or, at the very least, those beliefs which they will allow, can be used to guide further planning steps.

The procedure would follow this sequence of events:

(1) Each participant would be asked to write a statement of beliefs related to such matters as the role of the parents and community in planning for an educational institution, what and how children should be taught and treated, what is expected of the teachers and administrators, what the world of 2020 should be like, and other topical areas that should be explored. The nature of the beliefs considered will be shaped by the planning level selected.

(2) The beliefs of each individual would then be copied and distributed to all other individual participants.

(3) Each participant would then be asked to indicate the items with which they agree and the items with which they disagree, and these are returned to the educational institution.

(4) The beliefs are then listed in two columns, one for those which are agreed-upon (with the number of persons agreeing indicated) and the other for which agreement has not been found. These listings are then provided to each participant with a request that those not agreed-upon by the majority be restated in such a way that the respondent would then agree to the belief.

(5) The procedure listed in step 4 is then repeated until consensus is achieved.

THE FISHBOWL TECHNIQUE

The Fishbowl Technique is one where the planners divide a large group of stakeholders into sub-groups of six to eight persons who meet to reach consensus on a statement of beliefs. When each of the sub groups (for example, eight sub-groups) has finished its belief statements each group elects a representative to present its beliefs to the total membership of the large group. This is generally accomplished by having the representatives seated in a circle facing one another. All other members are seated outside the discussion circle. However, to permit those persons who are not selected as the sub-group representatives to address any topic as the dialogue among the representatives proceeds, an empty chair is placed in the circle.

Assuming that all sub-groups have completed their belief statements, this procedure then proceeds to discuss each of the subgroup's belief statements until consensus is achieved. An example might be the belief that all students can learn.

In this example, one group states the belief that all students could learn. The spokesperson for this group explains that the group members believe that all children, regardless of their intellectual capacity, can learn what the school chooses to teach. The spokesperson from another group states that certain severely handicapped youngsters cannot learn anything. A very excited member of the audience jumps into the empty chair and loudly states that though it may take longer for some children to learn than others, all children can learn what the school chooses to teach. A spokesperson in the circle from another group states that the school may wish to select different presentation styles and different content depending upon the needs and characteristics of the child or group of students being taught; but, indeed, all children can learn what the school decides to teach.

This dialogue continues with a discussion on the quality of the learning that takes place, and a whole range of individual student differences are discussed. Eventually, the entire membership agrees with the belief that all children can learn. The members then go on to discuss another belief that is to be included in or excluded from the belief statement once consensus is achieved.

As the representatives negotiate meanings and beliefs with one another, a member of the larger group may enter the circle and make any comment or statement that she/he wishes to make. The comment may be a clarifying statement, a compromise suggestion, or anything that she/he wants to present. Immediately upon making the statement, however, the person occupying the previously empty chair must leave the discussion circle and cease to participate in the discussion.

This process, as was true with the Delphi Technique, has to be continued until final general consensus is achieved. Consensus can sometimes be quickly reached, while at other instances a significant amount of time and effort is necessary to achieve consensus.

THE TELSTAR TECHNIQUE

The Telstar Technique is similar to the Fishbowl Technique, but it differs significantly in the method of involving all participants and in the degree of involvement that non-representative participants are afforded.

The initial process is to divide the large group into sub-groups. If the process is designed for a school district, the planners may go through the process with each school. They have each school nominate two members to serve as its spokespersons to the district-wide group, which has the ultimate responsibility to reach a consensus on a list of beliefs. This list will guide the district's representative stakeholders' planning group when it continues the work of strategic planning. In this case, let's assume that the number of persons involved at the school building levels varied from forty persons to six hundred persons, and there were eight school buildings in the district. The schools are composed of elementary, middle school, and senior high. If the planners so desire, the larger schools could be allocated a larger number of spokespersons to the district level group.

Also, in this situation, we assume that all buildings have achieved their listing of beliefs, and each building's group of participants has selected a spokesperson and an advisory committee of six persons. This configuration would provide a consensus-reaching discussion group of eight spokespersons, an advisory group for each spokesperson, and as many members as wished to sit in the audience to view the consensus-reaching dialogue.

The eight spokespersons would negotiate with one another to achieve a final listing of guiding beliefs. During the process of negotiations, any member of any of the eight groups' advisory committees could temporarily halt the discussion by calling "time out". This pronouncement would signal an opportunity for all groups' spokespersons to have a caucus with their advisory persons. During the caucus the person calling the "time out" tactic, or any other member of the advisory group, could present a strategy, a proposal, suggestion, or directive to the spokesperson. At the end of the time required for the caucus, as determined by the person calling the "time out", that same individual will call "time in". After "time in" is signaled all advisory groups cease discussion, and the negotiations within the spokespersons' group continues.

This procedure continues, as in the case of Delphi and Fishbowl, until final consensus is reached. This may take a good deal of time, but the planners can be quite certain that they will have formulated a consensus of beliefs that will be supported by large numbers of the district's constituents. This fact, in itself, will enhance the chances of gathering support for the final strategic plan that is developed.

It seems appropriate, now, to provide a few guidelines that may be used for those persons responsible for the development of strategic plans for their university, school district, or school building.

Guidelines for Strategic Planners Who Are Responsible for Arriving at a Statement of Beliefs

- Strategic planning is a process that cannot be rushed. This is especially true when attempting to reach agreement upon a statement of beliefs.
- Involve a truly representative stakeholders' group in the planning process. The stakeholders' group should be representative of students, parents, community, teachers, administrators, businesses in the area, civic clubs, other governmental units, industries in the area, and any other influential organization or unit which has a stake in the programs and results of the schooling that is offered.

- Planning may take place at the Mega, Macro, and/or Micro level. If the university, school district, or school building planners choose the Mega level, they must make certain that the Macro and Micro levels are aligned with the Mega level.
- Encourage the Mega approach to strategic planning.
- Beliefs which focus on ends (rather than means) will be most useful in later planning steps.
- Techniques for consensus-reaching must be employed when dealing with large numbers of people. The consensus-reaching techniques identified as Delphi, Telstar, and Fishbowl provide three concrete example formats for this purpose. Other techniques are also available to the strategic planner.
- Existing beliefs should be examined for current fit with both external reality and other stakeholders' perceptions. If they are not relevant, they should be replaced with valid ones.
- Beliefs must closely be related to the desired vision, needs, and the institutional mission. They should serve as guidelines for arriving at strategic goals and objectives.
- Beliefs which are agreed upon by large numbers of stakeholders provide the bedrock foundation for the remainder of the strategic planning process. Thus, the development of a statement of beliefs must be considered a crucial step in the total strategic planning process. There will be opportunities to revisit and modify the derived beliefs as the planning process develops.
- The consensus-building techniques may be utilized at any of the data-collecting and planning steps.

Glossary

Belief: a statement based upon fact or one which is projected as becoming factual at some point in the future.

Macro Focus: strategic planning that begins with beliefs about the total organization as its goal.

Mega Focus: strategic planning that begins with beliefs about society as its goal.

Micro Focus: strategic planning that begins with beliefs about a subgroup within the total organization. It may be a college within a university, or it may be an individual school or course within a school district.

Strategic Planning: long term planning designed to achieve a future useful vision of "What Should Be".

Values: perceptions about the choices of methods, means, things, or conditions which are relatively stable and are held in high esteem by an individual or group.

Wish: something that an individual or a group desires to effect. It may or may not be based upon fact, and it may or may not be related to a value.

Exercises

1. Define strategic planning which includes beliefs and values.

2. Define a belief. Give five examples of beliefs. Classify these in terms of whether or not they target means or ends.

3. List three beliefs each from the Mega, Macro, and Micro foci. Determine whether or not the three levels of beliefs are in line with one another. If they are not aligned, what would you do to get them aligned?

4. Name three consensus-reaching techniques presented in this chapter. Identify situations wherein you would apply each of the techniques. Read the literature and identify two more possibilities.

5. Why, and under what conditions, would you choose a Mega focus when doing strategic planning? Present an example.

6. Why, and under what conditions, would you choose a Macro focus for your strategic planning? Present an example.

7. Why, and under what conditions, would you choose a Micro focus when developing a strategic plan? Present an example.

8. What are the possible payoffs and penalties for not using a Mega focus?

9. Why is it important to involve stakeholders in the process of arriving at a statement of beliefs? How would you proceed to do this for your organization?

10. Why might some of the stakeholders later choose to modify their beliefs? Provide two examples.

11. Why are beliefs, needs, and current missions considered BEFORE selecting strategies and tactics?

12. Where in the thirteen-step strategic planning process might consensus-building methods be used? Why?

Endnotes

1 For further belief exercises, see "The Personal Value Statement (PVS): An Experiential Learning Instrument" by J. E. Oliver, 1985. In L. D. Goodstein and J. W. Pfeiffer (Eds.), The 1985 Annual: De-

veloping Human Resources (pp. 107–116) San Diego, CA: University Associates.

2 There are many different terms for describing how an organization does things and how it sees itself. While not identical, some often used terms include corporate climate, corporate identity, and corporate personality.

3 Notice that the planners either ignored or chose not to use the wider-scoped "Academic Learning Time" which includes time on task *plus* performance and feedback to mastery.

4 While both of these products (a cure for AIDS and high-yield corn) have major contributions to mega level results, they themselves are micro-level results.

Identifying Visions

A vision is a clear statement of what the strategic planners desire her/his organization to look like and deliver, as well as describe the environment in which it will operate. Visioning is the process of identifying the "ideal" world or constructing the "best or preferred future" desired before injecting reality data. In the recommended "Mega focus," a vision is the description of the future world of education and social context as seen by the planning partners. It contains the basic elements of the entire system, including society, the school system, parents, learners, teachers, and other important elements.

The basis for visioning requires letting go of "What Is," and describing a desired statement of "What Should Be" and "What Could Be." A subsequent set of activities takes place after the planners agree on a vision: (1) reach consensus on beliefs, (2) conduct an internal scan of the organization, (3) conduct a scan of the external environment, and (4) identify the organization's Critical Success Factors (CSFs) in order to reach agreement on a preferred future from which a mission objective will be developed.

Using a Mega planning focus, planners follow a path to visioning. A few suggestions will suffice to start you toward developing a vision:

- Don't "hold back" on your vision merely because of practical considerations, politics, or present financing vehicles.
- Share your vision with others to identify: (1) common elements, (2) unique elements, and (3) trends and directions.
- Reach consensus on a vision that all important stakeholders can accept.
- Know that visions begin the development of strategies, tactics, and action plans.

Two vision-setting approaches are possible. The most usual one is to build a vision declaration in an inside-out (or rolling-up) fashion by

89

initially identifying current results, realities, and conditions before developing a "do-able" statement. The other, and recommended approach, is to first define an "ideal" vision, in an outside-in (or rolling-down) mode, and then derive the building-block objectives to get there. The recommended proactive approach will avoid limiting one's creativity and energies to only making the current system more efficient. The ingredients for both approaches, however, are presented in this chapter.

This chapter will discuss prerequisite activities as well as alternate and preferred futuring. In this way, alternate and preferred futuring may be done by conducting a trend analysis, or by taking a ten year (or more) leap into the future to conjure up what the organization can or should look like at that point in time. It is important to define the vision *before* employing "what is" data.

Vision

A vision is the statement of the desired or required community (and/or world) in which the educational system will operate and contribute (for it cannot do the "whole thing"). One useful approach to visioning is to ask the planning partners to define the type of community and world in which they want their children and grandchildren to live (see Appendix).

The vision statement identifies results (such as "no crime, everyone self-sufficient and self-reliant, each person and group will contribute to all others' well-being"). When developing a vision statement, it's difficult to keep people from inserting strongly held methods and means (such as values education, strict discipline, and computer education) but it is important—even vital—to reserve all possible how-to-do-its until the vision and mission have been selected.

Some planning partners might think it's "idealistic" to define a "perfect" world, and want to jump directly into the "practical, here-and-now, achievable" statements of purpose. We urge that since a human's reach exceeds one's grasp, that an "ideal" vision should be first derived, and then the "practical" stepping-stone milestones and objectives could be derived from that. A relationship between an ideal vision and the "practical" strategic planning objectives may be seen in the illustration at the top of page 91. It is also suggested that strategic planning start with setting the "ideal vision" (even if we are not likely to get there in the foreseeable

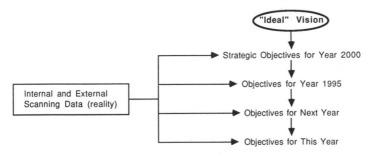

future) before collecting and using any of the internal and external scanning data.

After setting the "ideal" vision, and obtaining agreement on beliefs and values, the en-route or building-block objectives may be set. By moving in this suggested sequence, the planners will not be limited to a reactive set of strategic objectives. They will also set a course toward a better world that the partners desire . . . step-by-step towards a common "North Star."

After a consensus, for now, has been reached by the strategic planning group on a vision statement and a list of beliefs,[1] the group can turn to the next activity—conducting an internal scan. The scanning process allows perceptions about beliefs and visions to be compared with objective reality. From this, the preferred future (and related mission) may be selected.

Internal Scanning: Testing for Reality

It is important for strategic planners to collect data that may have an impact on the educational institution and on the society for which they are planning. These data may come from economic, political, demographic, or other sources. If we were to take as our planning base a local school building, some of the data that we might scan, and from which trends may be identified and projections made, could include: (1) student related data, (2) school climate related data, (3) human resource related data, (4) school board policy and other internal politics related data, and (5) finance and other resource related data.

STUDENT RELATED DATA

Such data, concerning learners, from a single year provide a status picture of "What Is". However, when these data are collected over a period of years, they form trends useful in making decisions. These trends can also be projected into the future; and, therefore, they become useful in deciding upon the "What Should Be" and "What Could Be" future scenarios.

Student data should be disaggregated in terms of sex, age, economic levels, cultural values, or other variables that may provide useful information. Student achievement data broken down into different categories allow planners to determine possible discrepancies in performance. For example, for learners in English classes, identify possible important relationships such as between male and female students and determine if students from lower socio-economic level homes are not achieving as well in reading as students from high socio-economic level homes.

Trends in test scores for the entire student body or for any subgroup can be helpful in identifying successful teaching strategies, and they can be useful in the identification of problem areas and down trends that require attention. In a school situation, these trends can lead to the formation of strategic goals to be met over time.

Some additional student related data that should be scanned includes:

- the number of students enrolled in total and at each grade level and in each subject or program
- the number and percentage of students who drop out of (or are pushed out of) school
- the number and percentage of students who go on to advanced education or training
- the number and percentage of students who participate in co-curricular activities
- follow-up surveys on prior graduates to determine the areas they feel were helpful and the areas they feel can be improved

SCHOOL CLIMATE RELATED DATA

School climate related data that are important to scan and identify trends over time, are related to variables which indicate the necessary components for a positive and effective school environment where students and employees are both productive and satisfied. School climate data can be collected by a systematic recording of direct observations. It can also be collected by a series of well-designed opinionnaires. Climate variables include such items as:

- a safe and healthy school environment
- a climate based upon the belief that all students can learn
- a climate which places high student achievement as an expectation, and which monitors results to determine the level of student achievement as a means of continuous focus
- a caring relationship towards students by employees and by the students towards one another
- evidence that a mutually trusting relationship exists
- an environment permeated by respect between and among students, employees, supervisors, managers, board members, and community members
- an environment encouraging meaningful input from students, citizens, and employees alike
- a climate where recognition of accomplishment is continuous

Taking the above statements, one could construct an opinionnaire that would look similar to the one below. (This example is of a high school student opinionnaire, but similar questions would be asked of middle school students, elementary students, teachers, or other groups associated with the school. Using a variety of schools and groups would allow comparisons of opinions among them.) If identical opinionnaires were completed by all the individual school buildings, the school climate between buildings could be compared. Then a composite of school climates across the entire school district could be arrayed and analyzed. If the same opinionnaire or a comparable one were completed yearly, trend data would become available. This trend data could identify discrepancies between "What Is" and "What Should Be"; then the needs, so identified, could be attacked by an action program designed to improve the school climate.

Your Opinions About Your School[2]

INSTRUCTIONS: Please fill in the information about yourself in Part 1 by placing an "x" in the correct box, or circling the correct answer, and then let us know how you feel about your school by circling the answer which best expresses your opinion to each question asked in Part 2. DO NOT PLACE YOUR NAME ON THE ANSWER SHEET.

Part 1

I am: ☐ female   ☐ male

I am in grade: 9   10   11   12

I participate in sports, band, or other activities: ☐ yes   ☐ no

Part 2

1. I feel safe when I am in school.   ☐ yes   ☐ no
2. I believe I can learn anything that I wish to learn.   ☐ yes   ☐ no
3. I believe that my teachers and the school prin-   ☐ yes   ☐ no
   cipal believe I can learn and they expect me to do
   well.
4. My teachers are always checking on my progress   ☐ yes   ☐ no
   and the progress of the other students.
5. The principal is concerned about the progress of   ☐ yes   ☐ no
   the students in this school, and she/he regularly
   checks on our progress.
6. I really feel that the teachers and the principal are   ☐ yes   ☐ no
   pleased that I am a student here, and they are
   very friendly towards me.
7. My teachers trust me to do many things, and they   ☐ yes   ☐ no
   give me freedom to make my own decisions.
8. Everyone in this school respects everyone else.   ☐ yes   ☐ no
   This respect is visible between and among stu-
   dents, teachers, administrators, school helpers,
   and parents.
9. Whenever I do something well, I am com-   ☐ yes   ☐ no
   plimented by my teachers and others.
10. Whenever I don't do well, they work with me   ☐ yes   ☐ no
    until I am successful.
11. When the principal finds out about some of my   ☐ yes   ☐ no
    accomplishments, he/she also seeks me out to
    congratulate me.

12. In this school, I have the opportunity to give my   ☐ yes   ☐ no
ideas and thoughts about things that might affect
me in the classroom, in activities, or on other
building level matters which affect students.

13. My teachers are more interested in my achieve-   ☐ yes   ☐ no
ment than they are in my compliance.

If one wished to find out why the students (or others) held the opinions stated in their answers, this could be accomplished by digging more deeply—asking the respondents to give reasons for each "yes" or "no" answer. This might lead one to develop an attitudinal survey or to interview the students. The key to attitudinal surveying is getting answers to the question: "WHY?"

Trending climate data allows strategic planners to identify areas of need (gaps between "What Is" and "What Should Be" for results). It also facilitates the development of intervention strategies and tactics designed to close the gap between "What Is" and "What Should Be".

HUMAN RESOURCE DEVELOPMENT RELATED DATA

Data related to human resource development assists strategic planners in identifying trending patterns about the quantity and quality of employees. These data, in turn, assist in identifying training and staff development requirements. The resulting requirements assist in the identification of the conditions which are prerequisite to hiring and keeping an excellent staff of employees. These data, and projections that can be made from the established trends, assist planners in determining employee placement, recruiting requirements, and the levels of knowledge and skill possessed by the current employee group. Once these projections are made, planners can determine the type of employee to be recruited, the conditions required to retain excellent employees, and the training and staff development opportunities required to maintain a high level of employee productivity.

A few examples of possible employee development activities provide a reference point and illustrate the action programs that strategic planners might put in place to meet the needs identified by a needs assessment (Chapter 7).

- training in technology for rapidly changing areas such as computer applications, robotics, and telecommunications

- training for teachers in such areas as curriculum development, delivery of instruction systems and techniques, curriculum mapping, instructional auditing, mastery learning, values identification, and results-based instructional planning
- training of auto mechanics in the area of electronic repairs for school buses
- training of special education teacher aides on methods usable with students having a wide variety of physical, emotional, and mental handicaps

SCHOOL POLICY AND INTERNAL POLITICS RELATED DATA

Data related to school policy and internal politics can impact the local school building in positive or negative ways. The building principal and her/his planning team can be proactively lobbying the board of education, the superintendent, or whomever is considering a new or modified policy. The proactive stance will enhance the possibility of getting the type of policy statement that is favorable to the building level. Lobbying may increase the probability of providing the building's planners with sufficient flexibility to allow the building level strategic planning to continue unencumbered.

Internal politics, in terms of non-policy activities, can be handled in much the same manner. Based on the data and payoffs, the building level planners can plant the seeds of desired changes in the minds of the district level's power brokers and decision makers. This is achievable through consistently obtaining information from the central decision-makers and by constantly providing input to the power brokers. By orchestrating two-way internal communication, the building level planners can enhance their strategic planning ability.

RESOURCE RELATED DATA

Resource related data involve internal financial support, internal equipment and supply adequacy, and internal allocation of human resources. One can classify issues over the past two decades as resource related when schools addressed such matters as: (1) female interscholastic sports, (2) occupational education, (3) special education, (4) gifted and talented education, (5) child care activities, (6) andragogical programs, (7) community education, (8) values and ethics, (9) work orientation and work habits, and (10) "excellence". It is important that attention be focused on these kinds of data, to determine the consequences each recommendation could have in the future.

Once resource related data has been reviewed, planners can identify which of the recommendations they wish to include in the school's programs, and identify the resources necessary to implement the desired programs. The strategic planners can identify "What Is" and determine the results-referenced gaps (needs) between "What Is" and "What Should Be" as we will see in Chapter 6. This permits strategic goals to be identified over a specific time span, and allows the vision of the future to include positive program changes.

There are also implications for strategic planners from local, state, regional, and national "blue ribbon" task forces (which could be made up of experts in education, demographers,[3] economists, political scientists, or a combination of experts from these various fields). Recommendations from these task forces should be studied to determine the impact each recommendation could have in the future. Once completed, planners can identify which of these recommendations they wish to include in the school's programs, and can determine the resources necessary to implement the desired programs.

Figure 5.1 demonstrates the necessary interrelationships[4] among: the Mega, Macro, and Micro planning scales; the beliefs and values; the

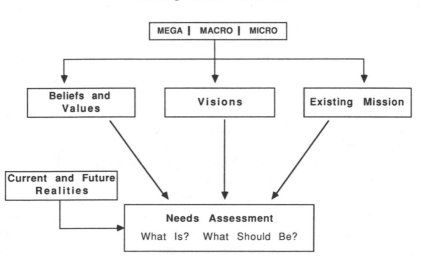

FIGURE 5.1 Relationships among beliefs, visions, existing missions, and needs assessment.

vision; the existing mission; current and future realities; and needs assessment.

While the planning partners might base their visions on beliefs and values, *the strategic planning process encourages a shift in these based on current and future reality and opportunity*. Simply because one comes to the planning process with facts, biases, and stereotypes, does not mean that these should be left unexamined and unchanged. Current and future realities (from internal and external scanning) supply both information and opportunity for constructive change. Openness, reality, and opportunity provide the basis for growth and positive change.

Now that some ideas relating to internal data have been presented and the importance of the scanning activity has been emphasized, we can turn to data from the external environment that could be helpful to scan.

External Scanning: Testing for Reality

The data to be systematically collected from the external environment should include: (1) demographics; (2) attitudes; (3) governmental laws, rules and regulations, and policies; (4) finances; (5) future forecasts and trends; (6) future opportunities; and (7) external political information. The discussion of external data monitoring, scanning, and projecting uses a *university* as its example case study.

DEMOGRAPHIC RELATED DATA

Demographic related data concern possible effects on the numbers and types of students who attend the university. The strategic plan must take into account such matters as the age of the student population. For example, are the students much older than traditional students, and do many of these students attend part time and in the evenings because they hold full-time jobs? Also, attention must be paid to whether or not minorities are appropriately represented within the student body.

If the university draws its student body primarily from one particular region, rather than nationally or internationally, it is important to discover through accurate scanning if the university-age population is diminishing or increasing in that region served. The strategic planners also must determine the character of the curriculum offerings based upon student and university requirements related to the future requirements for survival and contribution.

Some excellent sources for demographic data include: (1) the Census Bureau, (2) university and public libraries, (3) chambers of commerce, (4) the United Way, (5) many financial institutions, (6) numerous businesses and industries, and (7) research publications [38].

ATTITUDE RELATED DATA

Attitude related data are gathered by analyzing newspaper and professional reports; listening to conference and media presentations; and studying the pronouncements of scholars and blue ribbon study groups established by the federal government, the state government, philanthropic organizations, business and industry study groups, and the university itself.

In addition, university planners should carefully monitor legislative trends at the federal and state levels. They may also develop survey instruments designed to discover what the views of alumni, the students, and the taxpaying public are concerning the university's programs and plans.

Study and analysis of data trends provide opportunities for the planners to take two distinct types of actions when developing the university's strategic plan. First, if the attitudinal data indicate dissatisfaction with some program or operation and the university has evidence to support its excellence, the planners could build in a marketing[5] strategy designed to convince those who are critical that the program or operation is, indeed, high-quality. If on the other hand, the attitudinal data identify a weakness in a program or operation, the planners could develop action plans that will improve the weak area over time, and the specific actions to be taken within the time frame decided upon could be thoroughly publicized through the media and by letters to legislators and alumni.

Sources of information about public attitudes may be gathered from national polls, newspaper polls, legislative sources, university surveys, and business and industry surveys.

LAW AND POLICY RELATED DATA

Law and policy related data are crucial items to be scanned, because legislation at the federal and state levels, as well as the interpretations of the courts, sometimes dramatically affect the parameters within which the university administration must work. Policies adopted by the university board of control can also have a tremendous impact on actions by the administrators within the central university, as well as at the college and department levels.

For example, laws about affirmative action have affected every public university in the United States of America. Also, the policies of the university board of controls affect student programs, distribution of available funds, employee hiring and payment practices, and many other items that determine the operation and culture of any specific university.

An excellent source of future impact information in this area is the proposed legislation from the city, state, and national bodies affecting education. Of course, proposed rules and regulations by government regulatory bodies also provide important future impact information.

FINANCE RELATED DATA

Finance related data from such sources as federal funds, state funds, alumni contributions, grants, interest on investments, student tuition, and a myriad of fund-raising and other income-related activities must be monitored. They provide the lifeblood which allows the university to function. The ultimate health of the university is most times determined by the amount of funds available to it.

If the university is not successful in writing grants, many creative programs and much research may be eliminated or reduced. If the university is not provided sufficient funds from the state's budget, employees must be released, programs cut, or student tuition raised dramatically to make up for the shortfall in state tax revenues. If the university president or the university's board of control does something that alienates the alumni, a considerable decrease in alumni contributions will result.

By scanning finance related data sources, the strategic planners can project the intervention tactics necessary to reach the established strategic goals. Reaching these goals ultimately will allow the vision of "What Should Be" and/or "What Could Be" to be achieved.

Just about any financial institution has data related to future financial situations which may impact a given educational organization. Chambers of Commerce are another good source of financial data, as well as tax levying and property assessment units of government.

EXTERNAL POLITICS RELATED DATA

External politics related data identify attitudinal trending from such groups as political parties, alumni associations, philanthropic associations, lobbyists, professional associations and any other important groups which may have a positive or negative impact on the university. The consequences are dependent upon the degree of support or the degree of non-support that they provide to the university. Trends and projections of these data allow the planners to design intervention tactics that will bring support for the university's strategic plan.

In developing a strategic plan, it is clear to most planners that more information must be dealt with than simply that provided by beliefs, internal data scans, and external data scans. It is crucial that the planners also consider future forecasts and trends and future opportunities. There also must be some sense of the priority of items found most crucial to the organization's health. These priorities or basic items are those *Critical Success Factors* (see below) which are few in number, but absolutely necessary to identify in order to lay out the strategies over an extended time period.

Critical Success Factors (CSF)

Once the strategic planners have reached consensus on their vision statement and beliefs, and completed their external and internal scanning, they are ready to use these information sources to decide which items are, in their judgement, absolutely necessary for the organization to operate productively in a healthy and rewarding future environment. The strategic plan may involve many items, but the number of Critical Success Factors (CSFs) are usually very limited.

In a sense, the identification of CSFs serves multiple purposes:

(1) They establish those items which must be given highest priority.
(2) They focus planning efforts and resource allocations.
(3) They simplify communications by eliminating much non-crucial information and maximizing the two-way flow of information which relates to the CSFs.

An example of a school district's set of CSFs (arrived at through discussion, after review of the statement of beliefs), externally scanned data, and internally scanned data) will amplify and clarify these concepts. The strategic planning stakeholder's group for this district identified six CSFs.

(1) All students can learn, and student achievement is to be the focus of all schools in the district.

(2) Continuous stakeholder input and support is necessary to maintain the high quality of our school district.

(3) A well-trained and up-to-date group of employees is crucial to successful educational delivery; and the district is committed to providing the resources necessary to maintain a comprehensive, high quality program of staff development and training for all categories of employees.

(4) A good school climate is required for students, and a good Quality of Work Life (QWL) must be maintained for employees.

(5) High expectations must exist for students, employees, and parents or guardians for both school achievement and citizenship.

(6) Sufficient financial, human, temporal, and other resources must be provided to operate a high-quality school district.

Having identified the CSFs,[6] the district level strategic planners must consider these when deciding which actions to undertake, which cause the critical success factors to become realities. These will be useful when identifying and selecting possible methods-means (Chapter 11). Some activities that must be undertaken by the strategic planners, the superintendent of schools, the building and central administrators, and the board of education might well include the following examples of tactics:

(1) The action program related to student achievement will involve the building administrators and the central administration by continuously monitoring student achievement scores. These scores will be disaggregated by grade level, course title, sex, socio-economic level, and any other variable that will provide important detailed facts. For instance, it may be that the general test data in the areas of English and mathematics look excellent; but upon further study of disaggregated data, the administrators find that female students do more poorly in math than male students, and that male students perform more poorly in English than female students. This discovery can, then, alert the curriculum planners to address the problems of content and delivery systems requiring change.

In addition, student test scores, whether they be of the norm-referenced type or the preferred criterion-referenced variety, should be item-analyzed. This helps determine if students are achieving at a lower level than anticipated in any specific area and being masked by reviewing only general achievement results. If weak areas are discovered, the curriculum specialists can determine what has to be done to strengthen the areas of identified weakness.

(2) School climate and Quality of Work Life (QWL) surveys could be administered on a regular basis, and trends could be determined. Such matters as opportunities for input, a safe and healthy environment in which to study or work, a caring attitude, an attitude of respect, and a system of recognition all should be assessed. If the climate or QWL is not at the level desired, or if scanning indicates a decrease in any area, an action program to overcome the area(s) of concern must be undertaken. Hopefully, the action planning will involve those individuals who are affected by the decisions.

(3) An action program dealing with high expectations for students, employees, and parents can include clearly written statements indicating the expectations. They can be distributed to all by posting reminders in every school building and in school-related publications, by providing recognition programs for high achievers, and by creating a culture that expects and demands high achievement and citizenship. Once all parties accept ownership of this, the program will become a driving force in the organizational culture of each school building and of the entire school district.

(4) Stakeholder input and support can be enhanced by including representative stakeholders in any planning meetings or other important activities sponsored by the school district or the individual schools, by regularly asking for attitudinal feedback through surveys, or through reactions at school-sponsored events. Calling together focus groups for periodic assessments of the school district's operations can also prove helpful in this matter.

(5) Commitment to funding a comprehensive staff development and training program is an initial step to maintaining a high-quality staff. Other important action program steps include: (a) periodic values and beliefs assessments, (b) conducting periodic needs assessments, (c) revising the mission and related operational objectives, (d) conducting evaluations of every staff development or training program offered, as well as (e) conducting an evaluation of the entire operation and its community contributions.

(6) Action programs related to providing sufficient financial, human, temporal, and other resources to maintain a quality school are numerous. Some of the activities can include employee released-time for planning and staff development activities, citizen involvement in lobbying the legislature and other funding sources, citizen leadership of any campaigns requesting additional property taxes for any necessary support of the school district, development of volunteer

groups to serve each school building, and the formation of business and industry partnerships with the school district.

Once the statements of vision and beliefs are developed, the scanning completed, and the Critical Success Factors identified, the strategic planners can move to the very important task of identifying the preferred future vision for the district.

Developing Consensus: Selecting a Preferred Future

There are two basic ways of selecting a preferred future for your organization. One may use trend extrapolation and projection or alternate and preferred futuring. Both develop scenarios which describe the future in written form.

Trend extrapolation and projection is a technique which studies and applies the internally and externally scanned data to determine trends over time. These trends, once identified, are extrapolated and projected into the future. Once these projections are in place, en-route strategic objectives (year 2000, etc.) may be derived.

Alternate and preferred futuring is a technique that uses brainstorming, with or without the use of trend data, in order to develop multiple visions of the future. Once the alternative visions are developed, each vision is analyzed for predictability and desirability. Finally, the vision most desired is then chosen as the preferred future vision. This preferred future vision is then used for all subsequent strategic planning.

Scenarios are written descriptions of the predicted or desired future. In most situations, each scenario is analyzed on the basis of "what ifs". That is, potential variables which may effect the scenario are studied. The original scenario is modified when variables are determined to have a high probability of occurrence and a high probability of impacting the original scenario. Scenarios can also be developed without the collection of any prior information; the planners would merely project what the organization or school district would look like if it were to achieve the visualized situation. Two very abbreviated examples of scenarios for a school district might well look like those which follow.

EXAMPLE: ALTERNATE WORSE SCENARIO FOR IMPORTANT SCHOOL DISTRICT–DRIFTING INTO THE FUTURE

Based on a "things are getting worse" vision, data indicating trends toward less public support; increasing drop out rates; decreasing test results; decreasing school climate; decreasing property assessments which translate into less money for the school district; increasing labor/management problems; a rapid turnover of board members, administrators, and teachers; and the passing of many state mandates which hamper local control, the future scenario for Important School District would read:

- There will be an increase of "at risk" students in our district, and we are unable to handle this problem.
- No one cares about the school district.
- The climate for students, teachers, and employees in the schools is terrible.
- We have practically no supplies, the equipment is broken, the buildings are run down, and there are no funds to correct these problems.
- Student achievement is way below national norms and no one cares.
- Because of our very low salaries, we have to hire inexperienced teachers and administrators, and we have no funds to assist them in their training. It is no wonder they leave as soon as they can locate another job.
- Outside gang members come into our buildings all the time.
- The rich and high achieving districts, the city, the state, and the federal government aren't going to do anything to help us. We would be better off if we could bomb the place and go out of business.

Obviously, this is a very sad and damaging scenario. Yet, there are a few school districts in this nation that currently exhibit many of the characteristics of this worse scenario. But let's get on to more positive thoughts.

EXAMPLE: PREFERRED FUTURE SCENARIO FOR IMPORTANT SCHOOL DISTRICT

Our "let's make a better world" vision preferred future scenario, in contrast to the worse future scenario, capitalizes on the positives and anticipates eliminating the negatives. Some of the elements that are included in our preferred future scenario include:

- Student achievement in academics, vocation related activities, competitions, co-curricular activities, and social activities is very high.

- The school buildings are safe, clean, healthy, and aesthetically pleasant.
- The community is very supportive of the schools. Community members vote enrichment taxes, volunteer to help in many ways, and brag about their excellent school district to others.
- Area businesses and industries are anxious to form school/business and school/industry partnerships, and there is a waiting list for our "adopt-a-school" program.
- The students have high aspirations, and the faculty and parents readily assist them in achieving their aspirations.
- There are high quality and more than adequate supplies and equipment available to faculty and students.
- There are specialized and highly focused programs for students who are identified as "at risk", and the dropout rate among them and the student body as a whole is practically zero.
- The climate in all of the district schools is one of caring, helping, and mutual reinforcement among students, employees, and parents.
- The students will leave this school district upon graduation, and followup studies will show that practically all will become very productive, contributing, and caring citizens who hold high expectations for themselves, their families, their community, their schools, and for their country.

Is there any benefit to visioning and creating a better future? If the United States did not make a commitment to go to the moon and develop strategies to attain that vision and its related strategic goals, many of the technological by-products we enjoy would not exist. The political lift that it gave to the image of the United States around the world would not have happened. Also, if the environmentalists did not unite and lobby the various media and legislators, we would not have improvement in environmental controls – some of our lakes would be dead, some of our forests would have been destroyed, and many more of our people would have serious illnesses.

After studying trends, developing scenarios, analyzing the scenarios, and choosing the preferred future vision, the strategic planners must compare the "What Is" state with the preferred future vision (the "What Should Be" state). Any discrepancies or gaps between the two help identify the needs that must be addressed within the strategic plan. The strategic plan, once developed and acted upon, should lead to achievement of the preferred future vision.

Without developing the strategic plan, let's identify some items that could well be incorporated into the preferred future vision of the school district. Obviously, each element of this vision would be analyzed by comparing "What Is" to "What Should Be". The needs thus identified would be target foci for the strategic planners to address when completing the school district's plan.

The elements included in the vision of a school district may be many in number. Some of the more basic elements are:

- Students shall achieve at a high level (the word *high* will have to be clearly defined—put in measurable performance terms—to make this vision element operational).[7]
- Parents and community members and organizations will be supportive of the school district's efforts.
- The staff shall be of high quality, and staff members will maintain current knowledge in content and methods of instructional and managerial delivery.
- The schools shall possess safe and healthy environments for students and employees.
- A caring, trusting, and open communication attitude shall be evident among students and employees.
- Student achievement shall be the major focal point of all activities at both the building and district levels. The levels of achievement shall be continuously monitored by disaggregated detail in order that the data may be utilized for strategic planning.
- Sufficient financial, human, material, and temporal resources shall be made available to achieve the vision of "What Should Be".
- Graduates will be successful in both their future education and in their lives.

Although the planners have arrived at a vision statement, shared beliefs, and conducted the other planning activities that have permitted them to formulate their preferred vision of "What Should Be", future events could produce situations that—from the needs assessments and scannings—may well cause alterations in their original beliefs and vision. If extensive external and internal scanning is continuous, planners will gather data that sometimes will require changes to be made. Figure 5.2 demonstrates the basic functions involved in this process of revision.

In future chapters we will discuss the transitions from visions to missions to strategies to tactics to the details of operational planning. But, for now we shall turn to guidelines for strategic planners who hold the responsibility for creating and marketing a vision of "What Should Be".

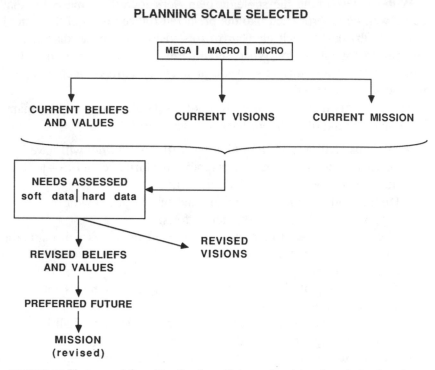

FIGURE 5.2 The general functions for determining and revising the mission based upon beliefs and values, visions, and needs.

Guidelines for Strategic Planners[8]

(1) In developing an organization's vision, it is wise to first reach a consensus statement of beliefs, and develop an "ideal vision" of the society in which you want your children to live. Then, you may conduct a scan of important internal data, do a scan of important external data, and achieve consensus on those few-in-number factors (Critical Success Factors) which are absolutely required to develop and maintain a high-quality university, school district, or individual school.

(2) By scanning data over time, from both the internal and external environments, the strategic planners can determine trends that must be considered when developing the strategic plan and the en-route (year 2000, year 1995, etc.) objectives.

(3) Identifying Critical Success Factors is an important step. It allows

the strategic planners to develop priorities among the multitudinous factors that exist in any organization's environment. The identification of the CSFs also allows the planners to allocate the available resources towards those really crucial factors.

(4) Although many methodologies may be used to assist in developing a preferred vision for an organization, two prime methods may be considered: (a) trend extrapolation and projection, and (b) alternate and preferred futuring. With either technique, the planners can take advantage of scenario writing—those descriptions of what the organization might look like in the future in order to choose a preferred future.

(5) Strategic planning is dynamic. Figure 5.2 shows how input and change builds during the process.

Glossary

Alternate Futuring: the process of identifying possible futures for an organization. Each alternate can be analyzed for probability and desirability. This is used after deriving an "ideal" future.

Critical Success Factors (CSFs): those few factors which are determined as vital for development and maintenance of a high-quality organization. They provide priorities which assist in resource allocations and determining information requirements.

External Scanning: the activity of collecting and monitoring data from the external environment encompassing the organization (school district or university) for the purpose of identifying trends over time to assist in planning strategies for the future.

Internal Scanning: the activity of collecting and monitoring data from the organization's internal environment, for the purpose of identifying trends over time. This assists in planning strategies for the future.

Preferred Futuring: the process of selecting the most desired future from alternate futures. This preferred future becomes the cornerstone for the organization's mission.

Quality of Work Life: the degree to which such factors as trust, caring, recognition, interesting work, and opportunities for input exist in the employees' work place. They are indicated by satisfaction, low absenteeism, and high motivation. The qualitative level can be assessed, and strategic plans developed to improve or maintain the qualitative level desired within the future vision of the organization.

Scenario: a written narrative describing a future. This technique can be helpful if a variety of experts are asked to develop a future scenario for the organization. Those consensus elements are identified and redistributed to the experts for additional comments, and this process is continued until a consensus scenario is agreed upon.

Trend Extrapolation: the process of using monitored data over a period of years to identify trends, and then using these trends to predict future directions that should be considered when developing the strategic plan for the organization.

Vision: a clear "picture" or written statement of what the strategic planners expect their community, society, and organization to look like, deliver, and accomplish at some future point of time. It is the description of the planners' determination of "What Should Be" or "What Could Be" at some future date.

Exercises

1. When viewing your school, school district, or university, which factors in the environment outside of the organization's control do you feel could have a significant impact upon your organization? What system could you develop to continuously collect data on these factors? How would you utilize these data in your strategic planning activities?

2. When viewing your organization's internal environment, what factors do you think would have a significant impact upon it? What structures would you put in place to continuously collect and analyze these data? How would you use these data when doing your strategic planning?

3. Do you think it is important to identify those factors which are most crucial to the "health" of your organization? What are the Critical Success Factors that you feel are crucial to your school, school district, or university?

4. Prepare an "ideal" vision statement. Why should you do this before collecting and using "reality" data?

5. What alternate futures could you foresee for your organization? Which of these would you select as your preferred future? What strategies would be helpful in achieving this preferred future?

Endnotes

1 See Chapter 3. Also see Reference [90] for other methods of identifying beliefs and analyzing organizations.

2 Again, we might provide the same format options as in Chapter 4. That is: (1) a five or seven point scale, (2) doing a "What Is" and "What Should Be" analysis, or (3) selecting the five most impacting and the five least impacting.

3 Demographics are increasingly useful and important [38].

4 Not all interactions are shown in this figure. In reality, some of the variables could have an effect on others (such as Beliefs and Values with Visions).

5 Drucker points out that you "sell" when nobody can use what you offer, while marketing finds the common area between what you have to offer and what the client could use.

6 Notice that no "Mega" CSFs were identified!

7 Realize that measurable performance indicators for all of these elements would also have to be developed.

8 This section also serves as the chapter's *Summary*.

Identifying Current Mission

Where are we going?
How will we be able to tell when we've arrived?

Education has purpose. It intends to supply learners with the skills, knowledge, attitudes, and abilities to be self-sufficient and self-reliant in an interdependent world. It aims at improving the world of learners as well as that of their fellow citizens. A mission states the over-arching educational purpose in terms which allow all educational partners to:

(1) Agree to that journey

(2) Decide what they want to spend — in time, resources, and effort — to get there

(3) Set their contribution "compasses" to enable them, individually and together, to steer towards that common goal

(4) Evaluate the extent to which they are progressing, and arrive at the shared result.

Educational purposes get stated in different ways — ranging from very precise declarations, which answer the two questions that opened this chapter, to very loose but inspirational pronouncements.

Unfortunately, the missions of educational systems are often stated in terms which are well intentioned, yet global and rambling, such as "It is the mission of this district to improve the achievement of all learners in a cost-effective manner." Such statements are much too vague to allow one to either plan how to get that done or evaluate success. When doing a strategic plan, the common "North Star", towards which all can steer has to be both precise and measurable.

Strategic planning depends on precise, measurable, valid objectives — mission objectives — which state the purpose of the organization along with criteria for success. Most often, a crucial task is to derive such a rigorous statement from existing pronouncements and intentions. This chapter deals with how to do just that: move from intentions — usually termed "mission statements" — to a precise and inclusive

113

measurable mission objective. Let's turn to see how one constructs a mission objective from more general mission statements.

Mission Statements, Measurable Criteria, and Mission Objectives

A mission statement is a broad and general description of purpose. It can be motivational, inspirational, and directional. Pull out the mission statement for your institution. They might be similar to these:

- "develop each child to her/his own capacity"
- "creating excellence in higher education"
- "better jobs"
- "learning for the 90's and beyond"
- "happy children make successful students"
- "a learning place"
- "higher standards for exceptional learners"
- "students come first"
- "building better students for tomorrow's world"

What's wrong with these? Nothing much if you like poetry and want to avoid accountability.[1] None of them will allow you and your educational partners to state in clear, concise, and unambiguous manner:

- Where are we going?
- How will we be able to tell when we've arrived?

An important strategic planning task is likely to take existing statements of purpose, and from them, derive mission objectives which will (a) answer the two questions, (b) add measurable criteria, and (c) provide the basis for both strategic planning and accountability for results.

A *mission statement* is a general, overall destination; an intended result or consequence.

A *mission objective* is a precise statement of where the organization is going and provides the criteria—stated as an Outcome, Output, or Product—for assessing when one has arrived.

If we are going someplace, we should know exactly where that "someplace" is located. A mission statement provides purpose. We must know the exact criteria[2] of where we are headed. The measurement of location, for both planning and evaluation purposes, is central to strategic planning:

Mission Statement + Measurable Criteria = Mission Objective

Most educational agencies already have mission statements. Often a strategic planner's job is to provide specific criteria—measurable objectives—for turning them into a mission objective. In a moment we will review four scales of measurement, which range from gross intentions to very reliable statements. If you have a mission statement which only names a result (e.g., develop competent vocational learners; all learners will be happy; meeting the challenges of the next century), or targets for improvement or direction for change (e.g., to improve citizenship; to encourage growth and development) you have to convert to an objective which is measurable in more reliable and precise terms. Precision and rigor are necessary for setting purpose and criteria which allow for the alignment of strategic plans and responsive management as you move from plans to programs to evaluating progress and success. Let's first turn to measurability, and methods for preparing objectives—including mission objectives—which have the proper specificity for planning, management, and evaluation.

A TAXONOMY OF RESULTS

As we report information about something (such as the purpose of an educational system or program) we can vary from precise to quite general descriptions of it. When we are uncertain, we can only name something vague (e.g., learning for the 20th century; readiness for life; professional competence), or only identify that something is equal to, greater than, or less than something else (improving our teaching; developing the skills for higher education). When better informed, we can measure our results and objectives with greater precision and reliability.

There is a taxonomy of results which allows us both to identify the relative reliability of our results and to distinguish between goals and objectives. There are four scales of measurement:

NOMINAL: names something (e.g., "rock", "Jan", "innovative")
ORDINAL: identifies things which are greater than, equal to, or less than other things (such as "Jerry is smarter than Bob"; "this cloisonne is better than this carving, and both are better than the portrait over here")

Table 6.1 A taxonomy of results.

Scale of Measurement	Description
Nominal Ordinal	Goal; Aim; Purpose
Interval Ratio	Objective; Performance specification; Measurable objective

INTERVAL: possesses an arbitrary zero-point to begin the measurement and has equal scale distances (such as means and standard deviations on an honesty test; score on the Utah test of mental maturity, temperature in °F)

RATIO: possesses a known zero-point and equal scale distances (e.g., temperature in Kelvin, weight, distance)

These four types of measurements—with ratio the most reliable, and nominal the least—form a taxonomy of results (Table 6.1). Refer to the list of mission statements we viewed earlier, identify which scale of measurement each displays, and compare with our sorting of them in Figure 6.1.

Not one of these intentions provide enough precision, rigor, or definition to serve as the basis for stating, without confusion "Where are we going" and "How will we know when we have arrived?" Each would have to be converted to a statement measurable in interval or ratio terms.

PREPARING USEFUL OBJECTIVES

A useful objective states:

(1) What result (or accomplishment) is to be achieved?
(2) Who or what will display that result?
(3) Under what conditions will the result be observed?
(4) What criteria (best in interval or ratio scale terms) will be used to determine success (or failure)?

A useful objective details the specifications, sometimes called *performance indicators*,[3] which can lead to the identification, selection, implementation, and evaluation of educational activities. When an objective has the four characteristics (above), confusion among the strategic planning partners will be avoided, and clear guidance is given to all who implement the plan.

Educational Intention	Scale of Measurment			
	Nominal	Ordinal	Interval	Ratio
Develop each child to her/his own capability	X			
Creating excellence in higher education	X			
Better jobs		X		
Learning for the 90's and beyond	X			
Happy children make successful students	X			
A learning place	X			
Higher standards for exceptional learners	X			
Students come first	X			
Building better students for tomorrow's world		X		

FIGURE 6.1 Some hypothetical educational mission statements and their associated scales of measurement. None are objectives.

MEANS

ENDS

FIGURE 6.2 Means and ends are related, but not the same.

Educational Intention	Means	Ends
Develop each child to her/his own capability		X
Creating excellence in higher education	X	
Better jobs		X
Learning for the 90's and beyond	X	
Happy children make successful students		X
A learning place	X	
Higher standards for exceptional learners	X	
Students come first	X	
Building better students for tomorrow's world	X	
Earn more than you spend or owe		X

FIGURE 6.3 Some hypothetical educational intentions and their dealing with means or ends.

An objective states the expectations of results to be accomplished. It does not target means, resources, procedures, or compliance. Objectives best aim at ends, not means. (Sometimes implementation-oriented "objectives" are written by planners, but this approach risks doing a job correctly when that job should not have been done in the first place [51]). Any useful objective, including a mission objective, requires the measurable proof essential to confirm that a venture has delivered an intended result.

Objectives have two fundamental uses, one proactive and the other reactive: (a) to identify what results (or mission) to accomplish, and (b) to provide criteria for assessing success or failure. Objectives can target any or all of the three types of ends (Products, Outputs, Outcomes) and thus Mega, Macro, and Micro levels of strategic planning.

"TEMPLATES" (OR PATTERNS) FOR DEVELOPING USEFUL OBJECTIVES

There are three characteristics of a useful objective. They:

(1) Differentiate means from ends (Figures 6.2 and 6.3)
(2) Measure results, ideally in interval or ratio terms
(3) Encompass the range of the three results—Products, Outputs, and Outcomes—of the five organizational elements (Figure 6.4)

Based on these, three "templates" (or patterns) may be used for preparing, reviewing, or converting intentions to measurable objectives.[4] Let's apply each characteristic.

Template ①: Ends and Means

The most important consideration in deriving a useful performance indicator is that it deals with ends—results not means, procedures, processes, or resources (Figure 6.2).

If an existing statement of purpose (such as a mission statement) identifies only a means to an end ("better curriculum for a better tomorrow"; "achieving excellence every day"; "schools of tomorrow today"), then change it to *include* the intended result. To convert a means-oriented objective to an ends-oriented one, ask "What would be the result if this means, process, or method were implemented?" Ends-oriented objectives should be used, for sooner or later, performance and results will be the basic rationale for assessing whether any intention, process, re-

Educational Intention	Organizational Element				
	Input	Process	Product	Output	Outcome
Develop each child to her/his own capability		X			
Creating excellence in higher education		X			
Better jobs			X(?)	X(?)	
Learning for the 90's and beyond		X			
Happy children make successful students	X(?)		X(?)		
A learning place	X				
Higher standards for exceptional learners	X		X(?)		
Students come first	X				
Building better students for tomorrow's world		X			
Earn more than you spend or owe					X

FIGURE 6.4 Some hypothetical educational intentions and their dealing with the five Organizational Elements.

source, or method is valid and worthwhile. If we are not very clear about where we are to go, we might end up someplace else [71] such as Antarctica, when we wanted to get to Chicago—without precise criteria to guide us, we might not recognize our mistake until we were very cold.

Looking at our earlier intentions, sort them into "means" and "ends" and compare them with Figure 6.3.

Template ②: *Measurability*

Recall the three levels of results (Products, Outputs, and Outcomes) and the four types of measurement. Any objective should be written in interval or ratio terms—regardless of whether it targets Products, Outputs, or Outcomes. Objectives written in interval or ratio-scale terms represent the most reliable bases for strategic planning and doing.

Sort the would-be missions by the scale of measurement to which they relate best. Contrast your findings with the comparison made earlier in this chapter in Figure 6.1. Use the four scales of measurement to calibrate your classification:

> NOMINAL[5]
>
> ORDINAL[6]
>
> INTERVAL[7]
>
> RATIO[8]

Template ③: Selecting the Correct Educational Focus

As noted earlier, what organizations use, do, and deliver may be seen in terms of five related organizational elements: INPUTS, PROCESSES, PRODUCTS, OUTPUTS, OUTCOMES.

To confirm that meeting an objective (including a mission objective) will in fact generate both individual competence and educational system accomplishments, and lead to the delivery of useful payoffs, you should next sort the performance indicators into one of the five Organizational Elements. Check your answers with those in Figure 6.4.

Unless only compliance is required, make certain that the indicator (or criterion) falls in one of the results elements (Products, Outputs, Outcomes).[9] Note that in our examples, only one of them ("earn more than you spend or owe") is Mega or Macro[10] in nature, and there might be some question as to whether there are any other examples at the Micro level.[11]

Using the Templates

Any of these templates may be used; ideally, all of them are. The relationships among the application of the three templates are provided in Figure 6.5. The steps are numbered, and include:

(1) Differentiate means from ends.

(2) Select the reliability of measurement.

(3) Classify by the primary organizational element upon which the project is focused.

Beyond Just Efficiency: Optional Template ④

Strategic planning is best when proactive, i.e., oriented towards creating a better future, not just making the current operations more effi-

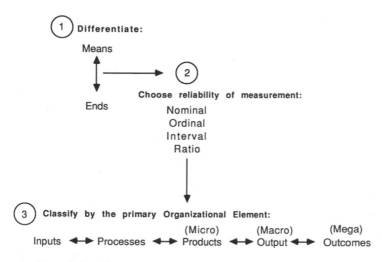

FIGURE 6.5 The relationship among the three performance indicator templates. Based on, with permission, Kaufman 1988: September.

cient. Some mission intentions (and other educational purposes) are framed only to improve current circumstances without examining their validity and usefulness — just improving "What Is". If you are confident of the validity and utility of current objectives and the educational mission, then the templates ①–③ will suffice. However, if you choose to respond to Drucker's advice [23,24], and ask if the objective/mission to be accomplished is worth doing in the first place, then template ③ may be extended to include the two planning dimensions of "What Is" and "What Should Be", as shown in Figure 6.6.

There is an added bonus for using this additional template surface when doing an evaluation. By examining both "What Is" and "What Should Be", an evaluation may be planned to compare three types of results (or levels) and then two types of means (resources and processes). This will allow a contrasting of "What Was Intended" with "What Was

Table 6.2 The areas of concern of Mega, Macro, and Micro planning for the organizational elements (including both "What Is" and "What Should Be").

	INPUTS	PROCESSES	PRODUCTS	OUTPUTS	OUTCOMES
MEGA-	X	X	X	X	X
MACRO-	X	X	X	X	
MICRO-	X	X	X		

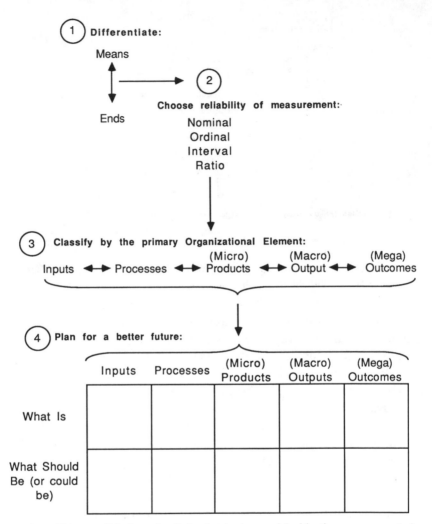

FIGURE 6.6 Four possible "templates" for developing useful objectives or corporate indicators. Any or (best) all may be used. The numbers ① to ④ show a recommended sequence.

Delivered" for each of the Organizational Elements, instead of lumping all means and ends together, or confusing different possible levels of evaluation.

Table 6.2 shows the scope of each of the three levels of strategic educational planning where each will be concerned with both "What Is" and "What Should Be".

A SUMMARY OF OBJECTIVES (INCLUDING MISSION OBJECTIVES)

Objectives, including mission objectives, should:

- relate to ends (or accomplishments) not to means, processes, or resources apart from the results they should deliver
- be measurable on an interval or ratio scale
- relate to a results chain which links all educational efforts, results, and societal consequences

When mission objectives are desired, planners have the opportunity to derive new and useful educational purposes, not only to increase the efficiency of existing ones. By assuring that there are indicators for the two dimensions of "What Is" as well as "What Should Be", you will shift from enhancing efficiency to improving effectiveness as well.

Given some guides (templates) on how to assure that any objective is measurable and useful, let's now turn to converting any stated intention into one which is measurable on an interval or ratio scale.

The Mission Objective

In accomplishment terms, a mission objective (mission statement plus performance criteria) precisely states the intended results of a mission. A mission objective often converts an intention—usually labeled a "mission statement"—into the most general yet inclusive assertion of the required result (mission) that can be made [48]. Recall the relationships among mission statements, performance criteria, and mission objectives as we move from intention to specifics.

Examples of poorly stated "missions"—actually intents—which might be available to strategic planners could include:

(1) Build an elementary school.

(2) Develop better citizens for the 21st Century.

(3) Develop the school system of tomorrow.

Although educational missions may be given us in these terms, such directives do not contain enough precise information to allow strategic planners to answer the questions:

- What is to be accomplished and delivered? (e.g., "An elementary school will be built on XZ3 site which will provide learning opportunities to 200 students initially and will be expandable to no more than 305 while meeting Board Code 55.6Y according to Board statement 44.5, on or before the contract deadline.")

- What will we use to prove accomplishment and delivery? (e.g., "The elementary school building and equipment will meet all city and Board codes as well as meet State requirements as certified by obtaining all local, Board, and State clearances and approvals as specified in Board Code 55.6Y and Board statement 44.5.")

We have to be specific if we are to proceed with any trust that our planned design and resulting efforts will be useful as well as efficient and effective.

Mission objectives stipulate results (ideally Outcomes—a Mega focus) to be achieved in measurable terms. Results are best measured in interval or ratio scale terms. Any mission objective, be it at the Mega, Macro, or Micro levels requires the same specificity as any other performance or behavioral objectives [71]. Reviewing, a mission objective must state precisely:

(1) What performance or result is to be demonstrated?
(2) Who or what will display the performance or result?
(3) Under what conditions is the result or performance to be demonstrated?
(4) What specific criteria will be used to determine if the performance or result has been achieved?

In addition, a fifth condition should be met:

(5) There will be no misunderstandings concerning what is to be accomplished. [48]

COMPONENTS OF A MISSION OBJECTIVE

A mission objective has two components—a mission statement and measurable performance requirements—which can be in a single assertion or can be composed of two distinct declarations. The following illustrates:

Mission Statement: Where are we going?

Performance requirements:[12] How will we know when we have arrived?

Or:

Mission Statement + Performance Requirements = Mission Objective

Beware the Means Trap

Most educators are "doing-type" people. They want to swing into action, and get things moving. Such "get-going" people find they cannot resist (at first) including *how* a result or performance will be brought about (methods, means, tactics, how-to-do-its). When a how-to-do-it is included in a mission statement ("using computer technology, prepare students for the 21st century") a solution is (prematurely) locked into place ("using computer technology . . .") before defining the overall results to be accomplished. As we will note in greater detail in Chapter 7, basic to practical strategic planning is the specification and selection of needs (defined as gaps in results, or ends) before choosing the how-to-do-its (means). No objective should contain or allude to methods and means for getting the results.

EVOLVING A MISSION OBJECTIVE FROM A MISSION STATEMENT

Mission statements identify intentions, inspiration, and general direction—an "umbrella" of educational purpose. Strategic planning often requires turning existing mission statements into mission objectives. Let's get some practice.

Consider the following hypothetical mission statements in terms of whether they provide enough specificity to guide strategic planning:

> *Unacceptable*: Develop better citizens for the 21st Century. (This is a statement of general intent, or a mission statement—not a mission objective.)

> *Better*: Before January 2, 2001, at least 90% of the learners who have completed the graduation requirements from our district will be self-sufficient and self-reliant as indicated by certified follow-up data (such as job tenure, credit levels, etc.) certified by the state university.

> (This objective is more specific and precise than previous. It expresses what is to be accomplished, under what conditions it will be verified, and to what degree the results will be obtained.)

In stating a mission (or converting an existing intent), we start by specifying what has to be accomplished: the statement of the mission (sometimes in general terms only) is the first step.

Some examples of general starting points might be:

(1) Develop each child to her/his own capacity.

(2) Reduce dropouts.

(3) Eliminate illiteracy in Sharphamton within ten years.

These, according to our taxonomy of results (in Table 6.1) are simply statements of goals, aims, or purposes. To be useful, our mission objective should be stated in interval or ratio terms (step 2 of the template in Figures 6.5 and 6.6). Let's see how we might move from the intentional to the precise by adding to our rigor and supplying performance requirements.

Ask, if we were to "develop each child to her/his own capacity, what would result?" If we moved to a results-oriented mode, we might respond "there would be fewer drop-outs and more completers." (This moved us to the Output level.) Take that reply, and again "If we reduced dropouts and increased completers, what would result from that?" A response might be "more jobs for graduates and fewer people would go on welfare."

By continually asking "so what would happen if we did that?" we move up the results chain from Inputs, to Processes, to Products, to Outputs, to Outcomes. We are rooting our strategic plan in current and future societal consequences. Continuing our development from the intention to "develop each child to her/his own capacity" we might come to a more complete example of a useful mission objective:

> Increase by at least 10% per year each year for the next 15 years the number of completers of the Janice School District who are self-sufficient and self-reliant as indicated by: positive credit ratings, no convictions for crimes, no commitments to mental institutions, full employment, less than 3/100 divorces, none on the welfare roles. Accomplishment will be certified by the Superintendent of Schools on the first school day of each new calendar year, and based upon actual independently verifiable data. The budget shall increase by no more than 5% per year after adjustment for inflation.

Notice that this mission objective contains both quantitative and qualitative aspects:

- What is to be accomplished? Increase self-sufficiency and self-reliance and reduce dropouts.

- Who or what will display it? Learners in the Janice School District.
- Under what condition? By at least 10% per year for the next 15 years within a budget of no greater than 5% per year increase, after adjustment for inflation.
- What criteria (how much or how well) will be used? Certification each year by the Superintendent and based upon independently verifiable data.

A mission objective has to successfully communicate to assure that all educational partners know where they are going (mission statement) and how they determine when they have arrived (performance requirements). Precision and rigor will help assure that reality. Another feature of a measurable mission objective and its results-orientation and precision, is that it must also include the criteria for evaluation. Loose or unclear terms such as "appreciate" and "understand" are not meaningful unless they are defined precisely. A mission objective has to be free of mere qualitative terminology. And let's always keep in focus a learner-orientation and her or his ultimate ability to be a contributing, successful member of today's and tomorrow's societies.

There are, then, four conditions stated in a useful mission objective and together they must show at least three characteristics,[13] as shown in Table 6.3.

AN EXAMPLE: Let's identify a hypothetical mission statement and "walk it through" as you and your strategic planning team might do in converting a mission intention to a mission objective.

Table 6.3 Conditions and characteristics of a mission objective.

Conditions	Characteristics
1. What is to be displayed in order to demonstrate completion?	Objectives must communicate success-fully to all users and evaluators. All of the conditions for measuring results must be specified and must contain the basis for evaluation; they must be in measurable performance terms which are valid and should leave no room for confusion.
2. Whom or what is to demonstrate completion?	
3. Under what conditions is it to be demonstrated?	
4. What criteria will be used to determine if it is done? (How much or how well is it to be done?)	

We might begin with a statement of the mission intention, revising and refining the intent until it has matured into a measurable mission objective.

1. "Achieve *excellence in education*". We have to refine this gross intent and make it precise and measurable on an interval or ratio scale.

2. "Increase student mastery of basic skills and knowledges and improve the self-concept of learners, by using state-of-the-art computer technology in teaching, so they will be successful in school and life".

In order to take this to a point where a strategic planning team will know what is required and expected of an "excellent" system, further refinement must be made—specifying the fundamental critical skills and knowledge areas that might relate to how a student perceives himself/herself, and further identify what will lead to success in and out of school. Notice that it inappropriately has a solution embedded (using state-of-the-art computer technology). This juncture is much too early to select how to get "excellence" delivered.

3. "To measurably improve student success and produce an increase of at least 13% per year in-school student mastery in reading, communication, problem-solving, consumer abilities, arithmetic, and self-esteem as measured on the Campos Test of Educational and Personal Accomplishment. Further, students should perform at or above national grade level norms, and also be self-sufficient and self-reliant in later life".

The strategic planner has moved closer to precision, completeness, and reliable measurement and is including major variables of required accomplishment. Note that the means (process) for assisting learners to perform—state-of-the-art technology—is now deleted.

Continuing:

4. "Increase Janice School District's learner in-school student performance as measured by The Campos Test by 13% mean improvement each year, so that:

- At least 90% of all learners are at or above grade level on all subjects, including reading, communication, problem-solving, consumer abilities, arithmetic.
- Improve learner self-concept significantly (.05 level of confidence or beyond) among these learners as measured within two years.
- After legal exit from the school system (reaching minimum age and/or graduation), at least 90% of all completers will be self-sufficient and self-reliant as indicated by applying the criteria of: no divorces; no unemployment; no arrests and convictions; registration for voting; no receipt of food stamps; no people on the welfare roles or receiving aid to dependent children".

The initial statement of mission intent ("achieve *excellence in education*") has been transformed into an acceptable objective by adding performance requirements, and this provides the basis for evaluation. By increasing precision, we derive a mission objective that is realistic, measurable, and evaluable. In addition, it communicates the results precisely with little or no misinterpretation. (Also note that as the rigor increased, Outcome/Mega indicators — external self-sufficiency — were included as part of the mission objective).

Recall that the mission statement, and its associated performance requirements, actually form a unitary package. Together the mission statement and performance requirements (measurable on an interval or ratio scale) provide the starting referent and the specifications for strategic planning and a basis for relating the beliefs, visions, and needs into a realistic, practical, and agreeable system plan.

A mission is the statement of intended overall results (usually an Outcome, but possibly an Output or Product) to be accomplished. It should be based on documented gaps between current results and required ones: i.e., needs.

The Missions of Other Educational Units and Their Relationship to the Overall Strategic Mission

We have seen that you can (and should) write an overall mission objective for an entire educational system. You may also prepare a mission objective for all of the other layers and components, from nursery school through higher education. Actually, each component of any system has major parts, each with its own mission. A trick of a successful education system is to assure that each part contributes to the whole!

Below are some mission objectives which were developed and used at Australia's Bond University [110].

On or before the end of 2010, the following minimal results will have been accomplished:

- At least 95% of graduates will be employed in a position of their first or second occupational choice (as per self-report).
- Of those graduates choosing public service, at least 60% will be in supervisory positions, and at least 10% will be agency heads or sub-heads (as per self-report).
- Graduates and former students who completed work earning Bond University credit, will have their courses accepted at full credit in

any overseas university which has a related program (as indicated by reports by such students).

- Less than 1% of the graduates will be on public charity or support (based on self-report and/or census data).
- At least 35% of the faculty will be elected as Fellows of their professional societies.
- The University will be fully accredited, at the highest level offered, by at least one accrediting agency for each of the following: (a) the entire University, (b) programs, and (c) disciplines.
- No promising students who would significantly benefit (as judged by a Bond University admissions committee) from attending Bond University will be turned away solely due to inability to pay fees as reported by the Director, Academic Services.
- Graduation rate of accepted students will be at 90% or better.
- Measurable performance standards (on an interval or ratio scale) for each academic program will be available, and updated at least once every five years.
- Bond University academic staff, depending on the nature of the profession or discipline (as stated by that area's Foundation Professor), demonstrate national and international scholarly standing through performance within the top 15% of academic staff of other universities in Australia as measured by appropriate (as indicated by the Foundation Professor) publication, patenting, consulting, and creative performance.

The teaching and research reputation and societal impact of Bond University will be such that:

- At least 95% of the students return for each subsequent semester.
- At least 20% of all Australian students place Bond University in the top three of their "university of first choice" as reported on the summary of student applications.
- At least 95% of our graduates are employed within three months in fields for which they qualify (as per self-report).
- Within the first 10 years, growth in demand is achieved by an increment of 150% every three years for undergraduate and graduate places at Bond University, both from Australian and overseas applicants, as reported by the Director, Academic Services.
- Bond University graduates are recognized for their

communication skills, business ethics, and their understanding of the Asian Pacific region and Australia's potential in an international market, as indicated by at least 95% employment in organizations (who state these characteristics as hiring criteria), and interview requests by such organizations.

- Bond University graduates the highest proportion of qualified women in technology of any university in Australia, as reported by the Director, Academic Services.
- Bond University attracts and retains faculty with proven reputations and develops their staff, as indicated by (a) no vacancies for approved lines which exist for more than six months, and (b) no resignations of faculty by those judged by the Foundation Professor as competent and desired to be retained.

An excellent example of setting secondary-level educational goals, deriving measurable indicators, making candid reports to one's public, and then using those for guiding further work is Fullerton (California) Union High School District's work since 1982 [27]. This district, in collaboration with its educational partners, derived (Macro level) goals, developed measurable indicators for each, and tracked and assessed progress and status. Based on the measurable expectations, the district reports results yearly, including: whether they are below standard, meeting standard, or above standard; and also what their weaknesses and strengths are. Being results-based is not only desirable and possible, it is actually being done in this case by caring professionals.

The Strategic Mission: Its Interrelationships

PUTTING PRECISION AND RIGOR INTO PRACTICE

For each component in your educational system, write a mission objective which meets all of the requirements for a measurable objective, and then make certain it contributes to the larger, overall whole, as shown in the relationship in Figure 6.7.

After preparing the individual mission objectives, find out if each contributes to the others and to the whole set of purposes for your organiza-

MICRO   +   MACRO   ⟶   MEGA

FIGURE 6.7 Mega planning incorporates Micro and Macro levels.

FIGURE 6.8 Do the Micro and Macro levels really contribute to the same Mega results? Compare results for rolling-up with those of rolling-down (see also page 276).

tion. If not, change one or more of them. Often, without realizing it, the various parts of the system actually interact negatively and cause the overall system to be ineffective.

In order to assure that the parts of an educational system are the correct ones, you should check to assure that the overall mission objective is at the Mega level, and that the subordinate parts will contribute to that. This is done by comparing, as shown in Figure 6.8, the results at the Micro and Macro level from rolling-up with those from rolling-down.

IDENTIFYING EXISTING POLICIES, RULES, LAWS, AND REGULATIONS

When identifying where your organization is going, also identify any current "ground rules" which are required to operate or accomplish its purposes. As part of the process of determining current mission(s), include the formal consideration of existing laws, rules, regulations, and policies—not that we will have to adhere to them blindly, but they might serve as a logical step for identifying what currently guides the educational system and its parts, and as a basis for negotiating required changes. The current legal limitations are part of "What Is" for the system. These specifications should be considered part of the performance requirements when developing the organization's mission objective. For example, some performance requirements for an educational agency could include:

(1) There will be no student or staff discrimination on the basis of color, race, creed, gender, age, religion, disability, or national origin as indicated by successful EEO or civil rights findings.

(2) The regulations covering State Nursery School operations (Code 45X7/33-89) will be observed, and there will be no successful legal actions taken by regulatory agencies.

(3) Each learner will have a signed medical release from a licensed physician in the State before beginning full- or part-time atten-

dance. The release form is #67-88 and has been approved by the Board. This form may be replaced or omitted only by recorded Board action.

(4) Attendance and performance records for learners are to be kept in the central office, and must be available to State Department of Education and/or Department of Health & Rehabilitative Service officials upon executive request.

(5) Etc.

During strategic planning, it might be noted that one or more existing rules, regulations, policies, or requirements are not useful—that is, they do not contribute to the revised mission objective. Based upon the data collected in the needs assessment and the visions/values analysis, a rational case may be made for changes. Even laws can be revised or modified if the reasons are strong enough.

Some Curriculum Considerations

There are some interesting curriculum considerations in this required interaction and facilitation among the various "sub-missions" of an educa-

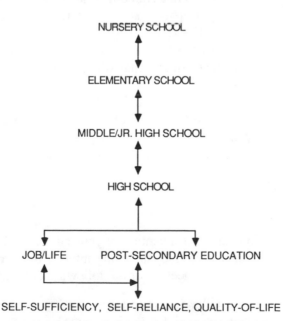

FIGURE 6.9 An educational results chain. Each level should link and contribute to the others.

tional organization. For example, the levels in the chain shown in Figure 6.9 should be mutually reinforcing—each level should contribute to the others.

Making it "all fit together" is a primary purpose of strategic planning. Assuring that all of the missions are (a) measurable, and (b) mutually reinforcing is a basic intention.

Glossary

Mission: The overall job to be done to meet the identified and documented needs; a statement of "Where are we headed", and "How will we know when we have arrived".

Mission Objective: A measurable declaration of the intended results and consequences including specifications for verifying when we have successfully reached where we have headed. An objective has four elements. It states clearly: (1) what results are to be achieved, (2) whom or what will demonstrate or display the result, (3) under what conditions the accomplishment is to be demonstrated, and (4) what interval and ratio-scale criteria will be used to determine if it has been accomplished? A mission objective has two parts: MISSION STATEMENT + PERFORMANCE REQUIREMENTS = MISSION OBJECTIVE

Mission Statement: The intentions about what is to be accomplished. A mission statement is often inspirational while providing general direction.

Taxonomy of Results: Classification of four different measures for results; a result or accomplishment which is measurable on a nominal or ordinal scale is called a "goal", "aim", or "purpose", and a result measurable on an interval or ratio scale is termed an "objective".

Exercises

1. Take the mission statement/intention of your educational agency and convert it to a mission objective (including interval or ratio scale performance requirements) to meet all of the following criteria:

   (a) What results are to be demonstrated?
   (b) By whom or what is it to be demonstrated?
   (c) Under what conditions is it to be demonstrated?

(d) What interval or ratio-scale criteria will be used to determine if it—the mission—has been delivered?

This four-part mission objective will state the exact Outcome (or Output, or Product) of the mission and contain the criterion basis for evaluation.

Performance requirements will contain exact (interval or ratio-scale) specifications, restrictions, and performance characteristics for results to be accomplished, and will identify measurement criteria.

Answer the Following Correctly

Fill in the Blanks

2. A mission objective must meet the following requirements:

(a) _____

(b) _____

3. Derive mission objectives for the major operating parts of your educational organization and identify the extent to which they are mutually enhancing. Identify possible changes which would improve their interactions.

Answer the Following Questions

4. What is the role of the mission objective?
5. What is the role of the performance requirements?
6. Why must a mission intent be converted to a measurable statement—a mission objective?
7. Write ten objective test questions that assess the basic concepts in this chapter.

Endnotes

1 Accountability—knowing what results are to be accomplished and assuring that they are achieved—is an important dimension and contribution of strategic planning.

2 We will use several different labels for measurable criteria, including "measurable objectives", "performance requirements", and "performance specifications". They all relate to being able to precisely measure the extent to which one has arrived at a specified destination, or result.

3 An *indicator* identifies a result which is typical of the total array of results which could be possible. For example, a weather reporter usually gives a temperature reading based on a single sample. Although people know it could vary from outside their window to that taken at city's center, the announced temperature is an "indicator" of the temperature for that area. We know there are differences, but we agree that indicators are "close enough" for our purposes.

4 Including mission objectives.

5 For example, "excellence in higher education".

6 For example, "improve learner performance in math and science".

7 For example, "improve learner performance on or before June 4th in addition, multiplication, subtraction, and division by at least one standard deviation on the Holly Math Skills Test".

8 For example, "on or before June 4th, 1999, reduce to zero the number of graduates of Fox High who are unemployed or not attending institutions of higher learning, as certified by the Department of Employment".

9 Make certain that there are linkages with each objective—including mission objectives—through all organizational elements. If there are no linkages for an objective with all five of the organizational elements, then you have due notice that the objective being considered probably isn't useful within and/or outside the educational organization.

10 Reviewing, Mega planning targets society and community as much the primary client and beneficiary as the school system itself. Macro planning views its primary client and beneficiary as the school system itself. Micro planning views the primary client and beneficiary as an inside-the-organization client, individual, or course.

11 Experienced and results-oriented strategic planners sometimes "project" consequences into existing statements, and thus give more credit than they deserve. For example, one might observe that the only way to "create *excellence* in higher education" is to meet valid performance standards, but adding such unstated criteria to one's understanding will be deceptive. If you want to have precise measurability, add it.

12 Recall, please, that we use such terms as "performance requirement", "performance criteria", performance specifications", and "measurable objective" interchangeably.

13 From Reference [48] permission granted.

CHAPTER 7

Scoping | Data Collecting | Planning | Implementation and Evaluation

Assessing Needs

What Is a Need?

Here is the basic "secret" of needs assessment and strategic planning:[1]

NEED IS A GAP BETWEEN CURRENT AND REQUIRED RESULTS

Simple? Absolutely! Ignored? Almost always.

Most people confuse ends and means, and select solutions before defining the needs and problems. Unsuccessful planning frequently comes from:

(1) Confusing means and ends

(2) Selecting solutions (methods, means, techniques, activities, resources) before knowing the needs and the results to be obtained

(3) Believing oneself to know the needs and problems just from experience (or from experts) alone

(4) Shifting from an ends-orientation when preparing objectives to a means-orientation when identifying needs (by using "need" as a verb)

Another way to view the differences and relationships among needs, means, and ends is described in Figure 7.1.

Needs assessments simply identify, document, prioritize, and specify the *gaps in results* between "What Is" and "What Should Be". A *problem* is a need selected for reduction or closure.

MISUNDERSTANDINGS ABOUND: CONFUSING ENDS AND MEANS

Because of common, everyday language, the word *need* is used as an imperative ("don't ask any questions, just do it") signal prescribing (no choices or options) a premature solution (methods, process, activity,

139

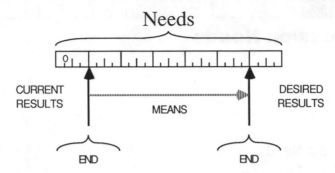

FIGURE 7.1 Needs are measurable gaps in results. Means are possible ways to close the gaps.

how-to-do-it). When used as a verb—need to, need for, needing, need-ed—"need" will slide you into a solution without formal consideration of the gaps between current and required results. Because its use as a verb has such a no-options message, it results in a loss of freedom—freedom to select a solution based on gaps in results, not based upon history, conformity, or intuition.

Strong? Let's see.

Means and Ends (or Wants and Needs) Are Not the Same (An Example)

Sam, who for five years has headed the office of planning and budget bumped into Sandy, the Associate Superintendent for Instruction's office, armed with statistics and a couple of recommendations:

> "The data are clear! We *need some changes here, and now*! A full 78% of all of the learners in grades 2–5 are below grade level in math and verbal skills as assessed on the North Dakota Assessment of Academic Abilities.[2] Of this 78% at-risk group, 87% of those are at least one standard deviation below national norms.

> "And just in case the Board might kid themselves into believing this is a transient situation, a trend has been going on here for the last seven years, and the levels are slowly decreasing, not stable nor rising."

Sandy shifted in her chair. These were important findings, but not ones which brought her any comfort.

> "Sam, I know you and your work well enough to have confidence in the reliability and validity of these results. I also know that the *North Dakota Assessment* is the best instrument available. You find, then, that the situa-

tion is with us, it is getting worse and not better, and you think we ought to fix it. Right?"

Sam straightened up. His message was received loud and clear.

"Without hesitation. The policy requires an increase in the basic skills of learners within our district in order for them to be successful in school and in life. We are going in the opposite direction with about 4/5 of our learners. We *need* some new programs here, and quick.

Based on the breakouts of who these at-risk learners are, I have several recommendations for you to consider carrying up the line."

Sandy was handed a sheet of recommendations labeled:

Draft: Executive Summary for Basic Skills Improvement

A second sheet of the report had a summary of the back-up statistics.

"Sandy, let me go over the recommendations with you. (1) Notify all parents of their children's positions with respect to the norms; (2) develop a remedial laboratory program for these learners—one for language skills and another for math abilities; (3) hire one specialty teacher and two certified technicians for each of the labs; (4) schedule each learner for an individualized program as soon as we get parent approval; (5) the first year of operation for these labs will have to be funded at $105,000 per year above the current operating budget. There will be a first year $37,000 start-up cost."

Sandy's brow was deeply furrowed now. She had heard this kind of response before—for these and other things over the last 25 years. And they weren't all that successful then. She recalled the "back-to-basics" movement, the "excellence" initiatives passed by the legislature three, four, and five years ago. All had been well-meaning, but still the results were obvious—performance wasn't improving. She drew a deep breath, knowing that she had to dignify Sam's initiative, technical competence, and desire to make a genuine contribution to both learners and parents. But she had to leap over the imperative message being delivered ("We *need* some changes here, and now! We *need* some new programs here, and quick.") and identify the basic, underlying needs before spending students' time and the district's budget. Sam might be right, but he also might be picking a solution (the remedial labs) before defining the needs.

"Sam, these data are undeniable. We have too many students performing lower than necessary, much lower. Before we recommend and start these labs, let's make certain that the source of the low performance will be properly considered when we swing into our program. Let's stand back for a moment and see what might be causing this performance discrepancy."

Sam seemed puzzled and a bit testy about this questioning.

> "Sandy, it's simple, they never learned the basics. We have to provide them . . ."

> "Let's look at some of your records. Are there any factors which might be contributing to these performance levels other than, or in addition to, the lack of basic skills? For example, any cultural characteristics, values, role models, parental factors, nutritional problems, physical ills, and such that might be bearing down on these students which might get in the way of their learning and performing?"

> "Come on, Sandy! Let's not get into that bleeding-heart nonsense. These learners just didn't get the basics and now we have to give it to them."

> "Sam, I just don't want to jump prematurely into a solution which, regardless of how well-meaning, will leave them in the same condition they're in now. How about finding out those answers for me?"

Sam went away, his shoulders hunched, and obviously not a bit pleased by this "rejection". He did do the homework, and two days later came back.

> "Sandy, the data are still the same. In addition, it seems as if the demographics have changed over the last ten years, and more and more of our learners don't have English as their first language. Also, when I dug, I found that most of the parents don't have much faith in formal education, and they get that message somehow to their kids who seem to have disdain for us and the whole process. In addition, about 25% of these kids are using drugs or alcohol, and that sure doesn't make it easy for them to learn the basics. Finally, I find that over 40% of these kids don't get enough food at home and the Government meals don't give them enough energy to pay attention even if they want to.

> "I guess you were right in telling me to dig further. We have to give them the basics all right, but we have to add some physical and mental support dimensions to whatever we do.

> "I have a meeting with the Department of Health & Human Services specialists today, tomorrow with their counterparts in the Department of Education and by next week at this time I will have a more complete report and recommendations for you. The problem is still acute, but you've pushed me to set it into a larger context. If we had gone ahead with the labs I guess we would have had a nice solution which didn't go with our learner's problems."

Sandy had learned that "needs" are gaps in results, not gaps in responses, programs, or initiatives. She applied this ends/means thinking to the situation which faced the district, and now she (and Sam) are more likely to be able to design a response which will be of value to the students.

The next week, in the class she taught at the local college, Sandy laid out the following exercise to the students:

Initial needs: (1) lower student performance than standards; (2)basic skills labs.

Defects in rationale: the basic skills lab (a means or solution) was not based on the detailed entry skills, knowledges, attitudes, and abilities of the learners. The analysis, in spite of the "need" to do something fast, and the "need for a new program" jumped from an incomplete identification of needs to the premature selection of solutions.

Actual needs: (1) lower student performance than standards; (2) physical capabilities lower than required; (3) values of parents and students different from those required for positive motivation to learn the basics; (4) drug and/or alcohol use rendered attention-levels below required levels for learning.

Why Do a Needs Assessment?

A needs assessment is an integral part of strategic planning (see Figure 3.1). The process identifies needs (gaps between "What Is" and "What Should Be" for results), places them in priority order, and selects the needs to be reduced or eliminated.

MAKING CERTAIN THAT PURPOSES, OPPORTUNITIES, AND THE SOLUTIONS YOU CHOOSE ARE USEFUL (OR AVOID-SOLUTIONS-IN-SEARCH-OF-PROBLEMS)

Needs assessments can provide direction for identifying and selecting the right job before doing the job right, as advised by Drucker [23]. By identifying correct and important needs before choosing any process or solution, we can improve our effectiveness and efficiency. By doing what's right, we have more confidence that what gets done will be good for everyone concerned—that we will be both effective and ethical. As a part of strategic planning, the identification of needs provides an empirical basis for planning—it adds actual performance data and consequences to the planning values, beliefs, visions, and existing mission information.

BEING PROACTIVE

Most planning efforts are reactive. A problem arises and everyone scurries to fix it. Rather than reacting to situational crises, using a needs assessment allows you to be forward-looking—proactive. Not only can we look at "What Should Be", but also at "What Could Be" as well. The world changes and is changeable, and we should help originate the change rather than simply becoming its victims. Creating a better future is a key function of a proactive strategic planning and needs assessment.

RESOLVING APPARENT CONFLICTS

A "bonus" for doing a needs assessment is that it enables one to resolve evident conflicts between various organizational partners: teachers (or professors), learners, legislators, citizens, management, and our shared world. A needs assessment, by examining gaps in results, can provide both the data base and the forum for comparing actual results with those which should be obtained. By involving three "live" partner groups plus one external results-based set of criteria in both identifying and selecting needs, we can include all of the important "actors"—the three human partners: organizational members; implementors of any program, project, or activity; clients, community, and society—and the actual results and consequences.

Often we see an initial conflict among partner "wants" (or demands):

- individual wants (e.g., promotion, power, pay, use of a favored approach, recognition, more teachers, course improvement)
- organizational wants (e.g., more budget, lower costs to deliver)
- societal wants (e.g., harder workers, smarter employees, better citizens, low pollution, social welfare, useful Outputs, lower taxes, more teachers, less red tape)

In practice, a needs assessment can find common ground and collective purpose so that a "win-win"—practical, agreeable, and mutually appropriate—set of results will happen.

Two-Level Organizational Elements Model (OEM): Three Types of Needs, Three Types of Needs Assessments

Figure 1.3 provides the five organizational elements (Inputs, Processes, Products, Outputs, Outcomes) on two dimensions: "What Is" and

"What Should Be". Three of these elements relate to results (Outcomes, Outputs, and Products). Because a need is a gap in results, and because there are three types of results, there are three varieties of needs—one for each Outcome, Output, and Product, or Mega, Macro, and Micro level.

Since there are three types of needs there are three types of needs assessments. The difference among them is in degree, not kind—the same general functions get performed. The only difference lies in the starting place.

(1) A Mega-type needs assessment starts with identifying gaps in the usefulness of what your organization delivers to its external clients and society (Outcome level).

(2) A Macro-type needs assessment starts with identifying gaps in the quality of what your organization delivers to its external clients (Output level).

(3) A Micro-type needs assessment starts with identifying gaps in the quality of what is produced within your organization by small groups or individuals (Product level).

Recall that the three types of results are related—nested, in fact—and actually interact one with the others. Therefore, a needs assessment at the Micro level actually has implications for needs at the Macro and Mega levels (Table 7.1).

ASKING THE RIGHT NEEDS ASSESSMENT QUESTIONS: FIVE NEEDS ASSESSMENT AREAS

The five questions first posed in Chapter 1 (Table 1.1) provide five alternative frames of reference for needs assessment. All five should be asked and answered. So, shifting these to a needs assessment context (gaps in results-oriented), Table 7.2 provides the questions to be asked and answered in a needs assessment or quasi-needs assessment.

When conducting a needs assessment, the gaps between current and required results for each of these questions should be identified and placed in priority order. The results chain which was related to needs (in Figure 2.2) also provides the suitable sequence for assessing needs.

Whether we recognize it or not, in a Mega sense, all of these five questions (and elements) lurk, waiting to be asked and answered, in every organization. None of the five questions are more "right" than the others, although each has a particular usefulness. The Mega option would provide a linked chain—composed of results, processes, and resources—of all the questions flowing from Outcome through Input.

Table 7.1 Three types of educational results, the primary level of their needs assessment and planning focus, and typical examples.

Types of Results	PRIMARY Level of Planning and Needs Assessment Focus	Typical Examples of Data Points
PRODUCTS	MICRO	Test score, course passed, competence gained, etc.
OUTPUTS	MACRO	Graduate, certificate of completion, licensure, promoted, etc.
OUTCOMES	MEGA	Individual self-sufficiency, self-reliance, collective social payoffs, etc.

Table 7.2 The questions to be asked and answered in a needs assessment and quasi-needs assessment.

Type of Needs Assessment and Quasi-Needs Assessment Focus	Questions to Be Asked and Answered
Needs	
Outcome/Mega	Am I concerned with closing the gaps in results related to the *usefulness* of that which my organization delivers to external clients?
Output/Macro	Am I concerned with closing the gaps in results related to quality—meeting specifications—of that which my organization delivers?
Product/Micro	Am I concerned with closing the gaps in results related to the quality of that which an individual or a small group within my organization produces?
Quasi-Needs	
Process	Am I concerned with the gaps in availability and/or quality of resources used?
Input	Am I concerned with the gaps in availability and/or quality of resources used?

NEEDS ASSESSMENTS, NEEDS ANALYSIS, AND CONFUSION

All that glitters isn't gold, and all that gets called a needs assessment isn't! Earlier we noted the tendency to call things we want, really want, or really *really* want "needs". Because of this, we often hear "What in-service training do we *need?*" not "What performances do we require?". There is the desire (almost, at times, the passion) to get a solution, or "fix"—and get it quick. So many things labeled "needs assessment", "training needs assessment", or "needs analysis" are really examining the desires (wishes, wants, demands, fantasies) for a particular solution.

Before picking a particular needs assessment model, ask the questions in Table 7.3.

Needs assessments provide the unvarnished results-based information required to identify the gaps between current and desired (or required) results. It uses both judgement-based and performance-based results. Much of what gets called "needs assessments" and/or "needs analyses" only tend to give part of the story. Many available formulations don't completely deal with the Needs Assessment Check List (Table 7.3) questions #1, 2, 3, 5, 6, and 7. In addition, most tend to rely on the perceptions of organizational players.

Table 7.3 A needs assessment check-list for selecting or designing a needs assessment.

A Needs Assessment Check-List
1. Does it target ends rather than means?

2. Does it cover the three levels or organizational concerns:
    — Micro (or Products);
    — Macro (or Outputs);
    — Mega (or Outcomes)?

3. Is it free from direct or indirect assumption concerning the solution (such as training, human resources development, management-by-objective, "excellence", etc.)?
4. Does it collect perception data about gaps in results from each of the three partner groups (recipients, implementors, and society/community)? (Recall the partners identified in Figure 1.6)
5. Does it collect and use performance-based results and not just the perception of the partners?
6. Does it identify the gaps in results in measurable performance terms?
7. Does it integrate the perception data with the performance data?
8. Does it place the gaps in priority order?

It is usually easier and less threatening to ask opinions about means, processes, and resources than it is to find out about gaps in results. Needs assessments are more than just questionnaires [54]. Both "hard" and "soft" data must be collected and compared before you can have much confidence in the needs identified. Let's get into that more.

Needs analysis comes after a needs assessment—in order to analyze something (break it down into its constituent component parts) you have to identify what that "something" is. Needs assessments identify the needs to be analyzed. Needs analyses find the causes and reasons behind the existence of the needs—they examine the linkages between adjacent organizational elements (see Figure 2.4) such as between Process and Products, Products and Outputs, and/or Outputs and Outcomes at either the "What Is" or "What Should Be" levels [62].

Hard and Soft Data

SOFT DATA

People's perceptions are, for them, reality. If they think something is so, it will be hard to change their minds. Any needs assessment will have to take into account perceptions of the partners.

One important source of perception-data in strategic planning is the collection of beliefs/values (Chapter 4) and visions (Chapter 5). Because this information is based on personal and private perceptions which cannot be independently verified, it is called *soft data*.

Many sources of perception data exist or may be constructed [55]. Frequently, questionnaires and interviews are used to collect this type of data.[3] This data is important so that (a) we take advantage of what is known by our partners, and (b) important partners and opinion leaders will identify with the results—that which Drucker [23] termed "transfer of ownership" from the planners to the partners.

There are other techniques allowing the planning partners to identify the perceptions and rationales of others, to share different views (if not biases) and to achieve a sensitivity to other perspectives. The art of negotiation is helpful here, especially if the planning partners first accept a common "North Star" towards which all may steer. Transformation—the complete shift from one position to another—is more difficult, but can happen when rationality is in focus within a context of a sensible and justifiable results-orientation.

HARD DATA

What happened is what happened. Performance is performance. Actual results and consequences which can be independently verified must be included in a sensible needs assessment. Possible data points (with their associated Organizational Element classification noted) might include:

- graduation rates (Output)
- drop-outs (Output)
- push-outs (Output)
- social class (Input)
- color (Input)
- race (Input)
- ethnic background/values (Input)
- primary language (Input)
- truancy rate (Product)
- accidents (Outcome)
- complaints (Outcome)
- grievances (Product)
- promotion to next grade (Product)
- promotion to middle school (Output)
- promotion to high school (Output)
- graduation from high school (Output)
- graduation from college (Output)
- lawsuits (Outcome)
- standardized test results (Product)
- criterion-referenced test results (Product)
- unemployment (Outcome)
- underemployment (Output)
- honors and awards (Products if internal, Outcomes if external)
- military service (Output)
- citizenship acts (Outcome)
- paid taxes (Outcome)
- etc.

USING BOTH HARD AND SOFT DATA

Using both hard and soft data provides the appropriate information when you decide on what to change and what to keep in your educational

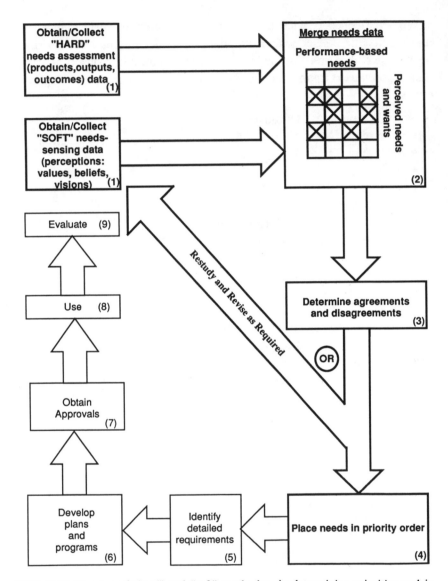

FIGURE 7.2 The use of "hard" and "soft" needs data in determining priorities and interventions.

enterprise as shown in Figure 7.2. Notice that the suggested process has you collect and use both hard and soft data. Once collected, determine the agreements and disagreements between them to distinguish what needs are to be restudied and which ones are to be prioritized.

The Nine Steps of a Needs Assessment[4]

The entire needs assessment process may be viewed in nine steps.[5] Following each of the nine steps are some ways and means for achieving them. The exact methods and tools you choose should be based on your particular situation. These are some guides.

Needs assessment is a major element in creating the data base for strategic planning. Chapter 3 (Figure 3.1) outlined a strategic planning process which involved the collection of planning partner information concerning (a) beliefs and values (Chapter 4) and (b) visions (Chapter 5). It also suggested stating the existing educational mission in performance terms (Chapter 6).

This data is potentially useful for the needs assessment. Belief and vision statements may serve as sources of soft data for the needs assessment. However, the beliefs and values as well as the visions and mission definition provide information that may also be considered during the PLANNING phase when the needs data is matched with the balance of the data from the DATA COLLECTING phase. The hard data and existing mission provide the critical "What Is" data. Figure 7.3 shows the ways in which beliefs and values, visions, and existing missions contribute to a needs assessment, either while doing a needs assessment or later in the first two steps of the PLANNING phase.

Here are the nine steps.

1. DECIDE TO PLAN USING DATA FROM A NEEDS ASSESSMENT

Selecting a Proactive Approach

Some people, unfortunately, choose to react to problems and situations. They gather problem data, examine gaps, and then simply try to close them. Still other approaches are: (a) having someone else tell you what to do, (b) doing what has been done in the past, or even (c) letting the problem go and putting faith in things turning out alright.

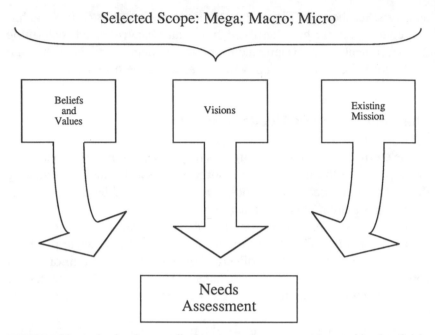

FIGURE 7.3 Strategic planning contributions to needs assessment (or provides data for the *Planning* phase).

One's first hunch might be that it is more time-consuming to take this needs assessment approach (and just jump right into a solution). It isn't. You can act in haste and repent in leisure. A proactive needs assessment (which begins by identifying and justifying the needs and problems) cuts down on having to go back later to repair the damage from not resolving the problem the first time around.

And consider the future—the past is not that wonderful. We should consider the past only as a prologue to the future. Strategic planning is one way to try to change what should be changed. The future is cloudy, erratic, and changeable. Anyone's crystal ball gets very murky even for this afternoon. Because of this uncertainty, some people behold planning with trepidation and seemingly want to "do yesterday over again—more efficiently".

Any rational needs assessment should look at "futures" in order to recognize where our society and organization is going, where it could be moving, and where it should be headed. Repeating yesterday ignores the risk that past mistakes might simply set the stage for future failure. We can, in a changing and changeable world, choose to be the victims or masters of change.

2. CHOOSE (OR CONFIRM) THE NEEDS ASSESSMENT (AND PLANNING) SCOPE (OR LEVEL) TO BE USED: (A) MEGA, (B) MACRO, (C) MICRO

Suggested: Use All of the Three Types of Results: Products, Outputs, and Outcomes

All results are ends, but all are not equally important in delivering individual, organizational, or societal success. Using the three levels of results is critical. By ignoring the differences and relationships among the three scopes of results we might (and probably will) improperly relate organizational efforts, organizational results, and societal payoffs. Restricting our planning to less than the Mega level should be done with the unmistakable cognizance that we either (a) have confidence that the result-chain (Figure 2.2) will be correctly accomplished, or (b) we are willing to risk getting here-and-now results which might not make an organizational contribution or have a positive societal/client payoff. If earlier planning (and needs assessment—remember that we are using "planning" in this chapter to include the element of needs assessment) selected the Micro or Macro levels, this is a good time to go back and reconsider that choice.

A useful way of keeping ends and means related is to use the Organizational Elements Model [47, 48, 49] covered in Chapter 2 and the templates in Chapter 6. To keep track of the three levels of results—and to help keep them from being mixed together or lost during planning—put together a format for listing them, such as the one in Figure 7.4

Each time an entry is made, check to be sure that (a) it is entered at the correct results level, (b) it is an end, and not a means, (c) you are including all of the levels of planning you selected, and (d) interactions and interrelationships within result-type levels (Micro to Micro; Macro to Macro) and between levels (Micro to Macro; Macro to Mega) are properly accounted for—don't get trapped at one level without realizing the interactions. If the Micro or Macro level has been selected, use of this format will serve as a continuing reminder that higher levels of results have been assumed.

The "Unit of Analysis" to Be Used

If we take on the Mega scope it becomes a holistic frame of reference. Macro plus Micro level concerns are organizationally focused, and working only on Micro is "middle-level".[6]

TYPE OF RESULT	CURRENT RESULTS	DESIRED RESULTS
OUTCOME (Mega)		
OUTPUT (Macro)		
PRODUCT (Micro)		

FIGURE 7.4 A format to track the three types of results (but don't forget the interactions between and within the levels).

Including Both "What Is" and "What Should Be" in Planning

Planning, after all, intends to create a better future. It aims to efficiently get us from a current state of affairs to a better one. Our planning could simply focus on improving our current efficiency—making "What Is" better—or it can also create a more responsive "What Should Be". There are two dimensions, or levels, for proactive, responsive, and responsible planning and doing:

- WHAT IS (our current situation)
- WHAT SHOULD (OR COULD) BE (an improved or "best" situation)

Successful planning formally considers both "What Is" and "What Should Be", and therefore planning using the three types of results should be bi-level, as shown in Figure 6.6. Knowing this, the planning group can decide on the appropriate frame of reference, or unit of analysis, for needs assessment, planning, and accomplishment. Review the now-familiar questions in Table 2.2.

Quasi-Needs Assessments

If your needs assessment and planning focus were to be on Processes and/or Inputs, you risk rushing to close gaps in processes and resources without knowing the results to which they relate. Because these relate to gaps in resources and methods but not to results, this type of concern is better termed "quasi-needs assessments" or "needs analysis" [62]. Many failures in organizational improvement come from picking solutions, interventions, or tactics before defining and justifying the underlying needs and problems first.

Evaluation Concerns

If your focus were to be on evaluation, the concern is with comparing your results with the intentions. While evaluation is a relative of needs assessment, it takes on a different set of after-the-fact issues (which we will talk more about in the last chapters).

3. IDENTIFY THE NEEDS ASSESSMENT AND PLANNING PARTNERS

Partners in Planning—Significant Others—Are Critical to Proactive Needs Assessment and Planning Decisions

The people important in making and supporting the results of any plan should be included in this decision. To identify them, list those who:

(1) Can and will participate in the planning
(2) Approve or support anything which comes from the needs assessment and planning
(3) Will be influenced by any plans and results

Such "gatekeepers" could involve:

- supervisors, managers, and executives who will use the plan
- important community members (or leaders)
- parents, educators, union leaders
- those who may be influenced by what might be planned
- other educators and professionals (e.g., State Department of Education experts, psychologists, health-care specialists, professors)
- those who could control the success of the effort

Including significant others—in proportion to their representation in the total population—in the planning process makes sense for many reasons:

- They will provide useful information which might be otherwise overlooked.
- It reduces the possibility of implementing a quick-fix.
- They will likely "own" both the planning process and its results, and will tend to become its proponent.

It is important that all planning partners and those who might have "go/no-go" authority over its results have a common frame of reference. The rationale in this book could provide them with a shared "North Star".

Including people as "planning partners" in the process is done both to obtain useful input and to get the significant others involved in the process and consequences of the resulting identified needs. Representative of three partner groups (Figure 1.7) include: implementors (those developing and who would likely deliver any interventions); recipients (such as teachers, learners, administrators, trainees, custodial workers); and society-clients-community (those who will be impacted by our Outputs external to the system). Also, active and genuine participation will develop ownership among the partners and their constituencies. Earlier, in the discussion of needs assessment step 1, there was a list of some of the gatekeepers who might be involved as planning partners. One way to view the planning partnership is as a triangle, as shown in Figure 1.6. This emphasizes that the perceptions of all the partners as to the gaps in results between "What Is" and "What Should Be" are important.

4. OBTAIN NEEDS ASSESSMENT PARTNER'S PARTICIPATION

When you are doing a needs assessment you can do without those who (a) were told to be there, (b) didn't want to miss anything, and (c) view participation as another opportunity to seek power and influence. There is too much to do without getting tangled up with these types of people. Useful planning (and needs assessment) depends on the right people doing the right things at the right time.

Get Commitment. Be Frank.

After identifying representatives who should be included, get them involved and committed. Contact each one and follow-up in communicating to them all of the facts and mutual understandings. Tell them definitely what will be provided (such as data, access, materials, human resources, transportation, expenses, payments). Relate exactly what they will have to provide in terms of time, travel, and levels of work. Give them a judgment about the form of their participation, who they will be working with, and what reports you expect.

Meetings can be face-to-face, or through questionnaires, teleconferences, a Delphi Technique (a method of getting group interaction without convening people in face-to-face groups), or computer-networking.[7]

Candidly discuss the implied criticism and threat carried by strategic planning and needs assessment, and provide assurance that there is none intended in this activity. Let everyone know that there will be no blaming, fault-finding, criticism, or scapegoating. The plan and the process is their property, used only so that they may become proactive in identifying which results are useful and which should be changed.

Many people come into a planning situation thinking that others will tend to hog the limelight, that a report has already been framed and they are intended only to rubber-stamp it, or that they are only being used for window-dressing. These are your partners in planning—be clear, precise, accurate, and truthful. Assure each partner that activities will be scheduled based on their requirements, not just yours. Deliver on your promises.

5. OBTAIN ACCEPTANCE (OR CONFIRMATION) OF THE NEEDS ASSESSMENT (AND PLANNING) FRAME OF REFERENCE: MICRO, MACRO, MEGA

Agreement on the level and scope is essential. Let the planning partners know the optional frames of reference (you might want to use some of the material in this book). The results chain usually reveals that the success of the organization resides in the linking and integration of all of the means and ends.

More than likely, one or two partners will want to zero in on a pet process, solution, or resource. Try not to let this business-as-usual orientation take the day. Revisit the total relationship among organizational efforts, organizational results, and societal and client payoffs. Discuss the importance of creating a better future, not just a more efficient mirror of yesterday.

Choosing the Correct Level for Needs Assessment and Planning

At center stage should be the commitment to a better future for learners, educators, and the society. If some partners choose to concentrate on Inputs (such as funds, facilities, resources, staff) or Processes (such as methods, courses, course content, training, scheduling, team-building) ask:

"If we were to implement _____, what results will we get?"

"If we do _____, what are the results we could get with the findings?"

"If we increased the number of teaching assistants, what would be the results and payoffs?"

"Increase of the budget to _____ will bring what kinds of payoffs?"

"If we were to close that school, what would happen to and for learners?"

"If _____ is the solution, then what's the problem?"

Show them where they are entering in the OEM and results chain, and ask them to describe the path through to the required results. Most educators and planning partners have never considered an organization as being a means to societal ends. Walk them through the OEM and the results chain so they will get comfortable with the ends-means relationships. Be tolerant, enduring, and patient.

Steer clear of the tendency to only improve the work environment, add perks, or work on would-be motivational possibilities. Recall the two dimensions of results ("What Is" and "What Should Be"), Self-Sufficiency-related, and Quality of Life-Related, and ask the partners to make certain that all are being included, in proper sequence.

If the planning team decides to restrict the effort to less than the Mega level, at least they did so with full knowledge of that which they were excluding or assuming.

6. COLLECT NEEDS DATA (BOTH EXTERNAL – OUTSIDE THE ORGANIZATION – AND INTERNAL – WITHIN THE ORGANIZATION)

When collecting data, there is information which came from both internal and external scanning (see Figure 3.1). This is the stage where that data is put to work.

Collect and Use Both Hard and Soft Data

A crucial component in successful planning is to identify the results to be delivered as well as to ensure that everyone involved is understanding and supportive. Perceptions must be weighed, and any differences between views and performance must be resolved. Both "hard" and "soft" data may be used to answer Mega, Macro, and Micro-related questions. (Recall that the Organizational Elements related to internal results are Products and Outputs, and the element for the external one is Outcomes.) Data collection methods, tools, and techniques abound for both hard and soft data. A number of books and methods are available. The best way to access them is through the questions you pose. The data collected must be reliable, so the selection of any data collection method should be checked.

Collecting Soft Data

There are useful data available from people's informal observations and experiences, i.e., soft data. Keep in mind, however, the notorious unreliability of personal observations by themselves. Soft data are the most trustworthy when they are supported by actual performance results (hard data), or at least by multiple observations or consensus of several different "soft" data sources.[8]

Needs Assessments: More Than Just Questionnaires

Want to collect data and not know how to use it? How would you like to send out questionnaires, obtain and reduce the data, find there is no rational way to assign priorities among the "needs," and just use questionnaires *alone* to assess needs [55]? To be sure, soft data concerning perceptions are important. But when you simply ask about (a) "What do you need" [sic][9] or (b) suggested solutions (such as resources, methods, support, course titles, etc.), there is not much you can do with the summary of respondent's wishes. Without knowing the gaps between current and desired results, there is no sensible and justifiable way to place priorities among the perceived needs. Questionnaires should:

- identify gaps in results, not gaps in resources, methods, or processes
- identify gaps for the three levels of results

- communicate clearly and without confusion
- not be biased by including (either directly or implied) solutions, methods, resources, or processes
- be relatable to hard data so that agreements and disagreements between hard and soft data might be found
- be long enough to give reliable results, and short enough to ensure that people will actually complete it

While questionnaires are quick, easy, and not difficult to assemble, and while there are various so-called "needs assessment" instruments available, all seldom provide crucial data for identifying gaps in results. Questionnaires, especially the off-the-shelf variety, usually only target wishes about methods, resources, and how-to-do-its—listings of desired resources and "fixes". Asked in the conventional manner, most people will speak to favored solutions and not even get to the underlying problems.

By collecting both soft and hard data, you may identify the agreements and disagreements between performance and perception. Figure 7.2 shows how both types of data can be used and orchestrated.

Needs assessments rely on planning partners' perceptions. People's perceptions are what they know and believe. Including soft data such as beliefs, values, and visions is a vital element in a successful planning effort. The important point, however, is to *combine* both sources of data in order to ensure validity.

Collecting Hard Data

In addition to the beliefs, values, and visions of the partners there should be a data-based "partner" supplying "hard", performance-based, independently verifiable indicators.

Data Exist

There are data already available. A useful way to find existing data is to:

(1) Prepare questions which target information defining where you want to go.

   Mega/Outcome level:

   - What is the financial status of completers? For which learners, and which majors or areas of study?

- How many employees hold jobs outside of our organization in order to make ends meet?
- Are there any deaths or disabilities which have been caused by us?
- Do our students enjoy their jobs and their lives?

Macro/Output level:
- Do our citizens approve of that which we deliver?
- Do our students get accepted to colleges and universities?
- Do our nursery school completers do well in the early grades?
- Do our graduates get into appropriate graduate programs?
- Are our faculty sought as consultants because of their expertise and stature?

Micro/Product level:
- What is the failure rate of students in various courses?
- What is the accident rate in our schools? What is our lost-time?
- Do our students get promoted?

(2) Identify *quantitative* indicators of actual (and later on, required and desired) results that lead to personal/individual performance measures impacting on both society and the organization. Such quantitative indicators are:

- positive societal impact by graduates/completers/non-completers might include: employer satisfaction; reduction in crime rate and criminal behavior; citizenship participation; improved quality of life for individuals and community; safety.
- self-sufficiency[10]
- mutual interdependence
- self-reliance
- health changes due to reduction in pollution
- reduction in neighborhood decay
- parent support
- contributions
- efficiency
- societal good (social spin-offs)

Some *personal/individual* criteria for use as indicators of self-sufficiency and self-reliance might include:

No person of legal age will, unless they are in school, be under the care, custody, or control of another person, agency, or substance, for example:

- health, both physical and mental
- not in a jail, mental institution, or on parole
- no substance abuse (as noted above)

An individual's consumption will be equal to or less than her or his production/contribution. This might include:

- credit rating
- not receiving government transfer payments (e.g., food stamps, unemployment, Aid For Dependent Children, etc.)
- citizenship participation and contributions (votes, public service, etc.)
- quality of life (marital satisfaction, enjoyment of work, socially active, takes part in the arts, does volunteer work, etc.).

When considering *organizational performance* within the educational establishment, other results could be used:

(1) Organizational/mission acceptance (e.g., public funding level)
(2) Accidents
(3) Grievances
(4) Lawsuits entered and sustained
(5) Failures of learners
(6) Drop outs
(7) Truancy
(8) Performance in higher grades
(9) Publications of faculty in refereed journals
(10) Books
(11) Committee memberships
(12) Contract and grants obtained

The societal impact indicators should be projected into the future so that they provide a tangible target. We may use them to define the "world" we wish to create, the kind of environment in which we want our children and grandchildren to live.

Quality of Life: An Important Planning Consideration

In developed nations and societies, we have pretty good assurance that most people will, at least, survive. Given that level of assurance, the quality of life for educators, community members, and students becomes increasingly important. The very basic and fundamental (to useful strategic planning) self-sufficiency and self-reliance criteria relate to whether or not we will survive. Quality of life indicators deal with "Now that we are surviving (or are now well on our way), how do we make this life worth living?"

Social Spin-Offs: Individual Plus Societal Payoffs

What's good for one person might not be good for everyone else. In the early days of mining, the risk of black lung disease was "paid-off" by increased salary, but later illness and its consequences were borne by all taxpayers. So, *social spin-offs*—the collective contributions made over and above (and sometimes different from) individual payoffs [102]—are very important strategic planning considerations.

When considering individual and social consequences, add into the mix the collective good (or harm) which might flow from any program, project, or activity. For example, will education contribute to community and social good, as well as allow an individual to get and keep a job? Indicators for individual and collective payoffs should be used.

Using the Organizational Elements Model (OEM) As a Needs Assessment and Planning Template[11]

The five Organizational Elements in the two level format (one level for "What Is" and the second for "What Should Be") provides a framework, or template [48,56] for:

- doing a needs assessment—identifying the gaps between current and desired results and consequences (Products, Outputs, Outcomes) plus considering the contributions of the two quasi-needs areas—Inputs and Processes)
- assuring that all Elements for planning are considered

This use of the OEM as a planning template is done by collecting the needs data and sorting them into the OEM in order to:

- identify data which is on-hand as well as that which is missing (noted as "empty cells")

- further ensure that the various contributors to planning and success are available and being used

As planning progresses, enter what has been identified and developed into the OEM framework and examine for completeness and linkages. Be certain that you have included the two dimensions of "What Is" and "What Should Be".

Past History—Why Things Are the Way They Are Now—Can Be Useful In Designing for Future Success

The past is a prologue to the future. We can use information about the past in developing our "What Is" data base. This forms the history/experiences of the past "bedrock" from which we must or could move. The study of the past offers the opportunity to understand today's problems and successes as well as tomorrow's opportunities. If we choose, we can be the masters of our future, not just the victims or spectators.

Include the Future

There is an abundance of "futures" projections and trends. Acquire and use these as you identify "What Should Be" and "What Could Be". Visioning, that which we discussed in Chapter 5, is a source for outward-looking planning. Together, as planning partners, we can "envision" the future that we would like to achieve for our society, our organization, our students, and ourselves; and we can include this in our mission objective and performance requirements. The future, after all, is the content of the Outcomes cell of the "What Should Be" dimension of the OEM.

7. LIST IDENTIFIED, DOCUMENTED, AND AGREED-UPON NEEDS

After collecting the data, enter it into a form to help assure that it is complete.[12] Enter it into a "needs assessment matrix" such as suggested in Figure 7.4.[13]

Keep perfecting the entries in the matrix until there is agreement about the data. Assure yourselves that it deals only with results. This might take several runs, or repeats. Stay consistent with the planning scale you have selected. Get agreement among the partners about the needs to be addressed. Ensure that agreement has been reached (the partners should select the level), and that the hard and soft data also agree. You may want to identify a time-frame for meeting some of the needs—a sequence for their elimination or reduction.

When there is disagreement, either between the "hard" and "soft" data, or among partners (or both), you must collect more data. To reconcile differences, look at the data in different lights, but don't go ahead until the disparities are resolved. Some sources for disagreements might include:

- incomplete or faulty hard data
- partner(s) still focused on means or resources
- missing hard data
- territoriality

When there are disagreements, collect additional hard data, and check with the disagreeing partner(s) to make certain their perceptions can be backed-up with external reality. Work together. No one can be sure his/her data is valid and reliable—so do more investigating. Reason together.

Frustration will be part of the scene at first as you watch some of the partners get preoccupied with means, solutions, and the way-we-have-always-done-it methods, in spite of data which shows the overall results clearly do not meet the needs. Be patient when a few people become resistent to change, or when they distort reality by calling "means" "ends", or argue that the system cannot be changed, or that the bosses won't "buy it" and . . . every excuse imaginable. Be patient, remember the integrity of the approach and calmly keep reintroducing rationality.

8. PLACE NEEDS IN PRIORITY ORDER AND RECONCILE DISAGREEMENTS

Have the partners rank each need (or related clusters of needs) on the basis of the cost to meet and the cost (both financial and social) to ignore each. With these rankings, the partners (or their representatives) should derive the priorities.

Techniques available for obtaining agreement on priorities include the nominal group technique (which fosters groups coming to a common view), vote-taking, role-playing, simulation, and open and objective discussions.

Agreements on priorities should be based upon what's "right" and not simply on adding up votes—that is why the needs data was collected in the first place. Stay with the methods and data that brought you this far.

When you have disagreements, don't argue and fight. Recall the usual ends/means confusion and realize that most differences come from people really believing that they are dealing with ends while really mired in means. Pose "If we accomplished _____, what would be the result? And what would be the result from that? And from that?" Use the results chain as the basis for tracking results, and for relating ends and means.

Another useful framework for understanding why people act the way they do is provided by Greenwald [29,30]. He advises that people do what they do because they receive payoffs which are important or valued by them, even if we outsiders don't realize or value those consequences. For example, to get attention, a student might misbehave, while most of us wouldn't use that method. When someone seems to be acting in an unusual or unorthodox manner, ask yourself "What payoffs might they be getting for their position and actions?" If you know what they find rewarding, you might use that information to facilitate their awareness of better consequences for different conduct.

9. LIST PROBLEMS (SELECTED NEEDS) TO BE RESOLVED AND OBTAIN AGREEMENT OF PARTNERS

This is now the easy part. List the agreed-upon problems (needs selected for resolution) along with their assigned priorities. The problems in priority order provide essential planning information for:

- developing, identifying, and selecting a preferred future
- preparing a possible new or revised mission objective
- completing a problem and needs analysis to reveal the characteristics, causes, and detailed specifications for eliminating or reducing each
- considering optional ways and means for meeting the needs, and then identifying the advantages and disadvantages of each possible methods-means
- selecting the best tactics, tools, and methods
- deriving a management plan
- beginning a sensible, justifiable evaluation process which use the needs, problems, and requirements to discover if (a) progress is being made, and (b) we have resolved the problems and met the needs

Quality

Many organizations, including educational ones, are using "quality" management programs. "Quality" seems to have many definitions, a usual one being "fitness for use". Others include conforming to specifications, and having no defects [92].[14]

In application, conventional "quality programs" often tend to hone in on Processes and Inputs (better teaching, less waste, more time-on-task, more cooperation and teamwork, higher wages, etc.) and assume that good results cannot be far behind.

We suggest educational "quality" may be improved at three levels: Mega/Outcome, Macro/Output, and Micro/Product. By identifying the gaps in results (needs) at these levels, appropriate quality programs may be tied to closing selected gaps.

By using such a results-based "quality" program, fitness for use may be accurately defined and delivered. Once again a focus on ends before means will improve the probabilities of success.

Needs Assessment, Strategic Planning, and Ethics

Quick-fixes might be fast, but they might not deliver the right results to the right partners. Some are often tempted to run away from (or ignore) the ethics and thus select a form of needs assessment which simply asks for solutions and desired resources.[15] To do so is self-deceptive and possibly dangerous.

Those who claim that most people (such as themselves) are too low in an organization or are powerless to seek "the right thing to do", are flirting with substituting rationalizations for ethics [7,45]. Like it or not, failures often publicly surface . . . along with generous portions of blame.

If something is not right, let it be known to those responsible. Give them the opportunity to do the right thing themselves. If the situation in question is crucial (safety, security, honesty), and the boss chooses to act inappropriately, then you have to decide either to take the matter elsewhere, leave, or both. Why get tainted by working for an unethical organization?

Summary

Figure 7.5 provides an algorithm[16] which summarizes the key considerations of a needs assessment.

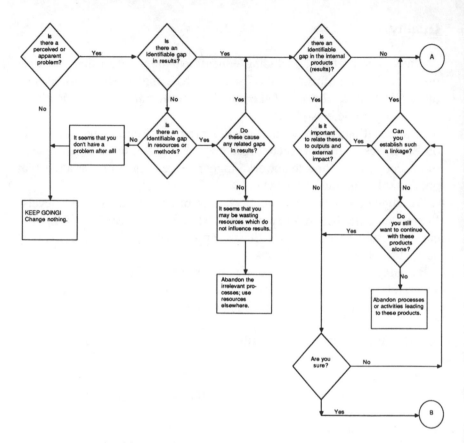

FIGURE 7.5 An algorithm which summarizes the key considerations of a needs assessment.

The nine steps of needs assessment—an essential part of planning—are:

(1) Decide to plan using data from a needs assessment.
(2) Select the needs assessment (and planning) level to be used: (a) Micro, (b) Macro, and (c) Mega.
(3) Identify the actual needs assessment and planning-partners groups.
(4) Obtain needs assessment partners' participation.
(5) Obtain acceptance of the needs assessment (and planning) frame of reference: Mega, Macro, or Micro.
(6) Collect needs data.
(7) List the identified, documented, and agreed-upon needs.

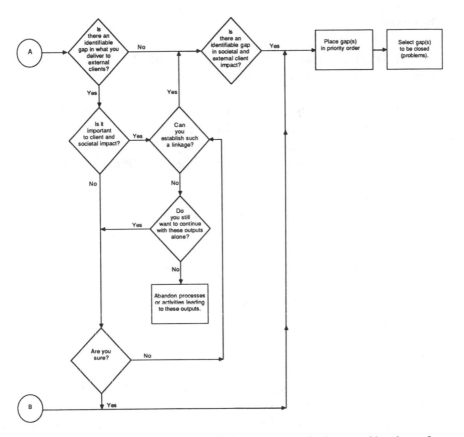

FIGURE 7.5 (continued). An algorithm which summarizes the key considerations of a needs assessment.

(8) List documented needs, prioritized in terms of their importance to be resolved (problems), and reconcile the disagreements among the partners.

(9) List selected problems (needs selected for closure) to be resolved and obtain agreement of partners.

These nine steps, when done, will allow you to:

- identify needs (as gaps in results)
- place the needs in priority order
- select the most important ones
- obtain agreement on both the needs and the importance of dealing with each

Glossary

Hard Data: performance data which is independently verifiable.
Need: (at least for planning purposes) a gap between current and required results.
Needs Analysis: an analysis to find the causes and reasons behind the existence of needs; the examination of linkages between adjacent organizational elements such as between Process and Products, Products and Outputs, and/or Outputs and Outcomes at either the "What Is" or "What Should Be" levels.
Needs Assessment: identifies needs (gaps between "What Is" and "What Should Be" for results), places them in priority order, and selects the needs to be reduced or eliminated.
Quasi-Needs Assessment: the identification of gaps between "What Is" and "What Should Be" for Inputs or Processes, but not related specifically to results.
Soft Data: data which is private, and thus is not independently verifiable.

Exercises

1. Why, at least for planning, is it important to restrict the use of the word "need" to a noun? What happens if a strategic planner is not clear about the differences and relationships between ends and means? Give some examples from your experience.
2. What is a needs assessment? What will it deliver to the strategic planning process?
3. How do needs assessments and needs analyses differ? Relate?
4. Give five examples each of "hard" data and "soft" data. How is each vital to strategic planning? How is each type of data used?
5. What are the nine steps of needs assessment? Briefly describe how each step could be accomplished for your educational agency.
6. How does the way in which you do a needs assessment relate to ethics?

Endnotes

1 Throughout this chapter, "planning" is meant to include (a) needs assessment and (b) strategic planning. The one word is used for both planning elements in order to reduce verbal clutter.

2 This, of course, is both a fictitious test and scenario.

3 Even though responses by a sample (or all) of educational partners are collected, tabulated, statistically analyzed, and reported in terms of means, standard deviations, and coefficients of concordance, does not mean that this is hard data. It isn't. Because each individual's responses are personal and not independently verifiable, this is a source of soft data.

4 The first five steps we suggest for doing a needs assessment could also be applied to the general strategic planning process. If you start with a needs assessment, use these nine as listed. If you start with strategic planning, use the first five steps below as a starting procedure.

5 This is based, in part, upon other work [48,55]. More detailed information is available in these and other referenced works.

6 Tools which deal only with Macro, Micro, Process, and Input level foci are usually called "needs analysis", "front-end analysis", "problem analysis", or "training needs assessment".

7 Also review related material in Chapter 4.

8 Many organizations rely on "soft" data. For instance, media, military intelligence, and marketing organizations piece together multiple independent observations to recognize a pattern and form a reliable conclusion. One frequently used technique is termed "triangulation" where three independent sources confirm a single phenomenon.

9 By asking "What do you need?" (using "need" as a verb) the respondents will almost always jump right into solutions, methods, and/or resources. Asking questions in this form is little better than asking people to "come sit on Santa's knee and tell him what you have always longed to get". Suggested solutions will be the overwhelming data collected unless you design otherwise.

10 One indicator for self-sufficiency expressed as Consumption equal to or less than Production is money (or any other medium of exchange). People tend to invest money where their values lie. They spend on what they value; for example differential amounts spent on teacher salaries versus legal and illegal drugs. Therefore, one proxy—the amalgamation of a number of variables—for self-sufficiency and self-reliance is that consumption is anything which causes an outflow of money, and production is anything which brings an inflow of money. Several sources discuss this and provide cases-in-point, including [63,69,102,113,115].

11 This was also discussed in Chapter 2.

12 Again, recall that this process may be used to consider only the needs data *or* it may include the additional data obtained from the DATA COLLECTING phase and thus may be the same as the first two steps of the PLANNING phase. The process of identifying matches and mismatches is the same, regardless of where in the strategic planning process you do it.

13 Also see Figures 3.6 and 3.7 in Chapter 3 of Kaufman [48].

14 Another important definition, because it is results-related, is provided by Taguchi [105] where quality is seen in terms of the loss imparted to society from the time the item (or product) is sent to the client. Notice that this definition has no "up-site" – it doesn't allow for a product to have positive societal consequences – only losses. We suggest that this is a limited, or partial, definition. A reasonable purpose for creating "quality" is an improved societal return (such as graduates who contribute to society), not just limiting one's losses.

15 As we noted earlier, questionnaires dealing with desired resources and means (programs, techniques, etc.) tend to lead one down this questionable path. Simply giving people what they want (and not identifying – with them – what they should have) might constitute a professional and ethical lapse.

16 From Kaufman [55] permission granted.

PART 2

Restructuring

Integrating, Obtaining Agreement, and Setting New Purposes

Restructuring—Possibilities for Positive Results and Payoffs

Based on our visions, data, and plans we can choose to restructure our schools to achieve useful results and payoffs (or merely to tinker with the status quo). While the term "restructuring" is often used loosely, we emphasize the importance of matching changes to needs and opportunities—a firm results base. Simply patching up an existing system or program, or adding a twist or a dimension is not functional restructuring [28,100].

Restructuring is changing what must be changed to get positive results and payoffs. Changes can range from full curriculum reform to school reorganization, from free access and choice to decentralization [106]. Any restructuring should be based upon firm information, not fads, quick fixes, or solutions-in-search-of-problems. Additionally, whatever gets restructured should stand the test of evaluation: if it gets required results, keep it, if not, change it.

Restructuring is to be based upon facts, not whims or fancy. In applying strategic planning as presented here, we have: (1) selected the scope for our planning (Mega, Macro, Micro); (2) collected our basic data concerning beliefs, values, and visions; and (3) identified our current mission and (if necessary) converted it from a mission statement to a criterion-referenced mission objective. We are now at the planning phase—we have to turn our collected data into overall strategic plans and associated tactics to achieve our visions and meet the identified needs.

Strategic planning is the process of designing a preferred organizational future which will energize the organizational attempts to achieve that vision. Besides developing the necessary tactics, procedures, and operations, to achieve that desired future vision, the strategic planners must identify matches and mismatches in order to reconcile any differences between what is desired and the existing beliefs, needs, missions and vision. Only then can they move smoothly on the road to achievement of the desired or preferred future vision.

175

Thus, we arrive at the point where we must reconcile what we have previously done with the current situation, and make certain that all is well-aligned. That is, all our previous work is revisited so we can determine the degree of fit among the various elements, and ensure that modifications are made if current variables so indicate.

What Do We Know?

Let's review what we know up to this point, and sort and coordinate our information. This is best accomplished by (1) listing our existing information, and by (2) comparing results by addressing a series of relevant questions.

Up to this point we have decided that the focus of our strategic planning efforts was a Mega (societal) orientation, although we could have chosen a Macro (organizational) or Micro (subgroup) focus. We also have collected and scanned for trends shown by hard (independently verifiable) and soft (attitudinal, non-independently verifiable) data to identify needs; derived visions; defined our beliefs and values; and we have turned our current mission statement into one which is stated in measurable performance terms. Thus, we have the following on hand:

(1) The beliefs, values, and visions of our various planning partners and stakeholders

(2) The identified needs (not wants or wishes) geared to the focal level of strategic planning selected. A need is defined as a gap or discrepancy in results between "What is" and "What should be" or "What could be".

(3) The organization's mission statement, written in a manner that identifies where the organization is going in measurable terms. The measurements will permit the planners to know if they have attained their mission.

These pieces of information comprise the substance used to identify how all of these fit together. That is, we can determine what is compatible, and we can discover where conflicts and differences exist. Once we locate the differences and conflicts, we can reconcile them so that all elements are aligned.

Comparing Results

Now that we have collected and organized all we know up to this point in our strategic planning process, our task is to sort it out and analyze it. The steps for doing this include:

(1) Making a list of all the data
(2) Identifying important categories within which to array the data in order to make them understandable
(3) Sorting the data into these various categories
(4) Analyzing the data to identify areas of differences, agreements, and points of confusion

First, make a list of that which you already have. Then organize this list. You can easily develop your own summary format, but make certain you have considered the following important variables.

VISIONS AND BELIEFS

Your data should be organized and stated clearly enough to answer these questions:

- Where should the organization be going?
- How will we know if we are being successful?
- How will we be able to determine if we are not successful?
- What, specifically, must our organization deliver?
- To whom must we deliver?
- When should we deliver it?
- What roles do each of the educational partners play?
- What are the responsibilities of each of the partners?
- What are the restrictions on what we deliver?
- What are the restrictions on how we deliver it?
- What are the values and beliefs relative to education concerning:
  —what?
  —who?
  —why?
  —when?
  —where?
  —how?
- How intransigent are the values and beliefs which are held?

- Who *is* responsible for: goals and objectives; funding; teaching; curriculum; courses; course content; buildings; grounds; management; learning and mastery; learner performance outside/beyond schooling; monitoring performance and achievement; evaluation; renewal?
- Who *should be* responsible for: goals and objectives; funding; teaching; curriculum; courses; course content; buildings; grounds; management; learning and mastery; learner performance outside/beyond schooling; monitoring performance and achievement; evaluation; renewal?
- Who wants the system to: change; stay the same?
- What are the rewards and punishments for: changing; staying the same?
- What are the assumptions about the: nature of people; motivation of people?
- What kind of educational system would each partner like to create?
- What kind of educational system would a consensus of all partners create?
- What kind of society would a consensus of partners like to create?
- What kind of graduate/completer success (beyond schooling) would they like to create?
- How do all of the above fit together?
- If there are areas of disagreement or poor fit, how is consensus and alignment to be achieved?
- What tradeoffs are possible or necessary to reach consensus?
- What impact will each tradeoff have on the vision, mission, and the organization?
- What impact will each tradeoff potentially have for the students?
- What is the time frame, in whole or in part, for accomplishing their vision?
- What, if any, are the en-route stages, and what is the time frame for each?

Second, gather the responses for all of these (or the variables you have selected) dimensions of beliefs, values, and visions for each major partner group. For example, you might pool the responses of educators, parents, community members, and learners. Or, if gender, cultural characteristics, or other demographic factors are important, you might want to cluster the responses under these demographic categories. Once having scanned the responses within and between the selected categories, you can begin to determine if there are any important differences between categorical groups.

A useful activity for the strategic planning partners to employ is that of reviewing the vision, beliefs, and values data, and analyzing them for: (a) agreements, (b) disagreements, and (c) points which require further clarification. This analysis activity could be quite structured and formal, using content analysis methods and rating sheets with the critical variables identified; or it could be done as an informal "arm-chair" analysis with each group of partners identifying important observations about their data. The partners, then, can see areas of misfit. "Scorekeeping" for this activity could use a form similar to the one in Figure 8.1.

Third, make a summary list of the areas of agreement and disagreement. This list should be carefully reviewed against the mega purposes by all partners. When disagreements are apparent, the partners must negotiate changes in order that the final list be one of consensus agreement. Most disagreements fall away when there is a consistent focus on (a) results, and (b) the Mega/Outcome level. Where the partners identify areas requiring further clarification, they must go back and collect additional data to clarify and bring into focus the unclear areas (perhaps utilizing some different methods and techniques than the originally used ones).

It would be helpful if you could develop a process with your strategic planning partners that would promote coming to agreement about emerging incompatibilities among the needs, beliefs and visions. Figure 8.1 can also be used as a "Concerns Matrix" for you to use—a check-list of the elements you should include in your process.

AREAS OF CONCERN	MEANS OR ENDS		BELIEFS	VISIONS	EXISTING MISSION
	M	E			
MEGA OBJECTIVES					
MACRO OBJECTIVES					
MICRO OBJECTIVES					
PROCESSES					
INPUTS/RESOURCES					

FIGURE 8.1 A possible format for tracking results of strategic planning and relating them to basic data collecting-phase activities.

INTEGRATION CHECK-LIST

(1) Identify areas of agreement and disagreement.

(2) Prioritize areas of disagreement.

(3) Take each disagreement area and identify the performance data which support or contradict it.

(4) Form conflict resolution groups and pick the conflict resolution method.

(5) Resolve the areas which can be resolved, and add to the "agree" list.

(6) For each disagreement area, identify soft and hard data which are missing and which would serve as the reasonable basis for resolution (e.g. "if the data says _____ I would shift my opinion").

(7) Collect the necessary hard and soft data.

(8) Attempt agreement, and add the new agreements to the basic list.

(9) Continue the conflict resolution, but perhaps using different methods, including expert opinion or some other new approach.

Conflict Resolution Methods

There are a number of sources for ideas on ways to reduce or eliminate conflict (The Annuals of University Associates, San Diego, are excellent sources for both methods and references). Some guidelines include:

(1) Keep the discussion targeted on ends/results, not means or resources.

(2) Listen to others, don't simply wait to speak.

(3) Relate each position to a Mega objective, or to the highest level of results your strategic planning team has selected. Ask "If we did that (what is suggested by a planning partner), what would the result be?" Keep asking that "what if" question until compatibility with the overall mega mission objective is obtained.

(4) If a planning partner keeps insisting on a means, method technique, or procedure, build a methods-means "place-holder" list for use when the "how-to-do-its" are selected.

(5) Serve as a clarifier of the disagreement and agreement areas.

(6) Serve as a mediator between disagreeing parties.

(7) Realize that the planning partners have been "means oriented" for most of their lives. Be patient and helpful. Don't judge or abuse them.

(8) If a planning partner gets defensive, "join the resistance". Quote her/his position back and attempt to find out the rationale for that position. Agree with it for the time being, and watch the partner start to join you. Sometimes people are only looking for acceptance and recognition, and after getting that, they "open up". Look for the rewards that any partner derives from her/his position, and seek for her/him alternative and more rewarding payoffs [29,30].

Once the areas of disagreement have been resolved, you can again review your organizational mission.

CURRENT ORGANIZATIONAL MISSION

By the time the existing organizational mission has been decided upon (and probably rewritten), it might be a page or more long. Whatever the length of the mission statement, it must be rechecked to see if it contains the crucial characteristics of any mission statement.[1] This can be done by following the steps outlined below.

First, check over your current mission statement to make certain that it has the following characteristics, and that it clearly states:

(1) Where the organization is going
(2) How success and failure of achievement can be measured in interval or ratio scale terms. (The four measurement scales are: (a) nominal—only naming something, (b) ordinal—determining that some things are greater than, equal to, or less than other things, (c) interval—stipulating an arbitrary zero point to start the measurement and specifying equal scale distances, and (d) ratio—starting from a known zero point and having equal scale distances between measurement points.

If your mission statement does not contain, as a minimum, the features listed in numbers 1 and 2, above, revise until it does.

Second, check to see if the statement of mission is compatible with the level of strategic planning selected for focus (Mega, Macro, or Micro). Revise the mission as required.

Frequently, current missions speak in broad general terms (such as "It is the mission of Crosby School District to provide *excellence in education*"); but missions must be accompanied by measurable criteria in order to be monitored, measured, evaluated, and accomplished. Also, in some cases the mission statement might contain some "Mega-sounding" words,

Mission Statement (or Objective) Elements (Existing)	Mission Statement (or objective) Elements (Desired)
1._____	1._____
2._____	2._____
3._____	3._____

FIGURE 8.2 A possible format for comparing existing mission statement (or mission objective) elements with desired ones.

but the details and performance indicators are at the Micro level. If this level-mixing occurs, then you must have the partners add the higher level data. For example, if the philosophical words are Mega and the performance specifications are Micro, go back and add the Macro and Mega elements to bring the mission into measurable terminology.

Third, take the desired visions, missions, beliefs and values, and compare them to the existing ones. You can devise many ways of sorting them into categories, but you might choose to build a matrix like Figure 8.2 for contextual mission comparison between the desired and the existing missions. This technique is also useful to determine desired and existing visions, beliefs and values. In addition, it could be utilized to compare "fit" (or alignment) between the desired vision and mission, the desired beliefs and vision, and for any combination of these items.

By filling in such a matrix, you might find areas which are missing— empty cells within the matrix. These empty cells will give you clues about potential trouble spots. Once identified, work can be completed on adjusting the alignments for a proper fit.

NEEDS DATA

The needs data have been collected through internal and external scanning, and the gaps between "What is" and "What should be" or "What could be" states identify the needs which must be addressed. In each case, the data should:

(1) Be stated in measurable terms
(2) Identify a gap in results (not in processes or resources)
(3) Relate to inside the organization's gaps (needs) as well as to outside the organization's gaps in results (also needs)

If done completely, the needs information will utilize both "hard" and "soft" data. Attitudes ("soft data"—non-independently verifiable) as well as objective facts ("hard data") are important to any strategic planning effort.

Let's now turn to the steps involved in organizing and sorting these needs data. The following general steps will allow you to make sense out of the needs data.

First, sort the needs data into the following categories:

(1) External—(Mega level) needs

(2) Internal—(Macro level) needs

(3) Internal—(Micro level) needs

Second, sort these into the matrix which you developed in the previous step using the existing (and probably revised) mission statement.

Third, check to make certain that all of the dimensions of the visions, beliefs, and values and the existing mission statement are included. If some of these are missing, collect and include them.

Fourth, make a summary matrix which contains the essential data. This matrix may be made from the earlier matrix; but here, superimpose the needs data on it (as if it were a 3-D format). In this way, you may identify where there is support for, or differences with the mission statement, beliefs, visions, values, and needs. Your matrix will now look something like the one shown below. An abbreviated example, provided in Figure 8.3 and based on a hypothetical university, will serve as illustration of this technique. The purpose is to discover which of the needs

Vision and Values Dimensions with Mission Elements	
Mission Comparing Elements	
	(example needs data below)
1._____	a. Increase the graduation rate of doctoral candidates from 78% to at least 95%.
2._____	b. Increase the minorities graduating at least from 21% to at least parity.
3._____	c. Increase grant funds by $5,000,000 per year over the next ten year period. It is now $100,065.
4._____	d. Decrease the non-graduation rate of athletes by 55%. It is now 64%.

FIGURE 8.3 A hypothetical format for comparing visions and values to a mission objective (or statement).

fall within each of the elements of the mission objective (or statement, if not converted with required performance criteria) and determine if some of the needs fall outside the mission. Ultimately, all mismatches will have to be corrected in order to provide a well-aligned road map (matrix) to be used for further planning.

Depending upon your level of educational interests, you might want to differentiate among various data sources relating to the different grade or accomplishment levels. For example, a Nursery school through Grade 3 system might want to see if there are differences among the parents' beliefs, values, and identified needs related to the different ages of the learners. On the other hand, a university might want to see if there are differences between entry classes and sophomores. The actual analysis, however, will depend upon: (a) your scale (Mega, Macro or Micro) of planning, and (b) the questions you want answered.

Fifth, identify the matches and mismatches among the sources of data. List the ones where there are agreements, and identify areas in which there are differences.

This analysis may be done by the entire strategic planning team. Again, the quality and completeness of the analysis will rely deeply on the objectivity of those persons conducting the analysis. If done well, there is likely to be very close agreement between the "soft" needs as-sessment data and the beliefs and values data—they both come from the perceptions of the educational partners.

At this point, let's pause and provide an example of how a school dis-trict identified the matches and mismatches, reconciled the differences, and aligned the vision, mission, beliefs, and needs, once the desired ele-ments were compared to the existing ones—that is, "What Should Be" to "What Is".

EXAMPLE: TOP-OF-THE-LINE SCHOOL DISTRICT

Current Beliefs Examples

(1) All children can learn what we decide to teach.
(2) The school environment shall be safe and healthy.
(3) Teachers and administrators should be knowledgeable and up-to-date.
(4) Students should have opportunities for input.
(5) High expectations of students and all employees should be a cul-tural norm.

Revised Beliefs after Determining Attitudes and Reality

(1) Most children will learn up to 80% of their capacities.

(2) The school environment can be made safe and healthy (after asbestos is removed).

(3) Some teachers and administrators can become knowledgeable and updated by the district offering staff development activities geared to identified needs.

(4) In-class and school-wide procedures will be developed to allow students to have input into decisions affecting them.

(5) Interventions will be undertaken by administration to develop the expectation of high achievement by students and employees as a cornerstone of the school district's culture.

Current Mission

It is TOP-OF-THE-LINE SCHOOL DISTRICT'S mission to provide academic, cultural, social and recreational activities to the students and to the adult community.

Revised Mission

It is the mission of TOP-OF-THE-LINE SCHOOL DISTRICT to offer academic activities to the students in a manner that will allow them to enter the world as productive citizens and to be self-sufficient for life, as indicated by employment, credit, voting, and social service records.

Identified Needs Related to Revised Mission (Examples)

(1) There is a 42% dropout rate in this school district. (It should be 0%.)

(2) Follow-up studies indicate that 18% of the high school graduates are unemployed (It should be 0%).

(3) Sixty-two percent of the teaching and administrative staff have not successfully completed any staff development or training activities in the last five years. (The faculty agreed it should be 0%.)

Current Mission Objectives Established Based on Identified Needs

(1) By the Year 199__ the student dropout rate will be reduced by a minimum of 5%.

(2) By the Year 199__ the school district's follow-up studies will indicate an unemployment rate for our graduates of 0%.

(3) By the Year 199__ the school will offer staff development activities on a continuous basis. These activities will be based on research on effective schools, effective teaching, effective learning techniques, and effective management. In addition, every teacher and administrator shall have successfully completed a minimum of two of these training activities each year.

In order to complete the picture, let's briefly discuss how we go from vision, mission, and mission objectives, to strategies, tactics, programs, schedules, and budgets. Using the mission objectives above, let's provide abbreviated examples which take one mission objective through the budgeting stage.

ATTACKING THE DROPOUT RATE

Strategy (What the District Intends to Accomplish)

The TOP-OF-THE-LINE SCHOOL DISTRICT will decrease its student dropout rate.

Tactics (How the School District Intends to Accomplish the Strategy)

The TOP-OF-THE-LINE SCHOOL DISTRICT will initiate the following programs to accomplish a reduction of the student dropout rate to a maximum of 5% within five years.

Program One: Additional competent counselors will be added to concentrate totally on this category of "at risk" student. Each high school in the district will have a combination of counselors who will have training in social work, vocational counseling, and individual counseling.

Program Two: A wide variety of co-curricular activities shall be put in place, and each student shall be required to participate in a minimum of one of these activities.

Program Three: A student placement service shall be added to each high school for the purpose of locating after-school jobs with businesses, industries, and other job sources which will provide student progress reports to the school's placement office.

Task	Time Target	($) Cost
YEAR ONE		
Hire nine compentent counselors	Sept. 1, 1993	270,00
Hire one secretary	Sept. 1, 1993	18,000
Remodel a classroom for counseling offfices at each of the three high schools	Sept. 1, 1993	120,000
Order and receive equipment and supplies	Sept. 1, 1993	30,000
Collect baseline data and establish a management information system	Nov. 1, 1993	800
Collect end of year data and evaluate the progress	May 1, 1993	400
Make modification in processes based on evaluation	August 1, 1993	0
YEAR TWO		
YEAR THREE:		
YEAR FOUR:		
YEAR FIVE:		
Conduct five year impact analysis which includes the percent of decreases in drop outs, the cost/benefit, and a process audit.	August 1, 1998	2,500

FIGURE 8.4 A hypothetical beefed-up counseling schedule and budget.

Program Four: A parent and/or guardian in-school and outside of school participation program will be initiated.

Taking the example of the "beefed up" counseling services (if later selected), let's follow through with an abbreviated example, shown in Figure 8.4, of scheduling and budgeting for this added program.

Identify and Select the Preferred Future

We know where we want to go, why we want to get there, and we have integrated and agreed upon our values (sometimes through some extensive individual and group soul-searching, data collection, and reconsideration). We have also derived (and perhaps even obtained substantial agreement on) visions. We have converted our mission statements from inspirational to measurable terminology, and we have collected data on the gaps between current and desired/required results (needs).

We have even gone through the partnership exercises and the experience of agreeing on values and visions, based upon the hard and soft data based results-referenced needs. Now, it is time to identify and select our preferred future.

There is nothing new, in terms of tactics and methods, at this juncture. We have earlier discussed consensus-building approaches, and now is the time to:

(1) Summarize and display all: (a) agreed-upon beliefs; (b) non-agreed-upon beliefs; (c) agreed-upon values; (d) non-agreed-upon values; (e) agreed-upon visions; (f) non-agreed-upon visions; (g) documented and selected needs; and (h) existing measurable mission objectives.

(2) Select an appropriate consensus-building technique.

(3) Provide the clear purpose of the consensus-building effort: to derive a common vision for the educational agency and for all of its partners (its communities and society, learners and internal staff members).

(4) Review with the strategic planners the importance of all partners — educators, citizens, learners, community—who have achieved a common "North Star" towards which all can steer and uniquely contribute.

(5) Identify possible: (a) visions to modify, and (b) visions to maintain.

(6) Select the vision (common "North Star") for the educational organization and its partners.

This effort must, repeat *must*, maintain:

- the selected planning frame of reference unless there is a shift upwards from Micro or Macro to Mega
- a results/achievement/accomplishment orientation

While it is tempting to resolve issues by mandating solutions, methods, resources, activities, and actions, it is counterproductive to do so—it prematurely selects methods and means before setting the destination. Methods-means analysis, force-field analysis, and solution identification and selection happens in a later planning phase (see Chapter 11).

It is vital that the selection of a preferred vision—where we are going—is agreed upon by the majority (and, hopefully, the vast majority) of the planning partners. Don't give in to satisfying one or two splinter groups. This is not the time for "playing politics". It is a time to target what is right to accomplish, not just what is acceptable or popular. Strategic planning is a leadership activity. As such, it selects where the organization and its people should go. It doesn't simply count votes or move to a popular destination.[2]

Identify Missions

Based upon the selected vision(s), it is now time to:

(1) Derive a new mission objective (a mission statement plus measurable performance objectives).
(2) Revise the existing mission objective.
(3) Ratify the existing mission objective.

With the Scoping and Data Collecting which has contributed to our getting to this point, it is quite unlikely that option #3 will be useful.

The ground rules for setting mission objectives are covered in detail in Chapter 6. Review that material for completing this strategic planning step.

This step should be fairly simple and straightforward because of the extensive data on hand: the accepted and/or ratified revised vision(s), and the hard and soft data from the needs assessment. Again, make certain that the mission(s) include measurable criteria which state, in unmistakable terms:

- What is to be accomplished?
- What criteria (on an interval and/or ratio scale) will be used to determine accomplishment?

Finally, it should be clear that methods, means, resources, facilities, equipment, and finances should not be part of the revised mission(s). Only results and accomplishments are to be included. Also, if a Mega level had not been previously selected, its use should be reconsidered at this juncture.

Summary

Your data are now ready to sort, and you can start making sense of it all as areas of agreement and disagreement are discovered. You should select a format for data analysis of the matches (agreements) and mismatches (disagreements) which meet your specific strategic planning requirements. Once completed, this analysis becomes the basis for reaching agreement with your partners on the organizational mission as well as the purposes of your strategic plan. You are now ready to consider tactics, and set time targets and resource allocations geared to your strategies.

After coming to agreement on visions, values, missions, and needs, it is appropriate to identify and select a new or revised preferred future. Then, based on this preferred future, you can prepare the "final" mission objective. This new mission objective states, in measurable performance terms, where we are going and how we know when we have arrived. The mission statement is a common "North Star" towards which all partners may steer and contribute.

Exercises

1. Categorize all of your strategic planning team's desired results as Mega, Macro, or Micro; and explain why each one is so categorized.
2. What steps would you utilize to compare the results and to decide which are valid?
3. List the type of questions you would use to determine the beliefs and visions desired by your strategic planning team for your school, school district, or university.
4. Why might missions, visions, and needs not be in the initial agreement?
5. Create a *concerns matrix* which will assist the planners in identifying and reconciling mismatches and matches among visions, beliefs, needs, and missions.
6. List and define ten means of resolving conflicts between and among the strategic planning team's members.
7. Develop a mission objective, and write an action program that is designed to achieve that mission objective. Be specific, and make certain that you have stated clear measurement criteria.

Endnotes

1 You might want to review Chapter 5.
2 Wess Roberts' book provides some very timely and useful understandings of leadership [95]. It could well be required reading for the leaders of a strategic planning activity.

Identifying SWOTs: Strengths, Weaknesses, Opportunities, and Threats

To get to this point in strategic planning, you have: (1) surfaced partner beliefs and values (and possibly reached agreement), (2) identified visions, (3) identified (and operationally defined) current missions, (4) completed an external and an internal environmental scan to identify needs, (5) decided upon the Critical Success Factors (CSFs), (6) extrapolated and projected trend data, (7) derived a new or revised mission in measurable terms (if required) based on alternate and preferred futures, and (8) chosen the preferred future of "What Should Be" as the vision for any plan to accomplish.

When the preferred future of "What Should Be" has initially been decided, the strategic planners must compare the preferred future to the current "What Is" state. The analysis of need data identifies the gaps (or needs) to be met, and possible causes and origins of the needs. This induces planners to modify their initial preferred future, replacing it with a data-based one.

Once the revised future vision is in place and a mission objective has been derived and accepted, it is wise to complete a SWOTs (Strengths, Weaknesses, Opportunities, and Threats) analysis.[1] This activity permits the planners to:

(1) Analyze those supports (*strengths*) that are available to implement strategies and tactics—**not selected now,** but useful later when actually developing the strategic action plan (Chapter 11)—which ultimately will achieve the vision of "What Should Be".

(2) Identify those *weaknesses* which should be corrected in achieving the desired vision.

(3) Identify the *opportunities* that exist in the environment which have not been previously utilized.

(4) Discover the *threats* that exist in the environment which can be avoided, or for which strategies can be developed to diminish consequent negative impact.

Sometimes SWOT is used in a manner that applies the strengths and

191

weaknesses only to the internal environment, while opportunities and threats are applied only to the external environment. For our purpose, the strengths, weaknesses, opportunities, and threats fully apply to both internal and external environments. Each of these SWOT factors must be objectively identified and carefully analyzed. They must be seriously considered when developing action plans. The action-planning strategies and tactics are developed in such a manner that they take advantage of the strengths and opportunities that exist in both the external and internal environments, while using strategies and tactics that avoid, minimize, or overcome the effects of the threats and weaknesses existing in the internal and external environments.

A SWOT analysis is a procedure conducted by the strategic planners to determine the strengths and weaknesses as well as the opportunities and threats that exist both (1) within the organization for which the strategic plan is being developed, and (2) within the external environment (support and restraint structures). The data from both the internal and external SWOT analyses allow strategic planners to deal with strategies and tactics that will enhance the probability of achieving the organizational partners' vision and mission based upon a thorough data analysis.

Examples of SWOTs Analyses

Let's look in on some of the SWOT items that have been identified by *Important University*, *Excellent High School*, and *Omnipotent School District*,[2] beginning with *Important University*. The SWOT analysis completed by the strategic planning group shall be highlighted, and some ideas for action will be presented.

EXAMPLE: IMPORTANT UNIVERSITY'S SWOT ANALYSIS

Strengths: Internal

The staff members of Important University provide services to other state agencies, businesses and industries in the state, governmental units within the state, local school districts, and the state's department of education.

The positive linkages created by Important University's previous service activities (such as business activity trending data provided to the state's business and industrial leaders) can and should be utilized in forming lobbying groups, as well as using individual power brokers, who will

speak on behalf of the university's justifiable requirements during budgetary discussions by the legislative bodies of the state. In addition, the staff
has learned the operational and policy realities of these clients to: (1)
identify emerging trends and requirements, and (2) have an early "warning" of changes and opportunities that will affect the strategies and tactics
utilized by the University.

The magnitude of the impact of Important University's service activities can be realized when one understands that over the previous five
years, the staff has worked with 508 school districts for a total of 10,016
person hours, in addition to serving on over 50% of state agency advisory
committees in such areas as financial aid to public institutions, demographic analyses, economic projections, health and safety regulations,
and curriculum mandates. Finally, the staff has worked with 28 of the
Fortune 100 companies to develop training and retraining programs for
employees, determine market analyses, analyze competitive status situations, develop policies, determine technological requirements, and produce basic and applied research of interest to over 350 corporations. The
magnitude of these service contacts places Important University in a
position to call upon linkages when dealing with support and/or lobbying
efforts that are in the interest of the University.

> Many research grants are received from federal, foundation, and associa-
> tion funds in the areas of engineering technology, medical research, and
> agricultural research.

(The contacts made by professors and grant writers in these areas can
be utilized to extend the research capabilities into other colleges of the
university. A specific plan to do just that must be developed by the university's planners. Over the past five years, the engineering, medical, and
agricultural staff members have received grants totaling $210,000,000,
while all other staff members have only garnered $18,000,000 over the
same time period.)

> The university insists that all senior professors teach classes even when
> they are involved in grant or service activities. This policy pays dividends
> as judged by 81% positive evaluations of professors registered by the stu-
> dents in those courses.

(Once the current students graduate, this high quality of teaching has
the advantage of developing a support group that can be utilized for multiple purposes. Therefore, it is clear this policy should be continued. One
of the most positive responses registered on student evaluation sheets is
the students' appreciation for being instructed by senior professors who

are sought and valued by outside persons or firms, rather than by graduate students or "has been" or "never will be" faculty.)

> Some of the university's professors are presidents or high-ranking officers in their professional associations, and many professors are highly regarded researchers, including three who have won Nobel Prizes.

(This fact can be publicized, and contacts the professors have with professional associations, as well as the prestige and name recognition of the researchers, can be important in developing supports for policy directions desired by the university. Currently, Important University's professors hold or have held the presidencies of six national associations, and sixty-eight professors serve in leadership positions in national associations. Also, 126 professors serve in leadership positions with state and regional associations, and ten professors head international research teams.)

Strengths: External

> The former governor—a graduate—is very powerful politically. She also has a history of being very supportive of the university's efforts.

(Even though the former governor will have to display an even-handed approach when dealing with the various universities within the state, it would be wise to invite her, as an honored guest, to any important university-sponsored event. It would also be prudent to present the governor with an "honored alumnae award" at a highly visible convocation. Finally, it would be a good tactic to get the former governor appointed to the governing board of the university. This would be a possibility since both the current and former governor are of the same political party, and the legislature is dominated by members of that same party.)

> The CEOs and board chairpersons of many major corporations are graduates of Important University.

(The university has many opportunities for appointing blue ribbon committees to study and advise the university's administration and board of control. As many of these CEOs and chairpersons as possible should be asked to serve on these blue ribbon committees. This procedure will keep important support persons in touch with the university, and will maintain strong linkages for other university purposes. It will also allow the university to know about the realities of current and future business environments.)

Opportunities: External

The Federal Government has announced RFPs (Requests for Proposals) for three $5 million medical research grants dealing with heart conditions, cancer, and AIDS.

(Since there are staff members in the School of Medicine at Important University already working on a federal grant related to cancer research, it appears that this research can be extended in another direction. Therefore, the university would stand an excellent chance of obtaining the $5 million grant for expanded and integrated cancer research. Since other universities have done much more with research related to heart conditions, this RFP will not be developed. On the other hand, because of the success of past research, the university will submit a RFP for the $5 million AIDS research grant.)

Many of the businesses and industries in the state employ less than one hundred people, and they have urgent requirements for training programs but cannot afford to hire their own training staffs.

(The university could fill this void by conducting a needs assessment with all the medium and small businesses and industries in the state, and possibly, by developing the training and human resource development intervention programs, could meet the identified needs and requirements. Training, responsive to requirements common to multiple businesses and industries, could be offered on a reasonable cost-per-individual basis for business or industry by utilizing the university's experts and by offering the training at the university or at some centralized site.)

The state legislature and the governor wish to appoint a committee to study ways of developing more equitable and cost-effective methods to finance the public schools of the state.

(The university can make certain that such persons as the professors of educational finance, demographers, sociologists, economists, and strategic planners are included as members of these study committees. This approach will provide service to the state, develop important contacts for the future, and have implications for the School of Education at Important University.)

Opportunities: Internal

Although many professors have received grants, there is no centralized support agency for professors who wish to prepare fundable proposals and conduct research in their areas of expertise. Some professors do not possess sufficient knowledge of research methodologies to compete successfully and do the work without additional help.

(The strategic planning committee could recommend that there be developed a centralized research support service available to any professor, department, or college wishing to increase the amount of research produced. The support could include assistance with: knowledge of grant possibilities available, methodology or design of the research, related literature searches, analysis of findings, and any other type of help that would be required or desired.

The success level could be determined easily by the number of professors who are successful in obtaining grants, and by the total grant dollars received when compared to a base year. The long-term trends of the number of grant dollars received and the number of professors receiving grants certainly constitute hard data that can be utilized for evaluative and marketing purposes.)

> Publication is seen as one of the four activities of Important University (the other three being teaching, research, and service). The 41% of the professors who do not publish or complete other scholarly activities (e.g., shows, recitals, presentations of papers, etc.) have indicated an interest, on a questionnaire distributed by the deans of the university, in participating in these professional activities.

(The university strategic planners see this as an opportunity to further strengthen Important University and to allow it to compete on a national scale. Two tactics appear as possibilities. The first involves creating an internal publications organization, and the second involves making publications a specific requirement for promotion or merit pay as related to the professors.

It is a rather straightforward matter to evaluate the success of this thrust over time. The number of professors who are published in refereed and non-refereed journals, the number of books authored, recitals, awards, shows, presentations at conferences, etc., are examples of "hard" data that can be used for evaluative purposes. Again, this may allow a secondary usage—that of marketing these accomplishments to enhance the prestige of the University.)

> The university leadership has expressed a high interest in creating advisory committees, composed of stakeholders outside of the university proper, which will function at the central university level and at the level of the individual colleges.

(Since the strategic planners feel that outsiders viewing the various elements of the university would be helpful in identifying strengths, weaknesses, and needs; they have requested that the board of control develop a policy related to using outside advisory committees.

Once the policy is adopted, it is the intent of Important University's Board of Control, which has accepted the recommendation of the strategic planning committee, to have each college dean establish both an internal and external advisory committee. The advisory committees will meet twice yearly, and advise the deans on matters related to the college's impact, image and curriculum requirements and opportunities.)

Weaknesses: External

Alumni support for the university has not been organized, and therefore the alumni financial contributions have been only twenty-five percent of the average contributions made to other universities of comparable size and status.

Over the past five years research funds of $62 million from the U.S. Government have allowed the university to pursue research on public health and safety issues. Because of the buildup and the doubling of expenditures in the area of defense, it appears that public health and safety research funds available to the university will be cut by two-thirds.

(External weaknesses, such as those above, always exist to some degree. It is crucial that strategic planners identify these weaknesses, and develop strategies and tactics which will take these situations into account. One response may be to sharpen current research programs, while another could be to integrate previously disassociated areas.)

Threats: External

Six major corporations are considering moving out of the state. Since the University obtains forty-six percent of its income through public state support, this is a very serious threat to the university's future well being.

During the last state legislative election, thirty-two anti public education legislators were elected by special interest groups.

Again, strategic planners must carefully consider these threats when developing their strategies and tactics. Ideally, the strategies will eliminate or seriously reduce the negative impact of these external threats.

Weaknesses: Internal

Within the next eight years, sixty percent of the university's senior professors and internationally known researchers will retire. There has been no sustained plan put in place to deal with the problem of acquiring high-quality replacements for them. In fact, the university's managers have attempted to hire assistant professors and beginning researchers in order to expend a greater percent of the total budget on capital improvements and meet reduced state budgets.

The university has experienced an eighteen percent vacancy rate in the number of students who live in the university-owned dorms. This fact is causing a $4 million loss in income while the expenditure for the maintenance of the dorms has increased twelve percent over the previous year.

Threats: Internal

The university's board of control is seriously considering a plan to eliminate high-cost graduate programs in favor of concentrating totally on undergraduate liberal arts education. Besides the complications of restructuring the university and changing its mission, acceptance of this direction would decrease the university's comprehensiveness (for which the university is widely known and respected) and would seriously weaken the ability to generate new and valid knowledge.

The classified employees' union has taken a strike vote, and the membership of the union intends to effectively close down the university operation. (In addition, the classified employees' union—unlike the rest of the employee groups—is growing at an 11% per-year rate). If this strike is successfully carried off, classes will not take place, tuition will have to be refunded, and thirty-two thousand students will be deprived of their education. In addition, parents, citizens, and area businesses will be greatly concerned; numerous non-striking employees will have to be laid off until the strike is over, and the faculty union has agreed to discuss the possibility of a sympathy strike.

It is obvious that these external weaknesses and threats must be considered seriously by the strategic planners. If successful intervention strategies and tactics can assist in lessening the potential damage to the university, these strategies should be developed and employed quickly.

Now that we have taken a look at some of the SWOT analysis items identified for a university, and we have suggested a few action strategies for these items, let's turn to another example. *Excellent High School* will provide the setting for this SWOT analysis.

EXAMPLE: EXCELLENT HIGH SCHOOL'S SWOT ANALYSIS

Strengths: Internal

In general, the teaching and administrative staff of Excellent High School is respected by the students, parents, and the community, as is indicated by yearly evaluations.

(Since the staff is respected, they can be used to solicit volunteers to assist the school. They also can be used to talk to civic groups, parents, and other organizations about their areas of specialty or about the goals, policies, and needs of the clients of the school. They also will be seen as knowledgeable representatives for the strategic planning process.)

Sixty people volunteered over 240 hours to the school as teacher aides, clerical aides, supervised tutors, outside speakers, or in other volunteer activities.

(These volunteers can be formed into a two-way communications network. By possibly publishing their phone numbers, parents or other citizens can call them to ask questions or get answers about anything related to school. They, then, will pass this information on to the school staff, get the necessary answers and contact the parent or community member who asked for the information. This group of volunteers can also serve as the nucleus of focus groups who, from time to time, may be called upon to explore or develop an issue with the principal or the school's staff.)

Overall student achievement is at the eighty-sixth percentile on standardized tests.

(As student achievement test scores become available and there is evidence that the student body is achieving well above state and national norms, a highly publicized media campaign throughout the community should be conducted. This can also be the approach to use if the school has National Merit Scholars, or if it has any other area in which individual students or groups of students achieve at a high level.

On the other hand, even though the student body scores well on standardized tests, the staff at Excellent High School should look at disaggregated and itemized test data analyses to develop special programs for individual students not achieving at the high level of their classmates. Special review and tutorial procedures are developed for those youngsters who have special instructional requirements.)

Strengths: External

The local university is interested in helping local schools improve their curriculum offerings and staff development programs.

(The principal takes advantage of this situation by inviting deans and professors of the schools of education and science to spend a highly publicized day visiting the school and discussing ways of arriving at cooperative programs that will be mutually beneficial to the university and to Excellent High School. A discussion agenda is agreed upon, and the university offers the principal and her staff a return visit to continue the dialogue and develop action plans.)

The speaker of the house and some legislators live in the school's attendance area.

(The principal and her staff capitalize on this fact, by inviting them to speak at commencement and at other ceremonies where they will have access to a considerable number of voters. These dignitaries also "teach" parts of courses and this procedure allows students to see government in action as expressed by those who are actually responsible for the governmental functions. Also, involvement of these high-profile officials in activities programs such as homecoming games, induction into the National Honor Society, and career day activities can turn into positive media events for the politicians and for Excellent High School.

Also, when the politicians are on-site, the principal and staff can make certain that they see the many positive things that are taking place at the school. The staff can also make sure the politicians are aware of the needs and related resource deficits which exist in order to continue the responsive comprehensive programs of the school.)

Opportunities: External

The Accrediting Association is due to make its once-every-seven-years accrediting visit.

(This provides an opportunity for the principal to organize the entire staff into year-long study teams which will investigate every aspect of the school's programs and their contributions. It also provides the opportunity to showcase positive things taking place within the school, as well as an opportunity to have outsiders identify areas that can be improved.

Once the school receives its final accreditation for another seven-year period, news releases and bulletins, created and distributed by the school, can explain the process utilized; purpose of accreditation; and value of accreditation to the school, students, and community.

This situation also provides the staff and planners with the opportunity to rethink emerging needs and opportunities. Since schools function as open systems, it is always healthy to rethink and reorder, if necessary, the goals, objectives, missions, and visions of the school. Realignment of each of these must be made as conditions change.)

A survey distributed within the community indicates, among other things, that parents and community members want to assist the school.

(The identification of this attitude allows the principal and her staff to begin extensive action planning in this area. One of the critical elements of the school's vision was to develop a strong and positive two-way relationship with the parents and community members. Some of the action programs developed by the principal and her staff include having community members and parents serve as advisors in their areas of expertise —e.g., a medical doctor assisting a health teacher, a newspaper editor assisting the high school's newspaper staff; these and many other possibilities can be capitalized upon—utilizing community members as lecturers for classes, involving them in creating and maintaining academic and other booster clubs, and involving them in any positive manner that will assist the school.)

Opportunities: Internal

A teacher on the staff has a spouse who is a nationally recognized computer expert.

(The principal and the teacher have agreed to ask the spouse to provide a series of six two-hour workshops for the teaching staff in the areas of setting up student test item banks, student record systems, and classroom management. They will also be provided suggestions on how to better transfer computer/high tech abilities to learners.)

The social science students are interested in establishing a global education club.

(The principal and teachers seize upon this interest to advance the cause of cross-cultural enlightenment for the entire school-related community. This interest also leads to the initiation of a foreign student and teacher exchange program.)

Weaknesses: Internal

> From the analysis of test data, it appears that some students do very well in advanced mathematics and in science classes, while 51% of the students have a very difficult time in those classes. There exists an obvious bimodal distribution among the students' test data.

(A solution being considered by the teaching staff is to organize the students into vertical cooperative learning teams wherein the students can learn from one another as well as from the teacher. Sometimes knowledgeable students can relate better than a regular teacher to students having difficulty. Furthermore, student team members can attend to one another on a more concentrated basis than a teacher who has twenty or more students in class.)

> Only 17% of students are involved in after-school co-curricular activities.

(Since co-curricular activities, such as clubs, intramurals, and other school sponsored after-school activities are considered important to the social, physiological, or intellectual development of the students, the staff has decided to do an interest survey of students. This survey will become a basis for the activities offered, and for the times the activities will be offered. Success will be measured by the percentage increase in participating students.)

> The student dropout rate has increased 7% per year over the past five years.

(A committee of students, parents, and staff members have interviewed numerous dropouts to determine causes of the problem. From the data collected from students interviewed, it was determined that additional counseling should be provided to those students who displayed a profile similar to students who have dropped out of school. Also, a series of parenting classes, to be offered in the homes of parents, was initiated.)

> Thirteen percent of the students have been arrested on or off campus for substance abuse, including seventeen cases of hard drug abuse and thirty-eight cases of alcohol abuse.

(A SADD—Students Against Drunk Drivers—group has been organized within the school. A blue-ribbon committee has been organized to work with a representative group of students to develop teams that will work with peers to lessen or alleviate the student substance abuse situation.)

Weaknesses: External

Very few community members show up for school-sponsored events, with the exception of athletic activities.

The State Department of Education is considering increasing the number of Carnegie Units required for graduation from 16 to 24 units.

Threats: External

The superintendent of schools and the board of education are considering adopting a policy that would suspend students for periods of from one to ten days for several rule violations.

A no tax increase group has been organized in Excellent High School's attendance area.

Threats: Internal

There is an indication that two small student groups within the school are about to engage in a serious confrontation—a gang war.

A group of parents have hired an attorney and requested a meeting of the board of education for the purpose of overturning the decision of the basketball coach and the principal who removed three regular players from the team for breaking the sports code of conduct.

When studying Excellent High School's vision statement, one finds such items as: high-achieving students, high-performing employees, broad-based community involvement and support, and a two-way communications system for stakeholders included. A SWOT analysis helped Excellent High School's staff to identify and take advantage of the strengths and opportunities they discovered in both the internal and external environments. In addition, it was important the staff of Excellent High School identify and deal with the weaknesses and threats that existed in the internal and external environment. These data were utilized to assist the staff in arriving at strategies and tactics, making both the internal and external environments conducive to ultimately achieving the school's vision of "What Should Be".

Now that we have presented examples of a SWOT analysis for Important University and Excellent High School, let's turn to an example of a SWOT analysis for *Omnipotent School District*.

EXAMPLE: OMNIPOTENT SCHOOL DISTRICT'S SWOT ANALYSIS

Omnipotent School District's vision statement contains the following components. This vision becomes the basis for strategy decisions. The SWOT analysis identifies factors which may have an impact on the strategies, and, thus, the basis for identifying possible routes to be taken to achieve the vision. Again, the SWOT process actually identifies the variables which will be used when deciding upon the strategies and tactics to be utilized (see Chapters 11 and 12).

- High student achievement in academic and co-curricular activities is the primary focus of Omnipotent School District in order to make self-sufficient citizens.
- Communication should be open and two-way with all categories of stakeholders of the school district.
- A highly trained and updated group of employees is necessary to an excellent school district. This implies that the school district shall allocate sufficient funds to provide opportunities for comprehensive staff development and training activities.
- Parent and community support is required.
- A safe and healthy environment must be provided.
- Adequate human, financial, material, and temporal resources must be provided to maintain an excellent school district.
- Employees and students should display a caring, respectful, and open attitude towards one another.
- High expectations should be a cultural foundation within the district for students, employees, and parents or guardians.

Strengths: External

Businesses and industries within the school district's environs have indicated an interest in the school district. Many of the management officials have children who attend schools in the district.

(The district's officials can capitalize on the interest of these individuals by asking them to speak to classes, make presentations at the district sponsored vocational day, serve on advisory committees to review the curriculum offerings in vocational subjects, technology areas, cooperative education, and other areas related to their expertise. They can also be asked to share their companies' staff development and training activities by allowing a few teachers and administrators to attend pertinent company-sponsored sessions. Finally, they can be asked to "adopt" one of the district's schools. In case of school adoption, the firm usually will donate some equipment and supplies, provide learning experiences outside the school's environment for students, allow learners to "shadow" employees to get interest and knowledge in the world of work, and serve as a booster or support firm for many of the school's activities.

Some words of caution to the school district's officials who are about to embark upon a partnership venture. First, when contacting a CEO of a firm ask her/him if there is something the school district can do that would help or be of interest to the firm. Second, make certain that if the partnership is formally agreed upon, the roles and responsibilities of the school and the firm are clear and acceptable to both parties. Third, listen to him/her and implement agreed-upon initiatives.)

A general attitude of support for the school district and its operations exists within the community (this has been verified by attitudinal surveys which are administered on a yearly schedule).

(The administrators and teachers can make certain that key opinion leaders are given personal invitations to attend every significant activity carried on by the district or by individual schools. Personal thank you letters should be sent every time any one of these important people take time from her/his busy schedule to attend an activity. Finally, these people can be asked to speak to civic classes, introduce guest speakers, take part in the school district's staff development activities, or become involved in other creative ways.)

Strengths: Internal

In general, student achievement on state and nationally normed tests is at the 69th percentile rank.

(This fact should be publicized in the media and in mailed-home information. However, the message also should be clearly given that the district is still looking for ways to improve its offerings to students.)

Many volunteers assist the school district in numerous ways.

(The school district can provide many ways of recognizing these volunteers. They can sponsor a district-wide recognition dinner at the end of each year, and awards can be given to each person who has actually contributed. Also, each school can publicize the individuals who volunteer and the specific work that they perform for the school district. The media can be provided with information regarding unusual group volunteer efforts, or unusual efforts by individual volunteers.)

Opportunities: External

There are many senior citizen clubs, and numerous at-risk individuals live within the school district.

(As possible responses, the school district could initiate an elective course for students in the area of community service. This course could be given Carnegie Units towards graduation, and the students could receive a grade that would depend on the types and magnitude of community service rendered. Some examples might be: driving the elderly to the hospital, shopping, or church; serving as a big brother or sister to some child; painting the homes of elderly couples; and a myriad of other excellent community services.

The senior citizen club members could be provided: free tickets to all school-sponsored events, buses for field trips, free or inexpensive adult education classes, free or inexpensive use of the school's facilities for such activities as swimming or exercise classes. They could also be asked to volunteer to tutor a young child.)

There are a wide variety of public relations, sales, and media firms housed within the boundaries of the school district.

(This fact provides the superintendent and the district strategic planners an opportunity to create an advisory marketing committee made up of talented people with expertise in the areas of publicity, marketing, and public relations. In this case, the district's superintendent should define marketing as reporting the good things that are happening within the school district, while notifying the community of action programs that are underway to improve any known areas requiring improvement. Ideas could involve asking stores to display excellent student work, providing informational placemats to area restaurants, arranging for performing groups to make presentations on cable TV, utilizing TV and radio service spots to sell the school, and involving successful graduates in publicly supporting the school's efforts.)

Opportunities: Internal

The classified employees are very interested in becoming a more integral part of the school's family.

(The superintendent can capitalize upon this interest by asking the classified employees' union to join the district's management in initiating a Quality Program wherein groups of six to eight volunteers help solve problems and improve the work environment at each work site. There can be numerous quality teams at each work site. The number of employees who volunteer to serve is the main determinant of the number of teams that are activated. Also, classified employees can be asked to help sponsor students, or individual school events. Additionally, a planned program of recognition for employees who perform well can be initiated.)

A teacher in the school district has been selected as the National Teacher of the Year.

(This happening provides an outstanding opportunity to emphasize within the community the high quality of teachers who are instructing the children and youth of the district.)

Weaknesses: Internal

Eight percent of the employees have involved themselves in advanced training or staff development activities.

(The district planners recognize this weakness, and commit significant funds to initiate and maintain a responsive training and staff development program for all categories of employees. The staff development programs offered will be determined by conducting and analyzing the results of a needs assessment. The results could possibly identify programs to be offered on school district time, or those for which the district could provide pay for attendance during non-school time.)

When student test data were disaggregated by sex, socio-economic level, and race, it was discovered that certain groups were not achieving as well as expected, even though the mean achievement scores for the total student body were significantly higher than state or national norms. (One area of weakness, for example, was the achievement level of male high school students in the English classes.)

(The school district's decisionmakers could organize a project team to determine potential cause-and-effect relationships (a needs analysis), and develop a program to correct identified weaknesses. One possible cause is that the material utilized in these classes is of greater interest to female students than to male students. The remedy considered is to develop teaching materials of greater interest to male students, while retaining teaching materials of interest to females.)

Weaknesses: External

It is very difficult to get the community to pass an important additional tax levy, and it has failed four times in a row.

(If an additional tax is not levied, the district will have to lay off teachers and eliminate some student programs. The district's decisionmakers should organize an all-school booster group to get out the positive vote; ask clearly identified opinion leaders to provide written statements of support to the various media outlets in the district; and have the superintendent, principals, and board of education members provide information on why the tax increase is necessary and what will be cut —without a threatening tone—if the tax levy fails.)

Governmental and other educational institutions in the district's geographical area very seldom cooperate on programs where collaboration would be of interest to the community and all institutions involved.

(The school district could invite all governmental and educational institutions, including university, community colleges, private training units, and other institutions with some common interests, to a dinner meeting. While there, all groups would be asked to separate into discussion groups of eight persons—including one representative from each of eight different institutions—for the purpose of developing a list of possible common interest areas. Once consensus is reached on this listing, a series of meetings would be established to attempt to develop cooperative action programs to bring possibilities into reality.)

Threats: External

The state legislature is considering a bill to superimpose a "novel teaching method" that would, in the judgement of the school district's decision makers, have a devastating effect on the curriculum.

(The principal, the teachers' union leadership, the board of education members, and the parent-teacher association leadership are organized to testify at a legislative hearing, establish a phone campaign to area legislators and to key legislators who are dealing with this bill, and develop an extensive letter-writing and telegraph campaign to dissuade the legislature from taking an affirmative action on the proposed bill. The superintendent and her staff develop a brief but powerful impact statement to be used in legislative testimony by the area legislators and to be distributed to the media.)

A no-tax-increase group has been organized in the community.

(The superintendent and other school leaders can organize a counter group which can write letters to be published in the area newspapers in support of the district. The counter group can hold coffee klatches in neighborhood homes during which they can review all the positive accomplishments of the school district's students and employees, they can explain how a good school district assists in maintaining high market value for their homes, and they can do a myriad of other activities to counter any negative effects of the no-tax-increase group.)

Threats: Internal

The district is experiencing very negative labor/management relations with its teachers' union, with two wildcat walkouts in the last six months.

(The superintendent and board president could ask for an executive meeting with the building stewards and the teacher union president to identify items of common interest and ways to cooperatively solve disagreements. At this meeting, the board president and superintendent should stress their desire to approach the differences from a "win-win" posture, and suggest a problem solving procedure, based on a Mega-referent, to eliminate any of the difficult items.)

Three newly elected board members ran on a program of reducing taxes and two denigrated "strategic planning" with knowing about the Mega level model actually used. This leaves the board with four experienced and long-term supportive board members, and three newly elected members.

(The superintendent and board majority, with a positive vote by the three new board members, could ask for establishment of a blue ribbon advisory committee on school district financial matters and strategic planning. The charge to the committee would be to investigate all aspects of the district's financial and planning operations, and point out areas in which the district can improve. Members of the blue ribbon committee might include such people as bank officials, auditors, corporate financial officers, a strategic planner, and taxpayer groups' representatives.)

Through the review of the SWOT analyses of a school building, a school district, and a university, it is clear that items discovered can have major importance for strategic planning strategies and the approaches utilized to reach the organization's vision of "What Should Be". A question remains: Where and how can one obtain the information to perform a SWOT analysis?

Locating Information to Complete a SWOT Analysis

A strategic planning group for a school district, a school building, or a university has an abundance of information sources available. Major sources of information can fall within categories which are demographic, political, social, financial, technological, and attitudinal. In most cases, the planners can obtain information from written documents, state and national data bases, discussions with knowledgeable persons, or well-designed attitude surveys. Make certain that the data you obtain is both valid and reliable. It is frequently wise to compare data coming from at least two different sources to ensure reliability.

Some prime sources of information and information that each source can provide are:

- chambers of commerce, which can provide data related to business and industry status and future plans
- state and university libraries, which can provide data from historical sources, as well as copies of current study reports related to pertinent community, state, and national variables
- state and federal agencies' publications and data bases
- financial institutions and major corporations in the district, which usually have demographic projections related to possible future markets, and data related to the financial and corporate requirements and markets
- legislative action summaries, which provide data related to impact statements of the various new pieces of legislation passed during the last session
- position statements from associations, political groups, economic groups and social groups, which provide directional guidelines that may impact on strategies and/or tactics to be utilized by the schools or universities
- records at the State Department of Education, which provide data on: student achievement trends; student population trends;

employee staffing trends; construction requirements and financial data on the state, program, and school district or university levels
- records of the U.S. Census Bureau, which provide data on all types of demographic variables related to age, sex, race, and so on (These data can be retrieved on a single or multiple census-tract basis to provide specific information related to the geographical area being served by individual school districts, community or junior colleges, and universities.)
- strategic plans that have been developed by such organizations as the United Way (The United Way of America has detailed demographic data related to their ability to generate charitable contributions.)
- real estate associations, which can provide data concerning types of housing and the numbers and categories of adults and children who live in the various types of existing and planned future housing
- the state bar association, which can provide information related to the impact of recent judicial rulings which may influence the operation of the school districts, community or junior colleges, and the universities

Once the information is collected, it must be analyzed carefully, and conclusions must be made. In making the conclusions, however, the strategic planners must integrate and synthesize all the discrete pieces of data, including that coming from the previous strategic planning steps. This provides a holistic view of the environment and the multiple effects that any and all of the data could have on their strategies and tactics. Once the synthesis is completed and the vision for the organization is clearly in mind, strategies can be decided that will maximize the probability of achieving the vision of "What Should Be" at the agreed-upon future point in time.

A simple example will demonstrate the interrelationship of these data and the use of the synthesized analysis by the strategic planners.

Example of Data Analysis and Synthesis

(1) The state legislature has recently passed an open enrollment bill allowing students and their parents to select the school district of their choice.

(2) At Great School District, a recent building boom has taken place due to the availability of inexpensive family housing.

(3) Industry, along with its local tax base, has been moving into rural areas of the state and away from the cities and first-line suburbs.

(4) Major manufacturing corporations have been lobbying for tax breaks, and they have threatened to move their manufacturing plants to other states where they will receive tax breaks and be able to hire less expensive labor. It is claimed that this action will make them more competitive and profitable.

Looking at these isolated pieces of information as a whole provides some serious variables to be considered in the strategic planning activities of any school district which may be affected by these variables. For instance, an affluent school district which has an excellent reputation and also houses industries which provide in excess of fifty percent of the district's tax base, may have to develop plans to temporarily house a large influx of students with a considerably reduced tax base.

On the other hand, a rural school district which is seen as offering mediocre programs, may anticipate the possibilities of making its curriculum more responsive and paying its competent employees a salary which will make the district more competitive in the teacher recruitment market.

Guidelines for Strategic Planners

(1) Once you have clearly defined your vision of "What Should Be" for your organization (school building, university, or school district) at some future time, and developed an accepted mission objective, it is important that you conduct a SWOT (Strengths, Weaknesses, Opportunities, and Threats) analysis of your external and internal environment. This analysis will alert you to the supporting and restraining factors which must be taken into account when identifying and developing your strategies and tactics.

(2) The sources of information are plentiful. Much information can be garnered from the data kept on file by your own school, school district, or university. However, there is a wealth of information available for the asking from such sources as: federal and state agencies, area businesses and industries, chamber of commerce groups, civic and social organizations, and professional groups of

many types. Publications, such as newspapers and journals, can also alert the strategic planners to issues for which data should be collected. Identify the demographic, legal, political, social, and financial data that will assist you in your strategic planning. It will be helpful to develop a checklist of the data you wish to monitor, and list these data under the sources from which they can be obtained.

(3) The major sources of data that should be collected include those related to demographics, finance, technology, attitudes, social matters, and political actions.

(4) In doing a SWOT analysis it is important to view all the data objectively and in detail. It is more important, though, to form a synthesis which the planners can utilize to estimate impact on the organization, and from which they can plan the strategies and associated tactics which will maximize the organization's potential to achieve its vision and make its external contributions.

(5) Finally, it is important to develop action programs which both capitalize on the internal and external strengths and opportunities, and which will nullify or counter internal and external weaknesses and threats.

Glossary

SWOT Analysis: a process utilized by strategic planners to identify, collect, monitor, analyze, and synthesize data about the strengths, weaknesses, opportunities, and threats that exist in the internal environment of the organization and in the external environment with which the organization interacts. These data are useful in planning strategies and tactics which capitalize on strengths and opportunities, and minimize or overcome weaknesses and threats in a manner that maximizes the possibility of achieving the organization's vision.

Exercises

1. When you view your school, school district, or university, what strengths and weaknesses exist? How can you overcome identified weaknesses so they do not hinder the ability to achieve your vision?

2. Show two examples from your organization, indicating how weaknesses or threats can be turned into opportunities.

3. When you view your school, school district, or university, what opportunities and threats do you feel exist? How can you capitalize on the opportunities and eliminate or reduce the threats?

4. Looking into the external environment with which your school, school system, or university interacts, which strengths, weaknesses, opportunities, and threats exist? How would you attempt to deal with them as you plan the strategies necessary to achieve your vision?

5. In conducting a SWOT (Strengths, Weaknesses, Opportunities, and Threats) analysis, what types of information would you collect? It is important to realize that your SWOT analysis is done for purposes of fact-finding and reality-setting.

6. What are some major sources of information that you could contact when doing a SWOT analysis?

7. How do you establish the reliability, validity, and completeness of the SWOT information? Why is it important to do so?

Endnotes

1 The SWOT process actually identifies the variables which will be used when deciding upon the strategies and tactics to be utilized (see Chapters 11 and 12). In many cases, strategic planners will identify possible strategies and tactics related to strengths, weaknesses, opportunities, and threats, *but it is very important that these serve only as "placeholders" for good ideas to be considered when the actual selection is made later*. Such *potential* (and possibly premature) ways and means for being responsive to the SWOTs are shown within ( ) in the examples which follow.

2 All of these examples, of course, are hypothetical.

Deriving Decision Rules and Performance Requirements

Once those involved in strategic planning have:

- selected the type of strategic planning focus to be utilized (Mega, Macro, or Micro)
- arrived at statements of beliefs, visions, and current mission
- identified those few basic CSFs (Critical Success Factors)
- identified and documented needs
- conducted internal and external environmental scans
- developed their vision of "What Should Be" at some point in the future
- identified and prioritized needs
- written and accepted a mission statement[1]
- conducted a SWOT (Strengths, Weaknesses, Opportunities, and Threats) analysis of both the internal and external environments

then they may derive decision rules—i.e., develop the *results-based policies* to use when making decisions.

Decision Rules and Performance Requirements

When strategic planners are dealing with multiple needs, goals, and objectives, they must develop a set of decision rules (or "policies") to assist them in selecting amongst the mass of needs, goals, and objectives. Decision rules should be few and clear. A recommended set of decision rules would include the following, as related to the items to be selected. They should:

- be related to the selected needs, visions, missions, and strategies
- provide the results-based criteria for making decisions
- be achievable
- be useful in terms of selecting required and feasible human, financial, material, and temporal resources[2]
- be evaluatable

215

The strategic planners must develop performance requirements (detailed measurable specifications) which are the basis for the decision rules. These specifications must indicate specific quantitative and qualitative performance indicators for determining accomplishment. Obviously, these performance indicators become evaluative criteria directly related to the mission objective of the school, school district, or university.

Performance requirements provide the measurable criteria for the results to be expected after an activity or function is completed. They include:

- specific result to be accomplished
- conditions under which they are to be accomplished
- design characteristics of the function or activity
- performance specifications, restrictions, or rules within which the result is to be accomplished

It should be clearly remembered that mission statement + measurable criteria = mission objectives (see Chapter 6 for a comprehensive review of this subject).

Examples of Deriving Decision Rules and Performance Requirements

Now that the decision rules have been defined and you have developed them, let's work through an example for a school district. The example shall artificially eliminate some of the steps in the total strategic planning process, but the strategic goals, and their related measurable objectives shall be written, and the decision rules shall be applied to a few example situations. Before plunging into the goals, objectives, and decision rules, we shall review the foundation beliefs that the Exemplary School District's strategic planners and decision makers have accepted for this school district of some 15,000 plus students.

EXAMPLE: EXEMPLARY SCHOOL DISTRICT'S BELIEFS (ORIGINAL LIST)

(1) We believe all children and youth can learn.
(2) We believe a safe and healthy environment is necessary.

(3) We believe the primary focus of all associated with the school district must be high performance. Student achievement must be measured, monitored, evaluated, and used for program decisions.

(4) We believe adequate and responsive human, financial, material, and temporal resources are necessary to the maintenance of an excellent school district.

(5) We believe both students and employees should display a caring, open, and respectful attitude toward one another.

(6) We believe two-way communication among students, employees, parents or guardians, and community members is crucial to understanding the school district's efforts and maintaining support for the school district's programs and plans. This provides a common purpose.

(7) We believe a well-trained and updated group of employees is a requirement for excellence. This implies an obligation on the part of the district to supply the resources and opportunities necessary to maintain a well-trained staff.

(8) We believe learners should be prepared to be self-sufficient, self-reliant citizens who operate in an environment of shared responsibilities and opportunities.

After reexamining this original list—based upon the realities of temporal, financial, and human resources available, and upon the readiness of the students, employees, and community to support multiple action programs related to these beliefs—the district's decision makers have decided to focus initially on two of these beliefs: (1) we believe all children can learn, and (2) we believe two-way communication and involvement among students, employees, parents or guardians, and community members is crucial to understanding the school district's efforts and maintaining support for the school district's programs and plans.

As an example using the belief that all children and youth can learn, let's rephrase this belief into a mission objective. Then, let's follow one strictly hypothetical and incomplete example objective through the required Inputs and Processes, and through the results chain.

An Example: Mission Objective, the OEM, and the Results Chain for Exemplary School District

Strategic objective: A minimum of 92% of the students of Exemplary School District shall graduate from high school by passing mastery tests in instructional areas we have chosen to teach. A five year follow-up study of graduates will indicate that, as an Outcome, a minimum of 92% of those graduated will be productive citizens (produce more than they consume).

Enabling objective:[3] Within three years the graduation rate from Exemplary High School shall be increased from the current 64% to a minimum of 92%.

Based upon this, they completed an analysis using the OEM framework to identify gaps between "What Is" and "What Could Be", to identify possible methods and means, and to select responses. For each "What Is" and "What Could Be" analysis they viewed (1) Outcomes, (2) Outputs, (3) Products, (4) Processes, and (5) Inputs.

Outcomes: Within five years of graduation from Exemplary School District a follow-up study will indicate that a minimum of 92% of the graduates will be productive citizens (produce more than they consume). Specifications for quantitative and qualitative hard and soft data to be used for evaluative purposes will include the following:

(1) A minimum of 92% will have qualified for a major credit card.
(2) A maximum of 8% will be on welfare or some other form of support (which could include prison, drug rehabilitation center residency, etc.).
(3) A minimum of 92% of the graduates perceived themselves having a good quality of life and producing more than they consume.

Outputs: A minimum of 92% of the students graduate from high school. (It would be possible to add other Outputs such as that each graduate shall accumulate a minimum of 22 Carnegie Units of Credit, 64% of the graduates will enroll in some form of higher education, and 28% will complete some type of vocational certification program after graduation from high school.)

Products: (1) The original completion rate in each course, as measured by mastery tests, shall be a minimum of 85%, and (2) A minimum of 7% of the students who are provided with additional help achieve mastery on the second exit testing.

Processes: A K–12 aligned curriculum for each subject area must be developed; an instructional auditing system must be put in place; mastery tests for each subject area must be developed and verified; a computerized management information system which profiles each student and monitors each student's progress must be developed; a strategy for developing Individual Educational Programs must be enacted; and intervention strategies (utilizing existing staff members and the new employees) must be decided.

Inputs: Twenty tutorial aides and four academic counselors are to be added. The office space, equipment, and supplies required for these added employees also must be funded. The additional annual expenditure required is $380,000.

Again, using these beliefs and associated mission as starting points, let's follow Exemplary School District's strategic planners as they develop a listing of strategic purposes,[4] and a series of enabling (or supporting) objectives (which are specific and measurable statements of Products and/or Outputs expected) related to each of the strategic goals.

STRATEGIC GOAL #1[5]

The aim of this goal is to increase ownership and support of the school district's programs and strategic goals by creating numerous opportunities for involvement by students, parents, community members, employees, and community businesses and industries.[6] This goal relates to Belief #6, which is incorporated into the district's vision. It also was a perceived "need"[7] identified during analysis of an opinionnaire survey indicating that all categories of stakeholders stated they wanted to be more involved in the school district's decision making. Also, after analyzing the degree of current involvement (performance data), it was clear that:

(1) Only ½% of the students were involved (student council members) in any decision-making role, and that role was limited to minor decisions.

(2) Parents were only involved in attending booster meetings of activities in which their children participated, and this amounted to a mere 3% of all parents.

(3) There was absolutely no planned involvement of business and industrial members.

(4) 12% of the employees were involved in curriculum development committees, and 86% participated in staff development activities, but in no case were they directly involved in planning activities with non-employee stakeholders.

(5) Community members were only called upon to assist the school district to run a campaign to increase taxes or to pass a bond issue.

Strategic Objectives Related To Goal #1

(a) Within five years a successful QWL (Quality of Work Life) program will be operational for all employee groups. The program will be initiated by union and management through establishment of a QWL central committee, bylaws, and program goals for Year One. By Year Three, all work sites will have quality management operating. By Year Five, a minimum of 700 employees will volunteer to serve on QWL committees, there will be a listing of a minimum of fifty pre-selected problems solved, and there will be a minimum of twenty centrally-sponsored QWL activities that were deemed helpful by at least 90% of the participants.

(b) Communication/governance committees will be functioning within the district by Year Five. These committees shall exist at each building level. The membership shall consist of at least twenty-five parents or citizens, working with the buildings' principals and staff, to identify needs, identify building level strategic goals and objectives, and develop action plans to achieve the building level goals and objectives. Measurement shall include the fact that each building has an operational communication/governance committee, and each committee shall have successfully completed a strategic plan, related to the district strategic plan, for its building which will be adopted by at least a 75% vote of the planning partners. Also, evidence will be available to prove that successful action plans have been implemented.

(c) By Year Five, a minimum of five successful business or industry/school district partnerships will be functional. Measurement will include evidence that at least five partnerships exist, and the quality and quantity of partnership activities will be deemed successful and meaningful by both partners.

(d) By Year Seven, a minimum of sixty activities involving a minimum of 5,000 citizens will be conducted. These activities can include: school advisory groups, school booster groups, school cooperative sponsorships of activities with such groups as the city recreation department, and citizen volunteer programs. Measurement will include proof that a minimum of sixty activities have taken place, involving a minimum of 5,000 citizens, certified by the Assistant Superintendent for Instruction.

(e) By Year Three, there will be an increase of student participation in student-sponsored activities, district wide, of at least 25% over the base year. This standard will also be applied to each school building.

(f) By Year Two, each school building shall create a student planning and advisory committee. This committee shall consist of representatives of all existing student groups, plus twenty members elected from the student body as a whole. The committee shall have adopted bylaws. Specific goals and objectives shall have been established. By Year Five, the student planning and advisory committee shall offer programs that involve a minimum of 95% of the student body.

(g) By Year Five, an opinionnaire distributed to students, parents, citizens, and employees will indicate a positive response of at least 75% of respondents from each of the groups to the question: "Do you feel more involved in the school district's programs and plans than you did in past years?" In addition, attendance at school district programs will increase by a minimum of 75% for the parent, citizen, and employee groups; and student attendance at school district sponsored programs and activities will increase by a minimum of 32%.

Obviously, each of the objectives can be further broken down into yearly in-process objectives, and there can be *a priori* measurements established for both quantitative and qualitative dimensions. Also, planners must determine which soft data and which hard data are applicable to each measured objective. Soft data are those that are opinion- or attitude-related, while hard data are those that are factual accomplishments. An example of soft data is that respondents feel more positive towards the school district. An example of hard data is that student test scores have improved by at least five percentile points.

Now, let's apply our decision rules to the above objectives.

Objective a: Quality of Work Life

- Related to selected needs, visions, missions, and strategies? Yes.
- Achievable? Yes.
- Affordable? No, not within the current budget.
- Evaluatable and evaluated? Yes.

Objective b: Communications/Governance Committees

- Related to selected needs, visions, missions, and strategies? Yes.
- Achievable? Yes.
- Affordable? Yes.
- Evaluatable and evaluated? Yes.

Objective c: Business or Industry/School District Partnerships

- Related to selected needs, visions, missions, and strategies? Yes.
- Achievable? No, the local CEOs have no current interest.
- Affordable? Yes.
- Evaluatable and evaluated? Yes.

Objective d: At Least Sixty Activities Involving 5,000 Citizens

- Related to selected needs, visions, missions, and strategies? Yes.
- Achievable? Doubtful. A much-reduced objective is required.
- Affordable? Yes.
- Evaluatable and evaluated? Yes.

Objective e: At Least 25% Increase in Student Attendance at Student-Sponsored School Events

- Related to selected needs, visions, missions, and strategies? Yes.
- Achievable? Yes.
- Affordable? Yes.
- Evaluatable and evaluated? Yes.

Objective f: Each School Created a Student Planning and Advisory Committee

- Related to selected needs, visions, missions, and strategies? Yes.
- Achievable? Yes.
- Affordable? Yes.
- Evaluatable and evaluated? Yes.

Objective g: An Opinionnaire Analysis Indicated a Minimum of 75% of All Respondents Indicated They Felt More Involved in the School District's Programs and Plans Than They Did in Previous Years

- Related to selected needs, visions, mission and strategies? Yes.
- Achievable? Yes, perhaps this should be only 25% for first year.
- Affordable? Yes.
- Evaluatable and evaluated? Yes.

When reviewing all the above, the strategic planning committee determines there are insufficient human resources available to the district to accomplish all objectives, even though the objectives viewed individually meet all or most of the decision rules. The committee determines that it will eliminate objectives *c*, *e*, and *f* which are related to Goal #1. (The reasons for the decisions are made clear, but they will not be discussed at this juncture.) For example, the strategic planners feel there are organized student groups that can be used for planning and advisory purposes without creating an additional group. Even though the added student group would be desirable, a slight change in activities of the existing student groups can somewhat serve the purposes intended for the student planning and advisory committee.

A Word of Caution to Strategic Planners

It is important that those individuals who are involved in strategic planning discriminate between means and ends. While these have been dealt with extensively before, the importance cannot be overemphasized. Means are the processes used to achieve a desired result. For example, the creation of citizen communication/governance committees at each school building can be classified as a means. Ends are the results desired or achieved—for example, an increase of third grade male students' achievement in reading as measured by a minimum increase of 5% by use of standardized test scores in reading, can be classified as an end.

Now let's turn to a few examples of strategic goals, and a listing of potential objectives for a single goal as these have been developed by the strategic planning committee for Universal University. The decision rules utilized by the strategic planners for Universal University are identical to those used by Exemplary School District.

EXAMPLE: UNIVERSAL UNIVERSITY'S STRATEGIC GOALS AND OBJECTIVES

Strategic Goal #1: Universal University shall increase the amount of grant funds received for each of the next five years.

Strategic Goal #2: The employees of Universal University shall increase the services provided to other institutions over the next seven years.

Strategic Goal #3: The staff of Universal University shall increase the number of publications in refereed journals in each of the next five years.

Strategic Goal #4: The staff of Universal University shall develop a series of telecommunications courses to be offered by each of the colleges which comprise the university. (Note: This really relates to a methods-means and not a results-related goal.)

Taking Goal #2 as an example, a series of objectives were developed, performance requirements for each objective were clearly stated in measurable terms.

Tactical Objectives[8] Related to Goal #2: An Increase in Services Provided to Other Institutions Shall Be Achieved within the Next Seven Years

Tactical Objective #1: The schools of education and science and technology shall develop partnerships with local schools by adopting a minimum of thirty schools within the next seven years.

Tactical Objective #2: The university shall provide paid leaves of absence to a professor of educational finance, a demographer, and a sociologist to serve as advisors to the State Blue Ribbon Legislative Committee on School Finance, which is charged with a five year study to develop a more equitable and effective formula for the distribution of financial aid to school districts within the state.

Tactical Objective #3: The university shall provide one hundred volunteers to serve on the boards of control for hospitals, the United Fund, and other service institutions within the university's service area.

Tactical Objective #4: Over the next seven years the Universal

University's School of Business shall develop a minimum of forty training and staff development courses to be offered the employees of small business firms within the state.

Each of these tactical objectives meet the four decision rules of being:

(1) Related to selected needs, visions, missions, and strategies
(2) Achievable
(3) Affordable
(4) Evaluatable

However, you will note that each of these objectives has a quantitative measurement, and that none deal with the quality of the service provided. Of course, detailed action plans would be developed to implement each of the objectives agreed upon by Universal University's strategic planners and managerial decision makers.

Now that we have explored some acceptable quantitative objectives, let's develop an example objective that has a qualitative measurement attached to it. Obviously, both hard data (factual measurements) and soft data (opinions, attitudes, etc.) can be utilized to evaluate achievement of objectives.

Qualitative Objective: Universal University's Medical Staff Will Develop, within a Ten Year Period, Medical Advances That Will Improve the Quality of Life for Patients of AIDS by Either Developing a Cure for AIDS and/or Providing Medication That Will Eliminate the Pain Associated with AIDS as Certified by the Surgeon General of the United States

The objective meets the decision rules as follows:

- Related to selected needs, visions, missions, and strategies? Yes, it scores at the top of the list in this category.
- Affordable? Yes, with grant money and university contributions.
- Doable? Probably.
- Evaluatable? Yes.

Now that we have explored both quantitative and qualitative objectives, let's examine another level of specificity: that of performance requirements.

Performance Requirements (PRs)—A Partial Review

After an activity or function is completed, a performance requirement (PR) provides the measurable criteria for the result to be accomplished. It includes: what specific result is to be accomplished; the conditions under which it is to be accomplished; who or what will display the results; and the performance specifications, restrictions, or rules within which the result is to be accomplished. An example for a hypothetical program will include the characteristics of PRs: (1) what result is to be accomplished, (2) who or what will display the results, (3) under what conditions will the results be observed, and (4) what criteria will be used to measure success or failure. Some examples are:

> A minimum of 92% of the students in Positive Senior High School's Advanced English Course 201, which features variable completion times, will score 85% or better mastery on the school district's approved criterion referenced test after completing the curriculum learning packages adopted by the school district for instruction in Advanced English Course 201.

> At least 90% of the students using the curriculum learning packages adopted by the school district for instruction in Advanced English Course 201, will complete the course at the minimum mastery level within thirty clock hours of study.

> The development of the curriculum learning packages and criterion-referenced test for Advanced English Course 201 shall not exceed $5,000. The school board will allow a weighted Carnegie Unit towards a graduation diploma for students successfully completing this course.

Now that we have discussed: (1) the writing of strategic goals and objectives; (2) development of detailed performance requirements; and (3) necessity of decision rules and examples which have been provided to illustrate and amplify the discussion points, it is time to provide some guidelines to strategic planners.

Guidelines for Strategic Planners

(1) When dealing with numerous goals and related objectives, it behooves the strategic planners to develop decision rules ("policies") which can be used to establish priorities for selection among the multitude of needs, goals, and objectives. It is crucial that any selected goal or objective fit within the vision and mission of the school, school district, or university. In addition, other decision

rules may include such guidelines as: "Is the goal or objective meaningful, achievable, affordable, and evaluatable in terms of human, financial, material, or temporal resources?"

(2) Strategic purposes[9] should be established after reviewing the previous activities of (a) arriving at a statement of beliefs, (b) conducting internal and external environmental scans, (c) identifying the Critical Success Factors of the organization, (d) developing a vision, (e) writing a mission statement (in measurable performance terms), and (f) completing a SWOT analysis.

(3) Each goal should be aligned with identified needs, the organization's vision, and the organization's mission. Expected Outcomes should be identified.

(4) Each objective should be directly related to a strategic intention, and it should be a specific statement of the degree of results expected over a defined time period.

(5) It is important that strategic planners can and do clearly distinguish between means and ends.

(6) It is also important that strategic planners be able to differentiate between, and use, soft data and hard data that can be used to determine whether or not objectives and strategic intents have been achieved.

Glossary

Decision Rules: those guidelines or policies that are used to prioritize and select among goals, objectives, and interventions as well as resources.

End: the result attained or desired.

Hard Data: those data that are based on observable or proven fact and are independently verifiable.

Means: the process or vehicle used to attain an end.

Need: the results-gap, or discrepancy, between "What Is" and "What Should Be".

Objectives: specific statements of the degree of results expected over a defined time period. They include: (1) what results are to be accomplished, (2) who or what will display the results, (3) under what conditions will the results be observed, and (4) what criteria will be used to measure success or failure.

Performance Requirements: provide measurable interval or ratio scale criteria for the result to be accomplished after an activity or function is completed. They include the result, the conditions, the specifications, and the restrictions or rules within which the results are to be accomplished.

Soft Data: those data that are not based upon observable, independently verifiable facts. Many times these data are of the attitudinal type. They are personal and not externally verifiable.

Strategic Goals: statements (measurable on an ordinal or nominal scale) of general results expected.

Tactical Objective: a results-referenced enabler linked to one or more strategic objectives.

Exercises

1. Develop a series of ten strategic purposes for your school, school district, or university. Make certain that they are aligned with your organization's needs, vision, and mission.

2. For each of the strategic intents you've developed, write a minimum of five tactical objectives. Check to ensure that they have the four characteristics of an objective.

3. Develop a set of decision rules which you can utilize to make choices within the developed goals and objectives.

4. Write a set of performance requirements for one of the goals you have written.

5. Define the difference between means and ends. Give an example of each.

6. Define the difference between hard and soft data. Give an example of each type of data.

Endnotes

1 Thus, they have established the parameters within which the detailed strategic planning takes place. That detail involves deciding upon strategic goals and specific objectives for each of the goals. Also, measurable criteria—performance objectives—must be written, needs must be prioritized, and decision rule policies must be determined.

2 While many discussions of "policy" link them to procedures and/or resources, we prefer to use the word to relate to decision rules for obtaining identified and required results—related to ends, not just means.

3 Enabling objectives are the performance specifications of what en-route results must be obtained in order to achieve the mission.

4 Such intentions can be either mission statements (general intent) or mission objectives (with criteria for judging accomplishment).

5 Again, the use of ends-related statements tend to get used interchangeably in the literature. When we use "goal" here and elsewhere in the Chapter, please keep in mind that the preferred statement of intended results should be an objective.

6 Because we are now starting to create strategies and tactics, the potential how-to-do-its (means) are starting to appear.

7 Shown in quotation marks because, dealing as it did with a means or process, it really represents a "quasi-need".

8 Tactical objectives involve identifying the most efficient ways to achieve a larger objective.

9 These may be in terms of goals (nominal or ordinal scale measures) or the preferred objectives (interval or ratio scale measures).

Scoping	→	Data Collecting	→	Planning	→	Implementation and Evaluation

Developing Strategic Action Plans

Strategic goals and objectives are statements of desired Products, Outputs, or Outcomes. They are not achieved as if by magic. Very specific actions, activities, and events have to be planned and carried out in order to achieve the desired results and payoffs.

Planners should develop alternative action plans from which they can choose the most promising one. The choice should be made after an analysis of supporting and restraining factors, as they relate to each alternative, is considered.

Action plans which take any substantial amount of time or are comprehensive, will probably require the identification of in-process milestones to determine progress achieved during operating them. In structure, a completed action plan will identify the Inputs required; the Processes to be utilized; and the Products, Outputs, and/or the Outcomes desired (Products are enroute results, Outputs are organizational results, and Outcomes are the effects of the externally delivered results of the organization on society).

An Example for Designing a Response

Let's follow through the decision line from the development of a strategic goal to a few typical objectives which might be subsumed under that goal; to the proposal (and thus transform it into a "strategic objective") of various alternatives; to the analysis of the various alternatives; and to the completion of the selected alternative by answering the What? How? Who? When? Why? and Where? questions. Our example will be that of Tremendous School District's action planning procedures.

EXAMPLE: TREMENDOUS SCHOOL DISTRICT'S ACTION PLANNING PROCEDURES

Tremendous School District's Strategic Planning Committee developed the following strategic goal (among many others which they developed).

231

A Strategic Goal[1]

Strategic Goal #8: To develop systems which will inspire greater citizen and community support for the school district's programs and procedures. Some of the criteria might include: support to be evidenced as a higher percentage of favorable votes when compared to past votes on tax increase issues for schools, an increasingly favorable attitude towards the school district on the annual survey instrument distributed throughout the community, the number of positive phone calls and letters received, the increased favorable columnar inches reported as an *indicator* of success about the school district's programs and operations registered in newspapers, and the degree of increase in the number of citizens who volunteer and the number of hours of volunteer time registered by citizens.

Sample Programs

The strategic planning committee next developed a series of programs which were subsumed under Goal #8. Four of these programs and a sample of their related objectives will illustrate this level of planning.

Program A: To develop a public information office that will cause at least a 100% increase in the positive information about the district covered in the area newspapers, when a comparison is made of the columnar inches published in the base year to the columnar inches covered in Year Five (the number of columnar inches provide "hard" data of a quantitative nature, and the judgement of "positive information" provides "soft" data of a qualitative nature).

Program B: To initiate a system of continuous citizen advisory committees to study and make recommendations about all of the district's programs and operations. The committees shall be established and all reports received by the board of education no later than Year Three. Attendance will be at least 85%, and there will be unsolicited requests by citizens asking to serve.

Program C: To initiate and maintain a comprehensive community and adult education program which will utilize all the school buildings after normal school hours, during vacation, and during the summer. By Year Five, there will be a minimum of 100 activities per year and a yearly minimum of 5,000 participants. A survey instrument over the five year period will show a minimum of 33% of the participants will indicate that adult education programs have assisted them in either obtaining a job or in getting a promotion; a minimum of 25% will indicate that their lives have been enriched because of adult education activities; and at least 40% of the participants who entered adult education health and conditioning classes will indicate their physical condition has been improved because of their participation.

Program D: By Year Five, there will be a minimum of 20 productive partnerships established between the school district and the businesses, industries, and service related organizations in the area. Measurement shall include: number of partnerships which are in place; specific results of cooperative activities undertaken; and degree of satisfaction with the partnership expressed by the CEO of each organization with whom the school district has achieved partnership status as indicated by financial and personnel support.

The four programs above have been selected by the strategic planners after completing a thorough methods-means analysis. This type of analysis identifies possible tactics and tools for achieving each performance requirement, and it delineates the advantages and disadvantages of each tactic. Thus, when a decision is to be made about which tactics or tools to utilize, the analysis is readily available to the decision makers. Let's now turn to *examples of this type of analysis when related to specific objectives*, and to the possible tactics and tools available to assist in achieving these objectives.

Program A: To increase the number of positive columnar inches of news about the school district's programs and procedures, including positive information about students and employees or school district management, by a minimum of 100% within five years. Potential alternate action approaches are then brainstormed. A few of these are: (1) Providing monthly and yearly summaries of the number of columnar inches of negative, neutral, and positive news about the district that is printed by each newspaper covering the district. The percentages of negative, neutral, and positive news are organized in such a manner that each paper receives its coverage report card. If the amount of positive news seems disproportionate to the negative or neutral, the editor of the paper is contacted for an appointment with the purpose of finding ways to increase the positive newspaper coverage about the school district. (2) Requesting that each newspaper editor assign a specific reporter to cover the school district. Arrangements are made for the superintendent and the school district's

information officer to meet with the reporters so assigned for the
purposes of: informing them of the potential stories (both positive
and negative); answering any questions that the reporters, editors,
and owners may have; providing any information which is requested; and offering to assist them by developing news releases they
may wish to receive or by arranging for them to meet with any student or employee of the school district or with any group within the
district. Asking the editors to form an advisory group to the district's
and individual schools' publications committees. (3) Asking key reporters and officials of the area newspapers to speak to the journal-
ism classes in each high school in the district, and (4) requesting
representatives of each newspaper to serve as judges for the annual
writing competitions held by the language arts, English, or journal-
ism teachers at each elementary, middle, and senior high school of
the district.

Now that four potential action approaches have been identified, the
strategic planning committee will decide those that have the most prom-
ise for achieving the objective. This may be accomplished by doing an
analysis—called a *Force-Field Analysis*—of the supportive and restraining factors, which apply to each alternative. To illustrate, let's follow this
analysis procedure for one of the above listed action approaches. (Of
course, such an analysis would be completed for each alternative before
choices are made as to which alternative or alternatives are to be made
operational.)

An Action Plan Example: Developing a Monthly and Yearly Columnar Inches Report Card of Positive, Negative, and Neutral News for Each Newspaper Which Covers the School District

Supporting Factors	Restraining Factors	Net Influence
Specific data would be made available.	Some editors would react negatively.	minus
Some editors would be pleased that the district is taking a serious interest in their newspaper coverage.	It would be costly to have someone clip and analyze each item reported, and this activity is not assigned or budgeted as part of any employee's job.	plus

Supporting Factors	Restraining Factors	Net Influence
Such an analysis would assist the district's staff in supplying more positively focused stories for the area newspapers.	There could be disagreement over whether or not the item is positive, neutral, or negative.	plus
It is assumed that the more positive news coverage achieved, the more favorable impressions citizens will have of the school district.	It takes quite a bit of employee time to monitor the newspaper coverage.	plus
Etc.	Etc.	

Such a *Force-Field Analysis* should precede the investment of resources in any of the potential alternatives suggested. Another helpful approach to analyzing alternatives is *methods-means analysis*.

Methods-Means Analysis

Once measurable objectives (at the Mega, Macro, and/or Micro levels) have been identified, it is time to determine if there exists, or could exist, one or more methods and means (or tactics and tools) by which they could be accomplished. The strategic planners should identify what has to be completed and in what order each tactic (or means) has to be completed, and they should have enough information to select the best possible means for accomplishing the strategic objectives.

In order to make the best selection of means (Processes) to accomplish each function, a listing of possible tactics and methods, along with the identified advantages and disadvantages of each, should be constructed. This collection serves as a data bank from which the strategic planning monitor or system managers will later on be able to make a cost-effective selection. The process by which such a data base is produced is called *methods-means analysis*.[2]

DOING A METHODS-MEANS ANALYSIS

"Methods" include the tactics for achieving functions and for meeting their associated performance requirements. A "means" is a way in which a tactic may be achieved. A methods-means analysis identifies the possible tactics and vehicles for meeting performance requirements for each objective and function. It includes a listing of the advantages and disadvantages of each optional possibility.

The selected missions, visions, and needs provide the specific objectives for which methods-means are to be identified and data obtained so that the most efficient and effective can be chosen. The methods-means analysis does not select how the requirement will be met; it only unearths the possible ways to achieve the performance requirements and thus to meet the objectives. The "how" selection is made after the possible ways and means have been identified.[3]

CONSTRAINTS

If an objective (and its performance requirements) is achievable by one or by combinations of how-to-do-its (processes, procedures, methods), further methods-means analysis continues. If not, then there exists a constraint that must be reconciled before we continue. The removal or reconciliation of a constraint may be accomplished by: (1) changing the performance requirement, (2) finding a possible methods-means to achieve the performance requirement, (3) redefining the limits within which the performance requirement(s) may be met, or if none of these are possible, (4) stopping the activity then and there [48].

The methods-means analysis supplies strategic planners with: (a) a data base of feasible "whats"—possible projects, interventions, activities, programs, and approaches—for meeting the strategic objectives; and (b) a data base of possible "hows"—tactics and tools—and the specific advantages and disadvantages of each.

WHAT ARE THE SOURCES FOR METHODS-MEANS INFORMATION?

Methods-means information is found in many places, few of which are difficult to locate. Many texts and journals—especially those from educational leadership, administration, curriculum, and instruction, and educational technology—discuss "means" at great length and in great detail. Planners might consult specialists, consultants, vendors, and the literature in education and other fields. Planners can also "brainstorm" possible ways for accomplishing a desired objective.

Considering many methods-means gives you the chance to be *creative*, and to get away from conventional wisdom and from "the way it's always been done" solutions. It is important to explore many ideas before deciding which gives the best fit. Sometimes the most extreme or unusual ideas initially presented become the best-fit final method or means.

Once you have listed all the possible methods-means for each objective and its requirements, the planners then compile and summarize them. Unless they are compiled and stored, many will be forgotten.

COMPILING AND STORING THE METHODS-MEANS DATA

Make a table which lists each goal, associated objectives, and the detailed performance requirements for each one. Give them numbers as a retrieval coding method [48]. Record each identified objective and associated requirements. List next to each requirement, the methods and means which could be used.

This registry will result in a compilation of possible methods and means. Next, prepare a methods-means summary table which gives a total listing of methods-means for each family of goals, objectives, and performance criteria.

The specific tasks to be performed when conducting a methods-means analysis are:

(1) On the methods-means identification form you have constructed, list a number for each goal-objective-criterion or related cluster.
(2) Derive a column for each item in #1, above, and list the results-based requirements that any methods-means combination must meet.
(3) Under a column you label "Methods-Means Possibilities", list any methods-means combination which will meet the requirements in column #2, above.
(4) For each methods-means combination identified, list the advantages (such as acceptability, availability, cost, time, reliability, transportability, and ease of use).
(5) As in step #4 above, list all the disadvantages for each methods-means combination identified. Note that Force-Field Analysis may be used here.
(6) Make up a summary sheet so that you may scan and find groups and "families" of both objectives and possible methods-means.

THE METHODS-MEANS ANALYSIS IS A FEASIBILITY STUDY

The Methods-Means Analysis serves several purposes:

(1) It identifies the alternative possible methods and means (or tactics, approaches, interventions, programs, and tools) and lists the advantages and disadvantages of each objective and criterion (or group of performance requirements).

(2) When used in an ongoing fashion, as the planning continues, it serves as a feasibility study.

(3) It forces consideration of alternatives for meeting the strategic objectives.

Selecting the Best Methods-Means

COST-RESULTS ANALYSIS

Basic to the success of any plan are the methods and means which are selected. The methods and means should be sensibly selected on the basis of "What do you get" and "What do you give". Important in the actual selection are the factors of time and cost [67].

Also useful is a criterion which relates results with money: relating cost and Product, cost and Output, as well as cost and Outcome [102]. Using the Organizational Elements Model, these alternative cost-results analysis have labels of cost-effectiveness, cost-benefit and cost-utility [48, 49,102].[4]

Cost-results analyses cannot be performed without the prior acquisition of data from a methods-means analysis, and from the alternative tactics, tools, methods, and activities which were identified. Note that cost results analyses are not the same as cost efficiency; in strategic planning we focus on payoffs and consequences (Outcomes, Outputs, and/or Products relating to the visions, beliefs, needs, preferred futures, and new missions). The simple achievement of efficiency without results-based benefits is a shallow victory. When doing the methods-means analysis, it is important to collect data concerning the time and cost dimensions.

Creativity, innovation, and methods-means analysis go together. To "force" moving from the simple and "safe" conventional wisdom to creative, inter-relative, useful options, at least two alternative methods-means should be listed for each objective. Doing this will likely force the consideration of new and innovative possibilities.

As a result of the methods-means analysis, we have identified and listed the possible methods and means (tactics, tools, procedures, interventions, programs) for achieving each objective. We have also identified the relative advantages and disadvantages of each possible methods-means. Based on this information, the strategic planner may select the best interventions from among the options. This tool for selecting the most efficient ways and means is called "systems" analysis [48].

Methods-means selection is frequently (and unfortunately) made by hunches, feelings, consensus, voting, historical precedence, and intuition. Often, the latest gimmick, "hot idea" or in-vogue method, or the most warm and comfortable solution will be chosen.

You may choose what is right and useful, not what is "in". Useful conceptual frameworks and techniques are available for assisting in the selection of useful ways and means [3,19,48,55,96,116]. Techniques for making sensible choices from an array of alternative interventions are also available and are called "systems analysis" tools. These include: cost-benefit analysis;[5] relevance trees; decision trees; Delphi technique; cross-impact analysis; queuing theory; cycle analysis; nominal group technique; and polling. Many others exist, and we suggest that you refer to some of the references at the end of this chapter. Because this book is not about implementation, operations, and evaluation in education, we provide very brief snapshot summaries of some of these approaches.[6]

PLANNING, PROGRAMMING, BUDGETING SYSTEM (PPBS)

PPBS is most useful for moving from the goals and objectives of the strategic plan, identifying alternative methods-means possibilities which could meet the objectives (based on a cost-benefit analysis for each possibility), and ranking the various alternative choices on the basis of their respective costs and contributions. After the choices are made, you may derive a related budget, based on the cost of achieving the objectives. It provides a network view of milestones and their interrelationships.

The usefulness of PPBS depends on the validity of the original objectives. Other techniques may be useful in the selection of methods and means. These include simulations, strategy trees, the Delphi Technique, cross-impact analysis, and polling.

SYSTEMS ANALYSIS

The technique of systems analysis may be seen as a methodical comparison of alternative methods-means (based on meeting the selected objectives) done on the basis of the input cost and the benefit associated with each alternative, and with the understanding that the payoff of any selection is relatively uncertain [3,19,48].

SIMULATION

The building and use of a model, from a real or predicted situation, will best define this technique. It can range from a model of a central office facility to a mock-up of a school or classroom in order to identify how it will work, when and if constructed. Other simulations are built on symbols, such as through the use of complex mathematical models with many interacting variables.

STRATEGY TREES

Strategy trees are used when one can identify hierarchies or distinct levels of complexity of events, with each lower level in a "tree" providing increasing detail. One can identify the associated pathways and/or alternatives by breaking down a series of a system's sequential component objectives and milestones into those programs, methods, tasks, or actions for major strategies. By examining the entire set of strategies and possible methods-means for each, you may choose the best ones. Then, you have the basis for preparing time lines and budgets. An example utilizing a strategy tree will illustrate this technique.

An Illustrative Strategy Tree

OBJECTIVE: Within five years we will have a comprehensive training tactics (staff development) program in operation for all employees of the school district, which will measurably improve: (1) relations; (2) classroom effectiveness, as measured by appraisals; and (3) learner accomplishments, as measured by grades and test results. Figure 11.1 shows a partial hypothetical strategy tree. Figure 11.2 details a part of that strategy tree.

From the example, it should be clear that this is a process which helps a planner to decide, in advance, what she/he must give and do in order to get the desired results. In other words, "methods" include the tactics for achieving the detailed functions and associated performance requirements; and "means" are the vehicles by which the tactics may be achieved. It is not designed to select "how" the requirements are to be

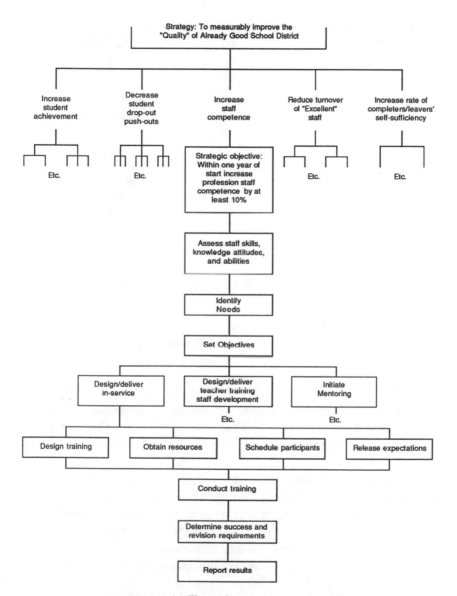

FIGURE 11.1 An illustrative strategy tree (partial).

OBJECTIVE

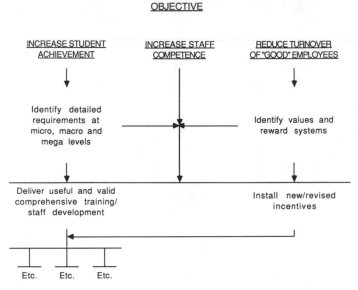

FIGURE 11.2 A detailed part of the illustrated strategy tree (Figure 11.1).

met; it only uncovers "possible ways" for achieving the performance requirements, and it identifies the advantages and disadvantages of each option to be considered [48].

Once the alternative approach has been decided, details of the action approach selected must be thought through and developed into a detailed and comprehensive action plan. That is, the finalized action plan should include answers to the questions: Why? How? Who? When? What? and Where?

This detail can be illustrated by providing the example of developing a community education program for the citizens of the district. The answer to the WHY question is to provide greater community support for the school district's programs and operations by involving many citizens in school district sponsored community education activities. The answer to the WHEN question is five years for the measurements of success, but there are WHEN questions to be answered for each task involved. The WHERE question is answered by the school's intent to offer the community education programs in all district schools. The HOW question is answered by the school's intention to offer a comprehensive set of community programs and activities. The details of WHO? WHAT? and WHEN? can best be described by completing a planning chart.

Table 11.1 An illustrative planning chart.

Tasks	Chronology	Who (primary person)	When
conduct a needs assessment	1	comm. educ. director	1st month
develop measurable objectives	2	comm. educ. director	1st month
hire a community education director	6	superintendent	3rd month
appoint a citizens community education advisory committee	3	superintendent	1st week
develop a listing of classes and activities	9	comm. educ. director & committee	6th month
estimate the budget required for each activity to be offered	10	business manager	10th month
decide upon the time schedule for the entire program	11	all administrators	12th month
assign the space required for each program	12	all administrators	12th month
check on the district's insurance coverage for such activities	13	business manager	12th month
locate the teachers and sponsors that will be required	8	comm. educ. director	9th month
establish fees, if any, to be charged to the participants	14	comm. educ. director & business manager	12th month
develop a board policy related to community education	7	board of education	2nd month
develop a board policy on school building usage	4	board of education	2nd month
hire the teachers and sponsors and initiate activities	15	comm. educ. director	2nd year
derive evaluative criteria and plan	5	comm. educ. director	2nd month
other	37	teachers & admin.	3rd year
other	58	comm. educ. director, admin., & adv. comm.	5th year
revise as required	N		

In order to save valuable planning time, the first step is to list all tasks to be accomplished, and the second step is to place these tasks in chronological order. If the planners attempt to list all tasks in chronological order while developing the list of tasks, much unnecessary effort will be put forth. Next, the planners will have to determine who shall be responsible for the accomplishment of each task, and when each task shall be completed. An illustrative planning chart, Table 11.1, demonstrates the usefulness of this approach.

It should be clear that arriving at a comprehensive strategic plan along with the action plans which are necessarily turned over to those responsible for management of the strategic plan, is no simple task or quick-fix approach to planning. Only if the time and resources necessary to produce quality planning are made available, will the school, school district, or university enhance the probability of achieving the vision of "What Should Be".

DELPHI TECHNIQUE, NOMINAL GROUP TECHNIQUE AND POLLING

The Delphi Technique is a method of obtaining group input and response without gathering the groups together (discussed in Chapter 3). It avoids biasing the results from the dynamics which happen during face-to-face meetings. This technique employs the conclusions and analyses of authorities acting as panelists. Each panelist is provided (in private) a series of questions which are distributed in rounds. Each round usually asks about future events and the expected consequences of each. Each of the panelists gives her/his expectations on the topic (e.g., when will all employees have to use problem-solving skills, when will traffic congestion require homework stations, when will street violence invade schools, and when will all learners have to acquire the skills of computer programming?). After each round and set of responses, the median response along with the range of individual responses (usually the center 50%), are provided each expert along with important comments of other panelists. After a few rounds (usually two to four), arrays of responses are clustered which represent the reflections of the panelists as they have been shaped by the responses of others [12].

The Nominal Group Technique is a structured process devised to stimulate new ideas and produce group accord. It usually encourages the participation of everyone, spotlights specific questions, and reaches accord through voting.

Polling is a structured process which asks representative people to provide preferences or predictions. This information then assists the strategic planner in devising her/his strategies.

One possible limitation of the consensus-building approaches lies in the risk of overlooking one, single, aberrant-but-correct position, by attempting to acheive consensus by leveling responses towards an agreeable center point. Agreement is not validity [48].

CROSS-IMPACT ANALYSIS

Things in our world don't happen in isolation from other events. This approach therefore intends to consider possible interaction effects among several variables and operations that are functioning at the same time. Each event is given a probability of occurrence and a time-line for its development. Prior events are used to determine the occurrence or non-incidence of future events. For example: scientific knowledge increases while cult values do so as well; state-wide competency testing increases while private school enrollments increase; teachers' salaries increase while computer-assisted instruction is demanded by students and parents; and drug program funding increases while student violence also increases. Given these multiple variables and occurrences, a cross-impact analysis can permit a planner to view an array of changes, time frames, and probabilities. She/he can vary each of the predicted variables so that optional possibilities may be determined [78,91]. This is an important tool because it does not assume the linearity of events—it considers the reality that many things interact at the same instance.

FORCE-FIELD ANALYSIS

A Force-Field Analysis is a technique which permits the identification of the supporting and restraining forces that are predictable for each alternative strategy and tactic considered as a potential means of accomplishing an objective.

Guidelines for Strategic Planners

(1) In order to implement a strategic plan, the planners must develop detailed and comprehensive action plans which, when completed, are turned over to managers and implementors for the operational phase.

(2) Action plans should answer the What? and Why?-related questions of How? Who? When? and Where?

(3) Possible methods-means may be identified from review of existing analogous programs.

(4) It is often wise to brainstorm a series of alternative approaches for meeting a specific objective prior to choosing those for which detailed tasks are planned. Once the brainstorming of tactics has been completed, it is useful to conduct a Methods-Means Analysis which assists in identifying the advantages and disadvantages of each tactic being considered. Then the planners can identify new possibilities, and determine which are and are not feasible.

(5) Two helpful (and possibly complementary) means of analyzing and choosing among a group of action programs are: (a) a Force-Field Analysis, and (b) a Methods-Means Analysis.

(6) When developing an action plan, it is wise to save a great deal of planning time by first listing all results-referenced tasks to be performed without concern for the chronology in which they are to be completed. Once ALL tasks are listed, they should be placed in chronological order; and the persons responsible for completion of the tasks and the timelines allotted can be listed.

(7) It is crucial that the planners be clear about the level of results they expect to attain. That is, they should be clear about the Products, Outputs, and/or Outcomes expected to be achieved.

(8) If the action plan is one covering a lengthy time period, the planners should predetermine some in-process milestone measurements.

Glossary

Action Plan: an operational plan which clearly and comprehensively responds to the What? and Why? questions providing answers to the questions of How? When? Who? and Where? as these questions apply to a specific set of tasks and procedures designed to achieve an objective.
Constraint: refers to a situation where at least one methods-means combination cannot be found which will meet performance requirements, and thus not meet the objectives and strategic goals.
Cost-Results Analysis: a technique which relates the costs of a result with the payoffs to be delivered by the successful associated results. Cost-Results Analyses ask the two simultaneous questions: "What do I give?" and "What do I get?"

Feasibility: the degree to which one can predict the probability of the action being successfully carried out and the objective successfully met. That is, one assumes the probability will be greater than chance.

Force-Field Analysis: a systematic procedure for analyzing the supporting and restraining forces that exist for each alternative action approach being considered.

Methods-Means Analysis: a systematic procedure for identifying possible tactics to be used in achieving the Products, Outputs, or Outcomes desired, and which is utilized to identify the advantages and disadvantages of each tactic being considered.

Milestone: refers to a certain in-process goal, objective, or product achieved.

Program Evaluation Review Technique (PERT): a network-based tool for planning the implementation of an educational system. This technique programs each detailed task and activity along an identified time-line, and identifies the person(s) responsible for carrying out the activity and accomplishing the event within the time frame indicated.

Systems Analyses: methods for *selecting* the most effective and efficient alternatives (ways and means) to meet delineated requirements. These usually compare costs and results among alternative ways and means for doing something based on optional resource costs and benefits and with consideration of the degree of uncertainty associated with the specific implementation.

Exercises

1. State two objectives that relate to a goal which you feel is important to your school, school district, or university. Turn two of your organization's goals into objectives.

2. Brainstorm a minimum of four action approaches for each objective.

3. Analyze these potential action approaches by use of a Force-Field Analysis or by use of a Methods-Means Analysis.

4. Select the action alternative which has the greatest potential and develop a comprehensive, detailed action plan which is responsive to the questions of What? and Why? by determining How? Who? When? and Where?

5. Take a *Mega level* mission objective for your educational system, derive (or use existing associated performance requirements) and perform a methods-means analysis meeting the criteria for methods-means analysis as stated within this chapter.

6. What is a method?

7. What is a means?

8. Name ten valid sources of methods-means information.

9. What is the product of a Methods-Means Analysis, and what data does it contain?

10. What are five methods for systems analysis? Give examples of situations where each may be applied.

11. Take an objective and a set of possible ways and means of meeting the objective. Conduct a Methods-Means Analysis and a Systems Analysis. Use a systems approach tool for the selection.

Endnotes

1 Please recall the conventional confusion between goals and objectives. While using both terms in our examples, we clearly prefer the derivation and use of "strategic objectives".

2 For details of doing a method-means analysis, see Kaufman, [48].

3 Sobel and Kaufman [102] and MacGillis, Hintzen, and Kaufman [69] provide guidance on selecting methods-means on the basis of societal payoffs.

4 While these definitions are not "standard", they attempt to relate to a "hard" metric for relating educational planning to societal consequences which are, at least partially, defined in terms of money. While money might, at first, seem to be simplistic, it is a very complex, multi-dimensional proxy for many simultaneous variables. A further discussion of this can be found in Sobel and Kaufman [102].

5 Or cost-benefit, cost-effectiveness, cost-utility. See Sobel and Kaufman [102] for a discussion of these.

6 More detailed descriptions and summaries are provided in Kaufman [48].

PART 3

Revitalizing

IMPLEMENTATION AND EVALUATION

Scoping	→	Data Collecting	→	Planning	→	Implementation and Evaluation

Putting the Strategic Plan to Work

This is the point at which the strategic plan is put to work; we go from plan to action, and from action to results. This step, strictly speaking, is *not a planning step* but a "doing" activity. Let's see, briefly, what's involved in going from plan to Outcomes.

Once the strategic plan has been developed, it must be implemented. Implementation not only involves operating the action plans, but it involves *strategic management*. That is, it involves monitoring and evaluating the plan during its operation. This process of *formative evaluation* alerts those responsible for strategic plan management to conditions that should trigger some in-process changes in strategies and/or tactics. Finally, those responsible for management should conduct a *summative evaluation* of the strategies and tactics utilized in order to assess the degree to which the vision has been achieved at a predetermined point in time. This summative evaluation is crucial to the development of a new strategic plan which will carry on where the previous strategic plan has concluded.

But before we discuss the details of strategic management and strategic evaluation, let's review all that has preceded the management stage:

- The strategic planners initially decided upon the type of focus to initiate their strategic planning efforts. They chose among *Mega* (societal), *Macro* (organizational) or *Micro* (sub-group) foci.
- A consensus *statement of beliefs* was agreed upon.
- A vision of "What Should Be" was developed.
- The *collection* of existing mission statements and the addition of measurable indicators (as required) occurred.
- An *internal scanning* was conducted. The data collected by this scan identified organization-related needs (the results-referenced discrepancies between "What Is" and "What Should Be") that were identified while developing the strategic plan.
- An *external environmental scan* was conducted. The data from the scan also alerted the strategic planners to societal needs and

opportunities that were identified while developing the strategic plan.

- *Revisions* to beliefs and visions were made as required.
- The strategic planners *identified matches and mismatches* among the vision, beliefs, needs, and mission. Any mismatches were reconciled until an integrated structure was developed.
- A revised *mission objective* was prepared.
- The *Critical Success Factors* for the organization were identified.
- A *SWOT* (Strengths, Weaknesses, Opportunities, and Threats) analysis was completed.
- *Strategic goals* and *objectives* were developed.
- *Decision rules* were developed for use in establishing priorities and making selections among the profusion of needs, goals, and objectives that were developed.
- Detailed *strategic action plans* were developed to serve as the road maps for those responsible for managing the strategic plan.
- *Strategic thinking* has become part of the organization's culture.

When management, evaluation, and recycling are added to the above list of activities, it becomes quite clear that *strategic planning is a continuous process*. Now that all of the strategic planning activities are reviewed, let's return to the focus of this chapter—that of putting the strategic plan to work.

Designing a Response

Putting the strategic plan to work involves: (1) developing structures within the organization which will achieve the strategies decided upon; (2) monitoring the activities and evaluating the activities and the strategies; (3) developing an integrated Management Information System (MIS) to aid those responsible for management of the strategic plan; (4) making in-process adjustments in strategies, tactics, or activities when the monitored data indicate that a change is required; and (5) ensuring the effectiveness of the activities and the success of the strategies employed.

Operating Conditions Affecting the Planning: Roles and Perspective of the CEO[1]

The Chief Executive Officer (CEO)—superintendent, president, chancellor—of the educational agency can experience, or perceive, different conditions which could influence the type of strategic planning which takes place; i.e., whether it has an emphasis upon Mega, Macro, Micro, or Processes and Resources (Inputs). Following are a dozen examples, Figures 12.1 through 12.12, of an educational CEO's possible roles and perspective for strategic planning. Each figure, in turn, depicts Roles #1 through #12.

WHAT SHOULD BE

Role #1: Ideal, What Should Be Role and Perspective (Shaded Area)

This role suggests that a chief executive officer would attend only to the planning elements of Products, Outputs, and Outcomes, delegating the elements of Inputs and Processes to others.

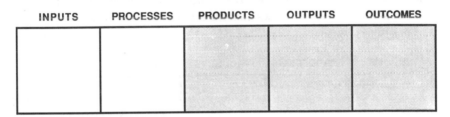

| INPUTS | PROCESSES | PRODUCTS | OUTPUTS | OUTCOMES |

FIGURE 12.1 Ideal, "What Should Be" role and perspective (shaded area).

Role #2: Pragmatic Ideal Role As Perspective

In this role, the CEO progressively spends more time and effort on the "results" (higher-ordered) planning elements, spending the greatest proportion of time and effort on the Outcomes element. In addition, a small amount of time and effort is expended on the lowest-ordered elements of Inputs and Processes.

Ideally, a planning role for a CEO should encompass only those results-oriented elements of the OEM. The results elements that should most occupy the CEO's planning attention are: (1) Products, (2) Outputs, and (3) Outcomes.

As is true in most real-life situations, an ideal state is a goal toward which one can strive. In reality, however, CEOs are ultimately held responsible for *all* activities, including planning, which take place in an educational organization. The CEO holds final responsibility for such matters as attending to the passage of a tax increase or bond issue, assisting (or guiding) the board in resolving labor/management problems, developing community support, and maintaining positive relationships with students and staff. Given these responsibilities, the ideal planning role should be initially modified to one of a pragmatic ideal planning role. This pragmatic ideal role would be one which emphasizes time and effort on the higher-order elements of Products, Outputs, and Outcomes, but one which does not omit (however it minimizes) the time and effort on the lower-planning elements of Input and Processes.

In other words, these are times when the CEO must be involved in the gathering of a very valuable Input—money. The role may be a marketer to the community, but it is a role that must be undertaken. Again, in times of crisis such as a teacher strike, a CEO normally and necessarily must attend to the Process elements necessary to overcome a possibly destructive situation.

There are pragmatic situations that must demand planning time and effort, even though they may require minimal time under pragmatic ideal situations. In comparison, let's analyze a few situations that veer far from the pragmatic ideal.

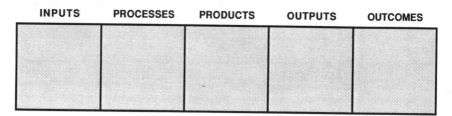

FIGURE 12.2 Pragmatic ideal role as perspective.

WHAT IS

Role #3: Crisis Planning Perspective

During a time of crisis, a CEO is pressed into an immediate planning mode. The situation requires a creative and quick positive solution. Practically all crisis situations focus on Input and Process—Quasi-needs (gaps between What Is and What Should Be) fixations on budgets and facilities, not upon learner accomplishments.

INPUTS	PROCESSES	PRODUCTS	OUTPUTS	OUTCOMES

FIGURE 12.3 Crisis planning perspective.

Role #4: The CEO's Planning Role and Perspective When Dealing with Immature or Inexperienced Groups

For the most part, the CEO is in a telling or selling mode when dealing with this type of group. Attention is focused primarily on the elements of Inputs and Processes, and perhaps the element of Products, Outputs and Outcomes may be introduced as a vehicle of measurement of the results of the resources (Inputs and Processes with some interest in Products, Outputs and Outcomes).

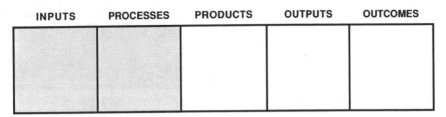

INPUTS	PROCESSES	PRODUCTS	OUTPUTS	OUTCOMES

FIGURE 12.4 CEOs initial planning role and perspective when dealing with immature or inexperienced groups (to slowly move toward a mega perspective).

Role #5: The CEO's Planning Role and Perspective When Dealing with a Mature Staff or Community Group

In this perspective, a CEO can play a delegator role, executive role, and a consultant role. Most of the CEO's efforts can be placed on the higher-order elements of Outputs and Outcomes, with much shared responsibility in the Outcome area.

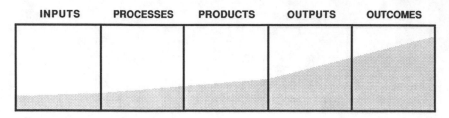

FIGURE 12.5 CEOs planning role and perspective when dealing with a mature staff or community group.

Role #6: Planning Role and Perspective of a CEO Who Is Ill-Trained or Lacks Skills in Dealing with the Higher-Ordered Elements

The significance and effectiveness of this CEO in a planning role can be greatly increased by skill training, if the CEO recognizes his/her weakness and chooses to correct it. Frequently, a fear of the unknown is the underlying block to change. If not trained, the CEO will probably have difficulty in demonstrating tangible results, first surfaced as Products. A symptom of unskilled operation here is a constant reaction to resource and procedures problems.

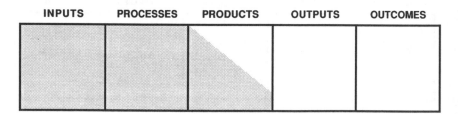

FIGURE 12.6 Planning role and perspective of a CEO who is ill-trained or lacks skills in dealing with the higher-ordered elements.

Role #7: Planning Role and Perspective of a CEO Who Is Afraid to Take Risks

The sad conclusion to this role is troubled and chaotic times ahead. Abandoning the planning field to others will not cause the need (gap in results between What Is and What Should Be) to disappear. In all probability, the need will be increased, and the CEO's leadership will and should be seriously questioned.

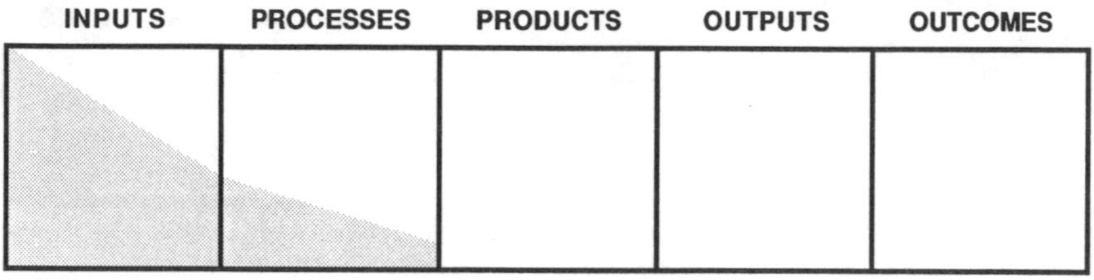

INPUTS	PROCESSES	PRODUCTS	OUTPUTS	OUTCOMES

FIGURE 12.7 Planning role and perspective of a CEO who is afraid to take risks.

Role #8: The CEO's Planning Role and Perspective in a Small District with Very Little Assistance Provided

Sadly, many talented and potentially productive CEOs are victims of the malady of serving too small an agency to support adequate assistance. In most cases, the CEO has all that he/she can do to deal with Inputs, Processes, and a few Product elements. Occasionally, a creative CEO can solicit some expert help, on a non-paid basis, from community residents or businesses. More often, the CEO must consolidate or seek suitable outside help.

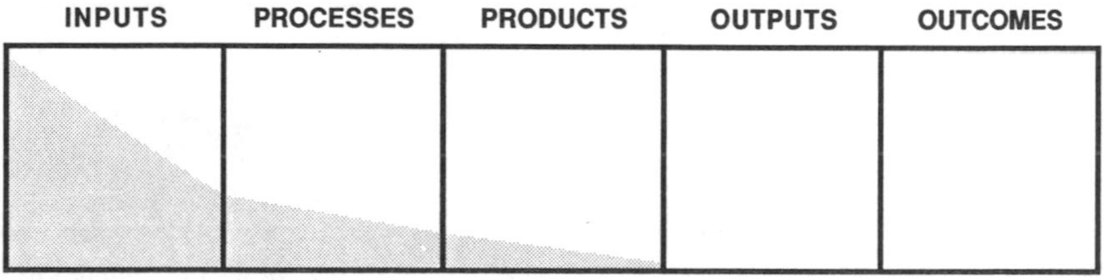

INPUTS	PROCESSES	PRODUCTS	OUTPUTS	OUTCOMES

FIGURE 12.8 CEOs planning role and perspective in a small district with very little assistance provided.

Role #9: The CEO's Planning Role and Perspective for One Who Is Well-Trained, Willing to Take Risks, and Wants to Contribute

Although the pragmatic ideal role is not attained, the direction of effort expended approaches that of the pragmatic ideal. There is much involvement in Outcomes and Outputs and very little involvement in the Input element.

INPUTS	PROCESSES	PRODUCTS	OUTPUTS	OUTCOMES

FIGURE 12.9 CEOs planning role and perspective for one who is well-trained, willing to take risks, and wants to contribute.

Role #10: The CEO's Role and Perspective for One Who Is Putting Out Fires, or Has Had His/Her Leadership Usurped by the Board, Union, State or Federal Legislature, Community Power Group, or Any Combination of These

This unfortunate CEO has reached a state of impotency which is likely incurable. A rapid change of scene or early retirement is highly recommended for a leader who has very little role in planning. Even the lowest planning elements of Inputs and Processes are little affected by the non-leader.

INPUTS	PROCESSES	PRODUCTS	OUTPUTS	OUTCOMES

FIGURE 12.10 CEO's role and perspective for one who is putting out fires or who has had his/her leadership usurped by the board, union, state or federal legislature, community power group, or any combination of these groups.

Role #11: The CEO's Role and Perspective as a Gatekeeper

This individual attempts to prevent change and the planning for it by spending his/her time attempting to control Inputs and Processes. No attention is placed on the higher-ordered elements of Products, Outputs, and Outcomes, because the identification of "What Is", "What Should Be", and needs will cause change to be openly addressed. This is a very high-risk, short-term survival role. It is for the executive who only wants to serve out a year or less.

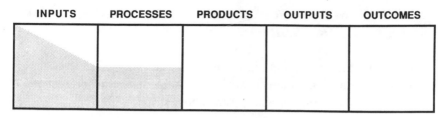

FIGURE 12.11 CEOs role and perspective as a gatekeeper.

Role #12: The CEO's Role and Perspective When Desiring to Be a Change Agent and Given the Resources to Accomplish the Change

Although this role is seldom seen in real life situations, a few CEOs are privileged to serve in this role. They parallel the pragmatic ideal planning role in that they spend the great majority of their time and effort on the highest-ordered elements of the OEM, and they spend a minimal amount of time and effort on the lowest-ordered elements. These are the most productive leaders (and are close to the #5 role).

INPUTS	PROCESSES	PRODUCTS	OUTPUTS	OUTCOMES

FIGURE 12.12 CEOs role and perspective when desiring to be a change agent and given the resources to accomplish the change agentry.

Developing Management Structures to Implement the Strategies

Converting from the belief that employees should be included in the decision-making process, and that their work environment should be of a very high quality, this belief (which is incorporated as an element in the organization's mission) the strategic goal of creating an excellent work environment for all employees, the strategic planners of Wonderful School District have selected an action plan to create a Quality of Work Life (QWL) program. Let's follow through on the details necessary to implement and manage this action plan.

EXAMPLE: WONDERFUL SCHOOL DISTRICT'S QUALITY OF WORK LIFE STRUCTURE

The steps that the action plan managers took relating to the strategic goal of creating an excellent work environment for all employees by creating a QWL program within the school district, were:

(1) Presenting an explanation of QWL and its potential benefits to the school district's board of education, administrative staff, and union leadership from each employee group, and relating the QWL process as contributing to the District's Mega mission objectives

(2) Adopting the measurable objectives and associated evaluation criteria

(3) Providing visitations to successful QWL programs which have been in place within other school districts and organizations

(4) Meeting with all district employees to obtain approval from the union leaders, the administrative staff, and the board of education, in an attempt to create a QWL program

(5) Conducting an orientation meeting with all employees, at which time the union officials and administrators support the idea of initiating a QWL program. At this meeting, the leaders ask for volunteers to assist in establishing the structure for an organization that will utilize employees to develop programs that will improve the quality of the employees' workplace. It was suggested that each group select four employees to work on this development phase.

(6) The board of education authorizes funds to hire an out-of-district QWL consultant to work with this volunteer group and to establish the format for the QWL program.

(7) The superintendent arranges financing to take the 30 employee volunteers, representing each union and each group of employees (food service, transportation, aides, central and building level administrators, custodial and maintenance, and teachers), to an out-of-district site for a three-day workshop. The superintendent attends, to indicate support, but the QWL consultant controls the developmental process. Developed by the end of the three-day workshop are: a draft policy to be presented to the board of education for adoption; bylaws for operation of the QWL program; and goals for the initial year which are related to the evaluation criteria.

(8) The entire school community is made aware of these developments, and the QWL group begins its meeting schedule.

The policy includes a desire of the board of education to involve the employees of the district in activities and decision-making that will create and maintain an excellent quality work environment for all employees. The policy also makes the superintendent responsible for approving an operational structure and providing a sufficient budget to allow the program to proceed successfully.

The bylaws adopted for the QWL program include the following:

- Anyone participating in the QWL central committee, or any work site Quality Team (six to eight employees who are given school district paid time to locate and solve problems at the work site) must be a volunteer.
- Any activity undertaken by any QWL group must be geared to the purpose of improving the work environment of employees, and to measurably improving the contributions of the employees to each other, the learners, and the district's mission objectives.
- An in-district QWL consultant will be made available to assist all the QWL groups within the district.
- Membership shall be for three years (with one third of the members rotating each year after they are initially elected, for a period of one year, two years, and three years).
- Each employee group (both unionized and non-unionized) shall elect or select two members for the central QWL committee. Two members shall also be selected from each work site.
- Prior to the beginning of each fiscal year, the QWL central committee shall determine: its yearly goals; specific objectives (either revised or new); action programs they wish to pursue to meet these goals and objectives; and the budgetary and other resources they project will be required. Each building level Quality Team shall present the building principal with a listing of problems the circle wishes to address, and the financial, human, material, and technical resources they anticipate will be necessary.

Also, prior to the beginning of each fiscal year, the superintendent and the board of education shall approve the budget for the central QWL committee. The building principals shall approve the budgets for the Quality Team groups.

- The Central Committee shall deal with issues of district-wide communication, employee wellness programs, employee assistance programs, employee recognition programs, and employee training and staff development programs.

- The Quality Team groups shall deal with any non-labor/management problem that affects the employees at the specific work site.
- The QWL Central Committee shall be responsible for developing a monitoring and evaluating system for its own operations and activities, as well as for those of each Quality Team group. The evaluation shall be conducted at least once annually, and the results of the evaluation, along with continuation and change recommendations, shall be distributed to all employees and to the Wonderful School District's Board of Education.

THE MANAGEMENT INFORMATION SYSTEM (MIS)

Once the structure has been decided, the planners and the QWL Central Committee develop a Management Information System (MIS) to monitor and evaluate all aspects of the employee work environment. Some of the data to be monitored and evaluated are of the *soft data* (attitudinal or non-independently verifiable) type, and some are of the *hard data* (verifiable) type. The development of data collection vehicles places special emphasis upon making the "hard" and "soft" data points comparable. Some examples of the types of data that are systematically collected as part of the MIS are as follows. These data are computerized, and trends over various time periods are available.

Hard Data

Hard data which indicate the degree of employee satisfaction with their work environment include: (1) the number of employee absences and tardies, (2) the number of grievances filed by employees or the number of complaints that are presented to the Central QWL Committee, (3) the staff turnover, (4) the reasons given for leaving employment with the district that are given at exit interviews with the personnel department's staff, (5) learner achievement (including graduation, work, and citizenship indicators), and (6) the number of employees and the number of hours they volunteer to be of service to other employees free of pay.

Soft Data

A *soft data* example is that of an attitudinal survey provided to a stratified random sample of each employee group on a regularized basis. The type of questions included on the survey instrument deal with such matters as:

(1) Do you feel that the board of education, administrators, and other employees care about you?

(2) Do you feel you have interesting and important work to perform?

(3) Do you feel you are given recognition for your contributions to the building in which you work and to the school district?

(4) Do you feel your opinion is asked for and listened to as it relates to your working conditions?

(5) Do you receive help if and when necessary?

(6) To what degree are you satisfied with your working conditions (very, some, not at all)?

(7) Do you believe you are now more effective in helping learners to achieve?

(8) Given a choice, would you choose to continue working in this school district, or would you prefer to work somewhere else?

The example of Wonderful School District's QWL program provided an example of a management structure decided upon, as well as presenting an example of a Management Information System (MIS) put in place. Let's now turn to the other activities involved in implementing a strategic plan.

Monitoring and Evaluating the Activities and Strategies Involved in Managing the Strategic Plan

Wonderful School District's QWL Program provided an example of the MIS elements put in place to monitor and evaluate a single action program which was directly aligned with: an objective, a strategic goal, and the vision. Monitoring and evaluating the responsibilities of those in charge of managing the strategic plan are much more comprehensive tasks than the limited example of monitoring and evaluating a singular action program. The management responsibility includes establishment of an MIS for all aspects of the strategic plan. The MIS should record, monitor, and evaluate hard and soft data from all of the following sources:

• beliefs, Critical Success Factors, needs, and the external and internal environments

- progress towards the district's vision, the strategic goals, and objectives
- progress of each action plan
- each activity that takes place within any phase of the strategic planning process

Most of these data can be computerized. Regular reports should be produced from these data, which provide: the hard and soft data; trends associated with them; and evaluative statements related to the data. These reports should be distributed to: all managers; the superintendent; all administrators; board members; all employees; all employee unions, and any stakeholder groups which have an interest and/or a stake in the district's strategic plan.

What are the uses of the data once they have been monitored, evaluated, and distributed? One of the primary uses is that of making in-process adjustments that are indicated by the data.

Making In-Process Adjustments in Strategies, Tactics, or Activities: Conducting a Formative Evaluation

In this section, we will provide an example of an in-process adjustment made because of data feedback at these levels: activity, action plan, objective, strategic goal, and vision. This procedure of *formative evaluation* is crucial to managing a successful strategic plan. Proceeding as if there is never a requirement to change the original decisions is either naive or mistakenly rigid.

The activity level can be demonstrated by the school district's sponsored wellness program. This program had only one tenth of one percent of the university's employees participating in any of the university-sponsored activities related to a stop smoking program. Once the data from the formative evaluation were reviewed in terms of participation and cost, the managers decided it would be wiser to use those resources for activities that have proven to be more successful.

The action plan level is demonstrated by the managers who discovered that sponsoring social activities for retired persons in the community, as a means of causing better two-way communications with that community group, was unsuccessful for two reasons: (1) the retired persons did not want to come to school buildings for social events, and (2) other institutions in the community were also unsuccessful in offering similar events to the community of retired people. The managers decided to replace this action plan with one which would cooperate with hotels in the district's environs in offering dances and special holiday events for the retired members of the community. This approach will also undergo a formative evaluation during year one of its operation.

The objective level is demonstrated through formative evaluation. The managers discovered that the objective of offering fifty activities each year sponsored by students of Excellent High School (under the goal of increasing student participation) was not cost-effective—perhaps because it, as a solution, was *not* related to a vision and need. The objective was eliminated, but the other objectives were retained under the goal of increasing student participation.

The strategic goal level is a general directional statement of intent. Objectives which are very specific regarding what is to be achieved are developed for the goal-level, and during which time period, (see objective level above) the goal-level is demonstrated by the strategic intent of involving businesses and industries in supportive partnerships with the school district. A formative evaluation demonstrated very little progress in interesting businesses and industries to initiate formal partnerships with the district. Instead, the CEOs suggested that the school district use its organizations for student visitations, and also that the school district cooperate with them in retraining activities for its employees. This proposal was broadened to state that relationships between area businesses and industries would be strengthened by assisting their organizations in conducting a needs assessment which would include the managers and union leaders.

The strategic vision was modified when the data from both the external and internal environmental scans indicated a serious trend change in the cultural, socio-economic, and educational level of the school district's residents and students. The vision was modified to include an element for promoting safety in a multi-cultural society.

These formative evaluations, and the resultant modifications, will do much to ensure the effectiveness of the activities undertaken, and the success of the strategies employed. Only through the collection of data, the in-process monitoring and evaluating of those data, and the in-process corrections which are indicated, can managers carry out their responsibilities in directing the overall strategic plan.

Once the formative evaluations identify that changes must be made, and modifications are made by the managers, the strategic plan is carried to completion for the time period previously decided. At the end of this pre-determined time period, the managers and the strategic planners must complete a comprehensive *summative evaluation* which will indicate the degree of success achieved in reaching the vision. It will assist the strategic planners in developing the vision of "What Should Be" for the extended future time period. The measurable objectives serve as the basic criteria for formative and summative evaluation.

Before leaving the topic of formative (in-process) evaluation, let's develop a format which will reinforce the concept. Remember, a formative evaluation is an activity that allows planners to make required or desired corrections *during the process*, rather than waiting until the planning/ doing cycle is completed to make these corrections.

FORMATIVE EVALUATION FORMAT

Example 1 (Vision Level)

Original Vision

The school district will offer many positive academic, social, and recreational activities to the day school students and to the community.

In-Process Event

Because of a decrease in the state's economy, the governor has decided to cut back the state aid to school districts by 25%.

Revised (Temporary) Vision

The school district will offer academic and social programs of high quality to all students attending during the normal school day so that they will be successful, self-sufficient, contributing citizens.

Example 2 (Mission Objective Level)

Original Mission Objective

By 1992 the university will obtain a minimum increase of $5,000,000 from the federal government for research related to teacher education.

In-Process Events

The President and Congress have agreed to a mammoth increase in funds allocated to welfare and health. One of the results was the elimination of 50% of the funds available for educational research. Also, the Congress reacted to public pressure and, with agreement of the President, the priority for research in education was changed to programs assisting "at risk" students.

Revised Mission Objective

By 1992 the university will obtain an increase of at least $5,000,000 from the federal government for research related to "at risk" students. It will also obtain another $1,000,000 from a combination of these funding sources to carry on general research in the area of teacher education.

Conducting a Summative Evaluation

A summative evaluation compares end-of-project/program results and consequences with intentions. Doing one will include the collection, monitoring, and evaluation of hard and soft data on all aspects of the strategic plan. The evaluation data will allow the partners to judge the effectiveness of that which was planned, and select what to change and what to continue.

Hard data should include proof of achievement of the strategic goals and objectives (such as reducing the number of high school dropouts, producing more basic research at the university, reducing unemployment, or improving the work environment for all the school district's employees). Hard data will include cost-benefit information (such as absolute increases in student achievement on standardized tests; increases in the university's staff; increases in the amount of grant money successfully brought into the university; and increases in low-achievers' incomes).

Soft data will include attitudinal changes during the application of the entire strategic plan. It could include such things as the opinions of experts on the health of the organization and the improvement in organizational health over the entire time period in which the strategic plan was operational. Of course, pre- and post-measurement would assume that baseline data were collected at the beginning and end of the strategic plan's operation.

Let's follow two objectives through this process, and determine what will be done during the next strategic planning cycle. If the objective is totally achieved, the decision focuses on whether or not to continue the programs or action plans that led to achievement of the objective. If the objective is not achieved, the decision possibilities include: (1) modifying the objective and attempting accomplishment during the next planning cycle or (2) dropping the objective from the next planning cycle.

SUMMATIVE EVALUATION FORMAT

Objective 1: Within Five Years the University Will Join in Partnership with a Minimum of Twenty School Districts in the State, as Certified by School Board Records

Results

At the end of five years the university has only been successful in developing school/university partnerships with three school districts in the state. Possible causes: (1) lack of trust by boards of education and school administrators regarding the assistance the university can offer the local district, and an attitude that "ivory tower" professors do not understand an operating school district; (2) the university powers would not agree to allow professors who are involved in school/university partnerships, to count the time spent on the partnership as a part of their professional load.

Decision Possibilities for the Next Planning Cycle

There are two decision possibilities that are being seriously considered, and they may both be acted upon favorably. First, is the decision to establish a strong lobbying activity with the help of staff, administration, and board members of the three successful project districts—to convince the university's powers to approve counting professorial activity related to school/university partnerships as part of their assigned load. Second, is the decision to request a fifty-member advisory committee of superintendents, principals, and board members. This advisory committee would study the issue of school district/university partnerships, and advise the university as to processes and conditions which would be favorable to both the university and the school districts.

If these decisions are favorable and agreed upon within Year One of the next planning cycle, the objective of creating an additional number of school district/university partnerships could be decided at the beginning of planning Year Two.

Objective 2: Our Nursery School Will Increase Its Profitability by 20% Each Year over the Next Five Years. This Is to Be Achieved by: Increasing the Number of Students by 12% Each Year; Increasing the Fee Charged Parents Each Year by 5% over the Actual Cost of Doing Business; and Reducing Legal Costs (Including Insurance) by 10% or More

Results

The number of students was increased by 12% each year for the five-year planning period. But because of competition from other providers, the increase in income from fees was only 10% over the entire five year period. Accidents were reduced by 34% and insurance fees dropped 11%.

Decision

To get out of the nursery school business because there isn't sufficient profit to warrant continuing.

Objective 3: By 1995, Success Elementary School Will Increase Student Test Scores in Grades 1–3 by at least 10 Percentile Points

Result

By 1995, the 1st–3rd grade students, as a group, have increased their test results on the Go-Go Standardized Reading Test by 16 percentile.

Decision

Keep the program design, action plan, processes, and activities that were used, and during the next cycle establish a similar goal and program for grades 4–6.

Guidelines for Strategic Plan Managers

(1) In order to manage a strategic plan you should set up a responsive MIS (Management Information System) which includes the collection of both hard and soft data. Much of these data can be computerized, and periodic monitoring of standardized reports should be produced. Hard data, validity, reliability, and accuracy are "musts".

(2) Formative evaluation is a crucial activity which a manager must conduct to discover necessary in-process changes in activities, tactics, strategies, objectives, strategic goals, or in the vision itself.

(3) Summative evaluation of the entire strategic plan should take place at the end of the predetermined time periods. The summative evaluation is done to calibrate the degree of success achieved in all aspects of the strategic planning operation. It should assist in developing the succeeding strategic plan which is to be operational in the future. This plan will also be based on a vision of "What Should Be" for the school, school district, or university.

(4) Strategic management thus includes taking responsibility for: collecting data; monitoring activities; evaluating data and activities, and making required in-process changes. A sample format is on pages 268–269. In some cases, the managers are also responsible for collecting, monitoring, and evaluating data which can be used for summative evaluation purposes. In many cases, the strategic managers join the strategic planning team in doing the summative evaluation, and they can suggest ideas to the strategic planning team, who will then develop the succeeding strategic plan.

Glossary

Formative Evaluation: the process of making quality judgments about activities, tactics, strategies, or other procedures or products which comprise the operational aspects of the strategic plan, *during the time when these are taking place*. It is important because it corrects for unsuccessful attempts and unimportant approaches, and thus assists in more closely achieving the strategic goals and the organization's vision.

Management Information System (MIS): a formal data system established to collect and disseminate information to be used by those individuals who are given the responsibility for decision-making and the management of the strategic plan. The MIS is specifically designed to meet the information requirements of the managers. The data collected by the MIS is frequently computerized.

Strategic Management: the process of monitoring and controlling the activities, tactics, strategies, and action plans that comprise the strategic mission-related plan. Management implies the ability to modify the initial activities, etc., if formative data indicates a requirement for in-process change.

Summative Evaluation: the process of making judgments as to the degree of success achieved at some predetermined point after the strategic plan was initiated. These judgments are based upon end results achieved, and are helpful to the managers and strategic planners in developing the strategic plan and vision of "What Should Be" at some predetermined future time.

Exercises

1. Determine the roles you would play if you were selected to manage the strategic plan that has been developed for your organization. How would you go about carrying out these roles?

2. What would you include in your Management Information System? How would your MIS be structured?

3. What is the definition of formative evaluation? What information would you collect? How would you use these data?

4. What is your definition of summative evaluation? How would you conduct a summative evaluation? What, in your judgement, is the purpose of a summative evaluation? How would you use data collected in a summative evaluation?

Endnote

1 Based, in part, on Kaufman & Herman [58] with permission.

Epilogue: Some Strategic Planning Considerations

Just using the suggested strategic planning framework does not assure you success. Following are some considerations which are useful in understanding not only how you go about planning, but also some of the responses you will get from others.

Strategic Planning and the Implied Criticism

When starting any intervention—strategic planning is no exception—many take the activity as an implied criticism [55]. After all, if you want to change things, or even offer the possibility, it means that the status-quo isn't good enough—and by insinuation, neither are they. The mere implication is sufficient to make some educational partners very nervous, frequently resulting in attacks upon the strategic planners, the planning team, consultants—in fact, anyone associated with the "implied" criticism [53].

Surface the implied criticism possibility very early in the preplanning, and deal with it openly and honestly. Realize that everyone is operating within the current reward system. Before the partners move, they must come to understand that a decision to change is accompanied by more appropriate payoffs [29,30]. Be patient with everyone in the earlier stages until others become comfortable with the rationality and usefulness of ascertaining where they and their organization should be headed.

"Realistic" Planning

Some might say that it is foolhardy (or "naive") to believe that any set of planners or planning partners would take the outside-in approach. Doing so could mean they might plan themselves out of their jobs. Indeed, their here-and-now case is made on the basis of what currently happens—planners usually seek to optimize on their own and their organization's survival and comfort. The consequent social viability and contribution is frequently alleged, assumed, or ignored. When they do look outside of the organization to confirm success, they overlook uncharted problems and opportunities. Sociologists for many years have noted that organizations tend to perpetuate themselves in spite of the rationalizations offered. Educational planners are not usually exceptions to this characteristic. But "What Is" is not the same as "What Should Be".

Actually, there is increasing evidence that successful organizations do care about both their world *and* their clients' worlds (not just about their clients' approval alone).[1] In addition, the "classical" struggle between union and management seems to be decaying in light of the rational shared seeking of common good [60,100]. Organizations are means to societal ends. The extent to which they appropriately improve the world—including payoffs for "all" partners—is the extent to which they will prosper or diminish. Schools which turn out illiterates or lawbreakers will ultimately suffer, along with the society which receives their defective outputs. Educational programs which provide incompetent students, inept workers, and inadequate human beings will be doomed to a slow but progressive extinction.

It is very, very practical for all educational organizations to take the outside-in frame of reference and see themselves as a means to current and future societal consequences, rather than simply "slicing off their splinter" and trying to improve on what is already delivered. In spite of some who might call such an approach "impractical", or even "Utopian",[2] stopping the planning frame of reference at "What Is" without moving, however slowly and methodically, toward a better "What Should Be" and "What Could Be" in the planning-vision [83,84] seems to be a pessimistic settling for the status-quo. There are many planning models available, but most tend towards the inside-out, or organization-as-client mode.

Asking the Right Questions

There are several questions, as we noted in Chapter 2, which an educational organization should ask and answer when doing strategic planning. These questions relate to who is to be the primary client *and* beneficiary of the educational plan and that which it delivers. These are summarized in Table 1.

Reactive and Proactive Planning

Planning can be either *proactive* or *reactive*. Reactive planning, the most usual variety, responds to the pressures of a changing world, political and/or economic environment, or value shifts. Proactive planning seeks to change things before there are pressures and problems — before the crises and before the damage. Proactive planning seeks to identify and bring about the kind of world in which we want our children and grandchildren to live.

One may conduct any of the three types (Mega, Macro, Micro) of planning in either a reactive or proactive mode.

Standard models of strategic planning tend to be reactive since they strive to maintain a "political focus" while attempting to develop a more successful organization. These conventional approaches are primarily concerned with such things as:

- reaction to competition for scarce resources
- obstacles
- demands of parents, community, and/or legislatures
- societal trends

None of these forces, or drivers, is likely to challenge the preeminence of one's own organization, create new collateral systems, or shut down existing ones.

Table 1 Three basic strategic planning questions and the type of planning with which each is associated, and each one's client and beneficiary.

Strategic Planning Question	Type of Planning	Primary Client
1. Are you concerned with the current and future self-sufficiency, self-reliance, and quality of life of the world in which we live?	Mega	Society
2. Are you concerned with the quality of that which your educational organization delivers to its external clients?	Macro	School System
3. Are you concerned with the quality of that which is turned out within your educational organization and is used by students, teachers, and staff as they do their educational "business"	Micro	Students/ Educators/ Staff

Proactive planning at the Mega level will identify the kind of world, for our internal clients, our society, and external clients that we want to help create. Instead of limiting ourselves by only reacting to crises, conducting damage control, or limiting our losses, the proactive approach builds a new and improved future, and does not simply respond to situations.

Rolling-Up/Rolling-Down: Two Approaches to Strategic Planning and Thinking

Most planning starts with what is known and prespecified. We simply design to get from where we are to a specific destination; consideration of what the destination *should be* is not contemplated. In standard planning efforts, where we are going is known, assumed or mandated (e.g., raise test scores, increase retention rate, cut costs, increase acceptance to colleges, increase graduates). When we don't question (or know) our destinations, we build from the bottom-up. We grow a tree from sapling to mighty oak. This is the bottom-up, inside-out, piece-by-piece approach. Most strategic planning models and approaches move in this way. But this isn't the only way. We don't ask if you want an oak tree, or even a tree at all.

Imagine this scenario. The captain of a merchant ship calls to his crew through the intercom:

> "I see the horizon from the bridge and am ready for us to set our course. I want each of you to identify the following: What is it you do and achieve? How fast can we go? What fuel do we have available? How long can we stay at sea without taking on additional provisions? How can we maintain communication with shore . . .? Next, I want you to examine your strengths, weaknesses, opportunities, and threats and then give me the strategic plan for your unit. When this is done, I want a representative group from each unit to 'roll-up' your individual plans and develop a strategic plan for all of us — the USS Public Ed."

Silly? Of course. The sailors in the engine room, like those in the communications center, cannot see where to go or what is on the horizon. They cannot even see each other. Those working in the depths of the ship can only provide information about their subsystem (how much fuel used per hour, clear channels, time to shore), but they cannot reasonably provide over-all sensible direction *only from their perspective and position*. Direction flows downward, information upward. It isn't that they don't have the potential to be the captain, and it isn't that their commitment to the mission isn't unequivocally necessary, the fact is—as sociologists have been telling us—that the whole is more than the sum of the parts. The whole has to take into account more than rolling-up all of the parts of the organization.

Educational strategic planning can start at the top—considering future opportunities and possibilities—and develop a responsive system downward, or it can start at the bottom,[3] and add up all of the plans and products for each operating entity and roll it all up to a plan for the total educational organization. How you progress—starting at the bottom or the top—may determine what ends you get. The approach you employ can determine the quality and usefulness of your strategic plan.

ROLLING-UP: THE INSIDE-OUT APPROACH

Many approaches to strategic planning move from inside-out. They build from lower levels of organizational efforts and results, and progress upward to the organizational mission—building a house of blocks from the lowest levels to the roof without a correct overall blueprint, or building the entire educational system from the learning objectives in each course to producing successful citizens. Using this typical tactic, each class, then course, then department, then school is asked, in turn, to do their "strategic plan". These, in turn, are used to build the levels above. In this sequential fashion, the whole array of individual strategic plans is "rolled-up" together to construct the total educational strategic plan. The consequence of this tactic is an internally consistent plan where each part is linked to all parts from lower to higher levels of the organization: from tests and courses, to buildings and teachers, to the curriculum and courses, to the school years, to the graduates, to the level of self-sufficiency and self-reliance. Typical of this approach would be an organization with several operating schools and levels (elementary, middle, secondary, vo-tech) where each part's strategic plans would be "rolled-up" together—like knitting a sweater piece-by-piece and then stitching the body and arms together and hoping the parts match. With this inside-out approach, you had better be sure you have the right destination before attempting to build an increasingly efficient educational system.

ROLLING-DOWN: THE OUTSIDE-IN APPROACH

Uncommon is the approach which defines the external environment and human condition to be achieved, and then derives—moving downward—what each part of the educational establishment must contribute to the whole, as well as the ways each part of the system must cooperate and contribute to the collective educational mission. Planning, using this tactic, might move from a desired self-sufficient society: from drug elimination and educated citizens, to incentive programs, to curriculum; from citizens who are healthy, down to the practices and procedures of hospital location and patient intake. By starting from the outside of the school system with the definition of what should be created (or maintained), the strategic planning is free from "how we always do our educational business here". It is thus released from the restraints of existing materials, approaches, content, and methods. Instead of only seeking efficiency, the rolling-down approach provides the opportunity to create a modified or even new organization, courses, methods of instruction, location, and content which will contribute to a more successful school system, including graduates and completers' survival and well-being, and an improved current and future world—perhaps making not a sweater but a running suit.

ROLLING-DOWN/ROLLING-UP: A CONSOLIDATED APPROACH

Most school organizations are currently successful in most of the things they do and deliver. They should keep operating and continue that which is successful while seeking what to change, modify, add, delete, or acquire. It is not probable (but not impossible) that entirely independent new school systems will be built. It is possible that new delivery avenues and techniques might be created and existing ones disbanded or modified extensively. As shown in Figure 1, it is reasonable to both roll-up and roll-down planning results simultaneously, compare the inside-out and outside-in perspectives, and revise as required: to develop the up-from-the-bottom strategic plan and, at the same time (ideally independently), develop the down-from-the-top plan and see if they meet and match!

If there are mismatches between elements of the plans, then changes should be made. For example, suppose the rolling-up plan calls for improving efficiency by increasing the school hours and number of school offerings of an inner-city school. This, in turn, calls for more teachers, more books, more media, and computers. Now, if the top-down plan shows that there should be no completers without job-readiness skills, abilities to identify and resolve problems, an increase of at least 70% in those who go to college, and an increase of 85% in those who get and keep jobs, then the rolled-up plan is likely incompatible with the rolled-down plan. What has to give? Based on the probabilities of

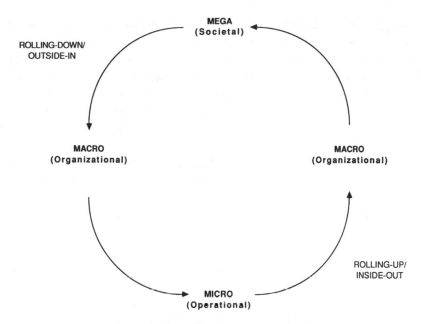

FIGURE 1 Integrating a rolling-down and rolling-up approach.

future happenings and consequences (tougher educational laws, increased educational activism, demands for nondiscriminatory hiring and school admissions, etc.), and the priorities the strategic planning partners have selected, alternative tactics may be identified, verified, and chosen. This selection of the roll-down results is because it is unlikely that the roll-up recommendations for throwing more money, time, and people at the existing situation will meet future realities [26,100].

A possible disadvantage of employing the roll-up approach alone is that new opportunities, targets, and visions, may be overlooked by moving from the bottom reaches of organizational efforts and results upward in increasing building-block fashion. By using both approaches—analogous to getting dressed by rolling-down a sweater from the top, rolling-up slacks from the bottom—and they both should meet in order to be properly clothed—you and your educational organization might get the best of all possible worlds by using both a proactive and reactive mode to identify a useful future for all concerned.

Holistic Strategic Planning: Not Simply a Linear Hierarchy

Strategic planning should not be a linear, lock-step, process. Simply because the organization is viewed as being composed of layers—1st grade, 7th grade, high school—does not mean that each part of the organization works as a system, where all parts work both independently and together to achieve a shared mission. When using a roll-down tactic, it is much easier to identify how and why each part of the organization contributes to the whole. Using the roll-up approach, one could easily overlook the interactions among organizational units—math and history can both require rigor and systematic thinking—and merely improve the efficiency of the various splinters.

When the organization employs strategic planning which begins at the Mega level, it is proactive. By setting its sights on improving the world in which it operates, and moving from outside to in (or rolling from top down), the organization will likely be both successful and efficient. It will be successful because it will be first to meet the current and future needs and requirements of its external clients, as well as the clients' world. It will be efficient because nonfunctional products and outputs will be spotted early and changed or eliminated.

Both the inside-out and the outside-in approaches can, or do, have concern for societal impact and consequences. The inside-out approach tends to project its current goals, objectives, and processes forward into society, while the outside-in approach tends to ignore all current organizational efforts, organizational results, and societal consequences until the questions of "What Should Be" and "What Could Be" are answered and prioritized. The outside-in approach is the more proactive of the two modes.

These two planning perspectives—inside-out and outside-in—have implications for the type or mode of planning you select and use. Holistic strategic planning—Mega/proactive—is a sensible and practical avenue to educational success.

Planning and Evaluation

The literature on needs assessment, system planning, strategic planning, management, and evaluation has become increasingly overlapping. Each set of specialists is adopting the territory of the others. While needs assessment, strategic planning, and evaluation are related and share some common data bases, there remain some important functional differences. Evaluation is retrospective, perhaps even reactive. It provides vital data concerning gaps between objectives and accomplishments. When planning for evaluation, there are additional questions to be posed:

"Are you concerned with how well we met our objectives?"

and/or

"Are you concerned with the value of the methods and resources which were used for getting required results?"

Needs assessors and strategic planners are consumers of evaluation data which supply the basis for the "What Is" baseline for planning. However important evaluation is, it is retrospective (even reactive) and deals only with that which exists. Needs assessment and strategic planning, on the other hand, are primarily proactive and deal with "What Could Be" as well as "What Should Be".

Glossary

Rolling-Down Strategic Planning: strategic planning which starts at the top—considering future opportunities and possibilities, and develops a responsive system downward.

Rolling-Up Strategic Planning: planning which starts at the bottom and adds up all of the plans and products for each operating entity in continuous fashion and rolls it all up to a plan for the total educational organization.

Exercise

1. What are the problems which might result from using rolling-up strategic planning alone?

Endnotes

1 Most of the newer "management" books on organizational success and behavior, starting perhaps with those on Japanese Management, emphasize attention to the client if not the society. Worth reviewing are References [41,42,86,87,88,89].

2 While "utopian" is often used in a derogatory sense, Ricoeur [93] shows that it can supply an important perspective for viewing existing systems and ideology in order to create a new and better reality. Even if something is not likely to be achieved, we still can attempt to get as close to it as possible.

3 Starting at the bottom and moving up usually assumes that everyone in the educational system understands and shares the vision and the final destination.

Appendix

Planning for Strategic Planning: What Was Done by a School District (A Case Study)

A school board member of Leon County (Florida) Schools,[1] along with several other central office professionals, became interested in strategic planning. She realized that while theirs was a good system, it could be better. The world was changing, but were the schools being responsive? She set out to learn more about strategic planning.

The election of a new superintendent and appointment of a new deputy superintendent provided the opportunity to do some results-based, futures-oriented strategic planning. The "initiating" school board member interested her associated board members and executive members of the district in investigating new educational directions. They were ready.

The superintendent and the deputy met with the strategic planning consultant. After much careful inquiry, questioning, and discussion, they realized that a Mega level approach was vital. The superintendent let the Board know of his perceptions, and asked that they consider such an approach. The planning consultant provided the board members with a briefing on the "Mega-model" and, after an active discussion, rendered a 5-0 vote to pursue it. (They were careful to get assurances that current district goals, and related programs, would not be disturbed until there was something better with which to replace them.)

A strategic planning committee[2] was formed (it was initially labeled "long-range planning" until the differences became apparent). They quickly set about planning to do strategic planning. Membership on the committee included the superintendent; deputy superintendent; two board members; the directors of public information, teacher development, curriculum, planning, and information systems; a secretary, and the chairman of the area university's department of educational research. A part-time graduate research assistant, assigned to help with the project, was funded equally by the district and the dean of the college of education. The planning consultant contributed his time on behalf of his university, research institute, and a local Rotary club.

First, a full briefing and explanation of strategic planning (using the tenets of this book) was provided, followed by much spirited discussion. Slowly, as people became increasingly comfortable with the rationale underlying the model and process, the format and materials for involving key educator, learner, and community groups were formulated. Then prototype agendas, materials, and approaches were developed, discussed, modified, and considered. The tactic selected was to identify representative community groups to serve as "direction-setting strategic planning partners". These representatives were to make the commitment to fully participate in at least two meetings, provide guidance on directions, as well as serve (if asked) as continuing contributors and reviewers while the actual detail planning progressed.

Next, a try-out group of five people was formed in order to get feedback from people typical of the "direction setters". Representatives from the five basic groups who would provide the initial "direction-setting" for the strategic planning effort were identified, contacted, and persuaded to help.[3] Thus, a student, a cafeteria supervisor, a parent, a teacher, and a principal went through a strategic planning workshop based on the preliminary materials developed. With their feedback, the final agenda, approaches, and materials were fashioned with the strategic planning committee. These were used with the several partner groups to help identify beliefs, values, and mission objectives—direction finding. Based on the input gathered from the publics, those data would form the basis for the Strategic Planning group (which was to be expanded to include representatives from the constituencies who participated in the direction-setting activities) for the actual strategic planning.

As the strategic plan is developed, representatives of the several partner groups will review and make suggestions in order to assure that the plan is holistic, appropriate, and accepted. Strategic planning is seen by all as an ongoing activity.

THE PLANNING PROCESS AND MATERIALS

The following are the agendas, activities, and materials used for the actual planning partner meetings. Also included are some of the products (unedited) that the parents group generated. They are provided with the agenda for each of the first two sessions. Notice that the strategic planning committee has deviated, in some minor ways, from the full strategic planning model presented in this book. They did so because they felt that these differences were important to communicate with their unique clients.

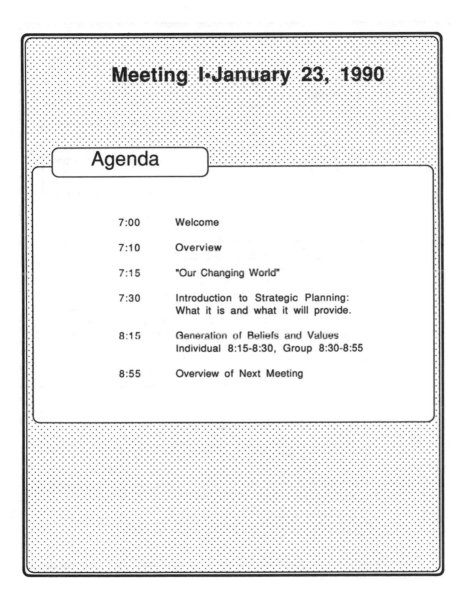

Meeting I•January 23, 1990

Agenda

7:00	Welcome
7:10	Overview
7:15	"Our Changing World"
7:30	Introduction to Strategic Planning: What it is and what it will provide.
8:15	Generation of Beliefs and Values Individual 8:15-8:30, Group 8:30-8:55
8:55	Overview of Next Meeting

WHY AM I HERE?

You have been asked to participate in the development of an action plan for Leon County Schools, which will be based on a clear mission and which builds upon the values, beliefs and vision of community representatives, school district personnel and students in order to build a better school and community.

WHAT AM I GOING TO CONTRIBUTE?

You will provide input at each of these meetings which is essential to the strategic planning process. **You will help identify: needs** which must be addressed in any strategic plan which we develop; **personal beliefs and values** about our community and the educational system which must be reflected in the plan; and finally a set of **mission objectives** which will help the planning committee determine what must be accomplished. This input will be used by the planners to develop an action plan which will be implemented by Leon County Schools.

WHAT WILL THIS PROVIDE?

This will provide a basis for a Leon County Schools Strategic Plan which will help create the kind of neighbors we want, and the type of community in which we want our children and grandchildren to live.

Meeting 1• January 23, 1990

WHAT AM I GOING TO BE DOING?

At Meeting 1, we will look at a variety of facts and figures about our community and will identify where there are needs that should be addressed. We will also discuss the strategic planning process that we are using. We will list some of our personal beliefs and values about our community and our educational system. Then, we will discuss them among ourselves.

We will:

• discuss the importance of becoming more proactive: planning now for future challenges,

• identify a list of needs, or gaps between what is the current situation in our communty and what we would like the situation to be,

• discuss the strategic planning process,

• write up some of our beliefs and values about people and our community and education,

• participate in small group discussions of these beliefs and values and find out where we agree.

"OUR CHANGING WORLD"

The FIFTIES

In the 1950's the typical American family (about 60%) was the Cleavers.   June Cleaver stayed home with Wally and the Beaver, while Ward went off to work.

The public schools were designed to meet the needs of the children of these families: most of them graduated and went on to succeed in the workplace. For those who were not successful in school, good-paying jobs awaited them in the factories.

Today the picture is different. Families are different, children are different, the workplace is different, and society is different.

The schools are not.

"THE CHANGING WORLD"

Today's family:

By 1985, only 7% of American families were the Cleavers. Mom no longer stays home with the children: in 55% of married couple families with children, both parents work: up from 36% in 1975. In fact in many families Mom is the only parent at home: 59% of all children born in 1983 will live with only one parent before reaching age 18. There are at least four million "latch-key" children of school age.

Today's children:

- Minority enrollment in public schools continues to grow dramatically. By the year 2000, one of every three Americans will be non-white.
- Many children are born into poverty. Almost half of the poor in the U.S. are children. Ninety percent of the increase in children born into poverty is from single parent households.
- Of every 100 children born today, 12 will be born out of wedlock-and 50% of these will be to teen-age mothers.
- Children are living with only one parent: 24% of our 63 million children.

289

- Work has become more knowledge-intensive. Three factors are changing the nature of work:
- New technologies are upgrading the work required in most jobs.
- Job growth will be mainly in high-skill occupations, requiring knowledge that wasn't necessary 20 years ago.
- New methods of organization for work are being implemented which require a completely new set of skills.
- Companies have to train workers even in basic skills. They are now spending some $30 billion a year on worker training.
- The workforce will increasingly be made up of women, minorities and possibly immigrants.

Today's society:

Finally, think about some of the problems we hear about on the evening news: drugs and violence, limited resources available due to the national debt, pressures on the environment, etc; changing family life, structures and values. Also consider that the information explosion is quickening: some say that the volume of the world's information will soon double every year!

Schools exist to serve the people and the community. If the people and the community have changed, then the schools must change.

"THE CHANGING WORLD"

WHAT IS (1989)	WHAT SHOULD BE	YEAR
GRADUATION RATE		
COLLEGE ENTRANTS		
DEATHS ON CAMPUS		
ARRESTS ON/OFF CAMPUS		
DROPOUTS		
UNEMPLOYED COMPLETERS/ LEAVERS		
COLLEGE COMPLETION		
MERIT SCHOOLS/SCHOLARS		
PREGNANT STUDENTS		
STATE ASSESSMENT TESTS (PASS RATE)		
JOB PLACEMENT		
PTO/PTA ATTENDANCE		

"THE CHANGING WORLD"

WHAT IS (1989)	WHAT SHOULD BE	YEAR
H.S. COMPLETION IN 5 YEARS		
CHILD ABUSE		
SUBSTANCE ABUSE ELEMENTARY MIDDLE HIGH SCHOOL		

Asking the Right Questions

Do you care about the impact and contribution that Leon County Schools makes to **society** through its students after they complete or leave the school program?

Type 1:
MEGA
LEVEL

Do you care how well prepared Leon County Schools' students are to enter our community and society upon completing or leaving the school program?

Type 2:
MACRO
LEVEL

Do you care about the quality of the educational experiences, i.e., courses, activities, instruction, that Leon County students have while in the schools?

Type 3:
MICRO
LEVEL

Do you care about the efficiency of the schools' operations?

Type 4:
PROCESSES

Do you care about the availability of adequate resources to help the schools achieve their missions?

Type 5:
INPUTS

293

TYPES OF RESULTS AT EACH PLANNING LEVEL

Planning Level	Description	Typical Examples
MEGA	The social impact and payoffs of results.	Individual self-sufficiency, self reliance
MACRO	Results which are delivered by the organization to society	Graduate, certificate of completion
MICRO	Results which are the building blocks for larger result	Test score, course passed

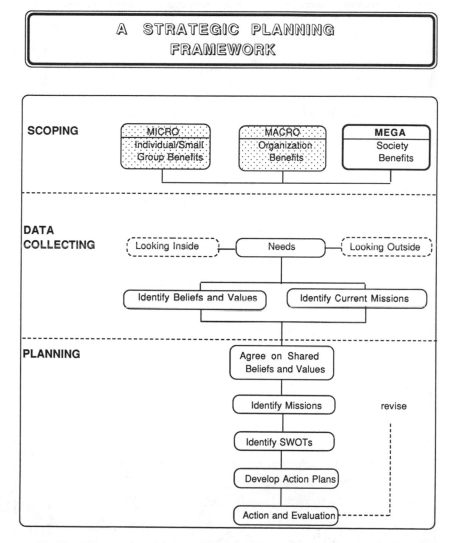

295

Guidelines

On the lines below, please write one thing that you feel the strategic plan must accomplish and one thing it must not do.

The strategic plan must_____

_____

_____

_____

_____

The strategic plan must not _____

_____

_____

_____

_____

Means and Ends: What's the Difference?

MEANS are the ways in which we do something. They are processes, resources, methods or techniques which we use to deliver a result.

ENDS are the results, impacts or accomplishments we get from applying the means. They are what is achieved.

Please classify each item on the list below as MEANS or ENDS. Put an X in the appropriate column.

ITEM	MEANS	END
1. All students in the 3rd grade scored above grade level on standardized achievement tests given in the Spring.	_____	
2. The current budget of $60,000.00 must be spent by June, 1990.	_____	_____
3. Orders are up 12% over last year.	_____	_____
4. Reading	_____	_____
5. Science instruction will be the focus of teacher education this term.	_____	_____
6. We should re-zone our schools.	_____	_____
7. Sidewalks should be built near our schools.	_____	_____
8. All of our completers will earn a good, honest living.	_____	_____

Examples of Beliefs and Values

I believe that all learners should develop an understanding of democracy.

I believe that parents should set high expectations for their children.

I believe that teachers should meet the individual needs of their students.

I believe that administrators should be strong instructional leaders as well as good managers.

I believe that schools must be an integral part of the community.

I believe values should be taught and modeled in the schools.

I believe that all learners can be successful.

Beliefs and Values

Below, write down some of your personal feelings about people in our society, our county school system and what you think schools should achieve.

I/We believe:

that learners:

_____
_____
_____
_____
_____

that parents or guardians:

_____
_____
_____
_____
_____

that a good teacher:

_____
_____
_____
_____
_____

education in Leon County:

_____
_____

Beliefs and Values

the schools must:

_____
_____
_____
_____
_____

that administrators:

_____
_____
_____
_____

that children in school:

_____
_____
_____
_____
_____

a good school system delivers:

_____
_____
_____
_____
_____

Beliefs and Values

that a successful graduate of Leon County Schools:

_____
_____
_____
_____

that the Leon County I want my children and grandchildren to live in:

_____
_____
_____
_____
_____

that dropouts:

_____
_____
_____
_____

arrests on campus:

_____
_____
_____
_____

that_____
_____
_____
_____

Beliefs and Values

On the lines below write down some of your personal feelings about people in our society and education and what you think schools should achieve.

_____

_____

_____

_____

_____

_____

_____

_____

_____

_____

_____

_____

_____

_____

_____

_____

_____

_____

Mission Objectives

On the lines below please list the mission objective(s) that you developed. Remember, these are the purposes of the educational system related to creating the type of community in which we want our children and grand-chilren to live. **Keep in mind the beliefs and values we have agreed on**.

Meeting 2•January 25, 1990

Agenda

7:00	Overview of Meeting 2
7:05	Rank Ordering of Beliefs and Values
7:30	Group Consensus
7:50	Individual Mission Objective
8:00	Group Mission Objectives
8:30	Group Sharing
8:40	Guidelines for Committee
8:55	Next Steps/Follow-Up

Meeting 2•January 25, 1990

WHAT AM I GOING TO BE DOING?

At Meeting 2 we will review the lists of beliefs and values that we generated at Meeting One. They have been combined and categorized. We will work in small groups to rank order them to determine an agreed upon list of the most important beliefs and values we hold about our community and the educational system.

We will also formulate some *mission objectives* for the educational system.

We will:

* participate in small group discussions of beliefs and values and will rank order them.

* get agreement on shared beliefs and values.

* identify missions of the educational system based on these beliefs and will generate mission objectives by answering: "Given this set of shared beliefs and values, what are the purposes of the educational system?"

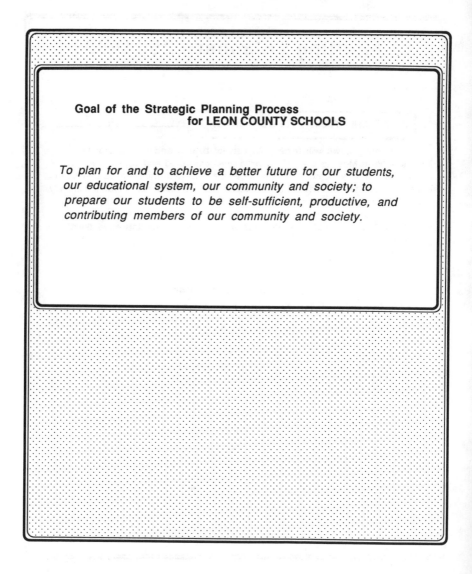

**Goal of the Strategic Planning Process
for LEON COUNTY SCHOOLS**

To plan for and to achieve a better future for our students, our educational system, our community and society; to prepare our students to be self-sufficient, productive, and contributing members of our community and society.

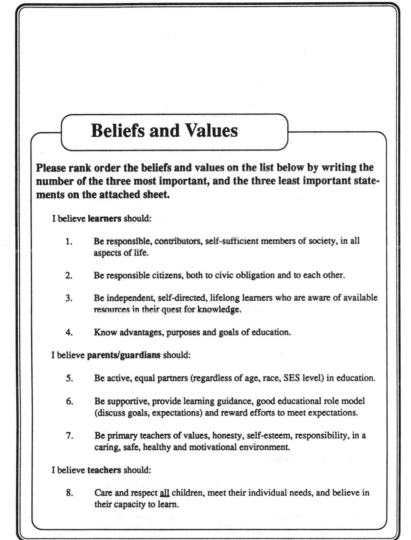

Beliefs and Values

Please rank order the beliefs and values on the list below by writing the number of the three most important, and the three least important statements on the attached sheet.

I believe **learners** should:

1. Be responsible, contributors, self-sufficient members of society, in all aspects of life.

2. Be responsible citizens, both to civic obligation and to each other.

3. Be independent, self-directed, lifelong learners who are aware of available resources in their quest for knowledge.

4. Know advantages, purposes and goals of education.

I believe **parents/guardians** should:

5. Be active, equal partners (regardless of age, race, SES level) in education.

6. Be supportive, provide learning guidance, good educational role model (discuss goals, expectations) and reward efforts to meet expectations.

7. Be primary teachers of values, honesty, self-esteem, responsibility, in a caring, safe, healthy and motivational environment.

I believe **teachers** should:

8. Care and respect all children, meet their individual needs, and believe in their capacity to learn.

Beliefs and Values

9. Build self-esteem, assist and motivate students in seeking out knowledge and in becoming lifelong learners.

10. Encourage excellence in education, creativity and individualism, and be a positive role model.

11. Encourage parent support and participation.

I believe **education in Leon County** should:

12. Give all students an equal opportunity in learning by providing the tools (books, equipment) which they require to be self-supporting, capable individuals.

13. Be of highest quality possible and be made available to all citizens.

14. Be a beginning, not an end to a person's learning.

I believe **schools** should:

15. Provide a clean, safe, drug-free, encouraging atmosphere for all learners which is conducive to learning, where serious business is taking place.

16. Be a vehicle for a student to maximize his or her potential, to develop a love of lifelong learning and be a place to explore interests.

17. Work with community, meet the needs of the community, be a focal point.

I believe **administrators** should:

18. Be skillful managers, facilitators, team players, who set high standards for staff.

19. Be responsive to the community.

20. Be committed to the goals of education.

I believe **children in school** should:

21. Come to school prepared to learn and have the opportunity to maximize their potential for learning.

22. Feel good about themselves as well as their schools.

Beliefs and Values

I believe **a good school system delivers:**

23. Programs and services that address the needs of the individual student, the community and the society in general.

24. Individuals with a positive self-image who are prepared to be self-reliant and self-sufficient with the skills to become contributing members in the community or continue into higher education levels.

I believe **a successful graduate of Leon County Schools** should:

25. Be prepared to enter a higher education program or the job market successfully.

26. Have an understanding of democracy and be a valued contributor to his/her community.

I believe that the **Leon County which my children and grand-children live in** should:

27. Offer equal access to jobs, homes and educational opportunities to all who live here.

28. Be sensitive to the needs of the total community.

29. Be clean, drug- and criminal- free.

I believe **drop-outs:**

30. Should be actively encouraged to complete high school or obtain their GED.

31. Are mostly poor, black, and faced with a future of low paying jobs, welfare, homelessness or prison.

I believe **arrests on campus** are:

32. Unnecessary

33. Inevitable as long as our schools are a reflection of our society.

I believe **that:**

34. A student's self-worth and self-concept should be the emphasis of our system.

BELIEFS AND VALUES

Please rank order the beliefs and values on the attached list by writing the number of the three most important, and three least important statements on the lines below.

	Your rank	Group rank
Most Important	___	___
	___	___
	___	___
	___	___
	___	___
Least Important	___	___

Examples of Mission Objectives

Increase to 100% the number of completers or leavers who get and keep jobs within five months of leaving the school program.

Increase to at least 85% the number of completers or leavers who maintain stable family relations as indicated by divorce rates, reported domestic violence, living with family, etc.

Reduce to at least 5% the number of completers or leavers who have been arrested and convicted of any crime carrying a fine above $100 for a period of five years after leaving the school program.

THE MISSION OBJECTIVE DERIVED BY THE PLANNING PARTNERS

The planning partner groups followed the process and developed their statements of values and beliefs, visions, and derived mission objectives. An integration of the consensus among them was derived (and is provided below). First is the mission objective at the Mega level, followed by some of the specific "supportive quotes" which were forwarded by some of the partner groups. Also included are mission objectives at the Macro and Micro levels, as well as suggested purposes for educational Processes and Inputs.

MISSION OBJECTIVE – MEGA LEVEL

The following mission objective is an integration of mission objectives generated by the planning partner groups involved in the Leon County Schools Strategic Planning Project.

Leon County Schools will increase to 99% the number of individuals leaving the school system who will be self-sufficient, self-reliant, caring and contributing members of the community as indicated[4] by:

(1) Gainful employment or college enrollment five years after graduation/leaving
(2) Increased voter registration and participation
(3) Freedom from care, custody, or control of another person, agency, or substance
(4) Increased involvement in community activities
(5) Maintenance of stable family relations
(6) A reduction in the rate of teenage parenthood
(7) A reduction in teenage suicide rate
(8) A decrease in crime rate
(9) A reduction in welfare received
(10) A reduction in incarceration rates

Supportive Quotes from the Planning Groups

"Leon County School System will provide for learners to become self-sufficient, contributing, and responsible individuals when the students have reached a success level of 98% by either entering and completing higher education programs within 8 years or by being gainfully employed and financially independent within 5 months."

"Increase to 98% the number of students graduating from high school who: enter college; enter specific vocational training, or are gainfully employed; a woman who chooses to be a housewife will be gainfully employed."

"By the turn of the century, reduce the crime rate, unemployment rate, teenage parent rate and suicide rate by a factor of at least four while increasing the citizen retention rate by a factor of two. Lifelong learning at work."

"To develop citizens who are productive, self-sufficient and caring as measured by: (a) have a job/or be in college 5 years after graduation, (b) be a registered voter and voted in most elections, (c) not be under the control of another person, agency or drugs, and (d) be a positive role model as demonstrated by: parenting skills; involvement in community activities; sustained employment and/or school."

"Provide a quality education for 100% of the students. This education should be designed to guide students towards a successful, responsible, fulfilled quality of life that will contribute to the well being of our society. As measured by: (1) per capita income regardless of any socioeconomic or discriminatory factors, (2) a decrease in number receiving public assistance, (3) a decrease in rate of crimes committed by Leon County graduates."

MISSION OBJECTIVES – LOWER LEVELS

These objectives are the products of the groups involved in the planning workshops.

Macro Level

Reduce leavers rate in Leon County by at least 50% by the start of the 1991–92 school year.

The Leon County School System will rank in the top 10% of school districts in Florida by 1995 and top 5% by the year 2000 as indicated by high school graduation rates, student achievement, employment of graduates, scores on tests of critical thinking, communication, problem solving, advanced classes and advanced placement, percent entering postsecondary education, and "parental involvement".

Graduation rate will be one of the top three in the state by June 1992 as documented by State certified statewide statistics.

Micro Level [5]

Meet the needs and be responsive to the characteristics of all students by providing a diversity of appropriate programs, increasing student's positive attitude — and decreasing dropouts to 0%.

Provide a well-staffed, well-equipped, positive learning environment to increase the number of graduates who are well-educated, self-reliant, contributing members of society as indicated by:

(1) At least a 10% increase in the graduation rate
(2) At least a 10% increase in those graduates either employed in a trade/vocation or accepted into a postsecondary/vocational or academic program

Process Level [6]

In order to increase student performance and development of self-esteem/self-concept, all (100%) parents and community partners will be involved with teachers and school staff as documented through records of parent conferences, volunteer hours, and other parent/school activities by 1992.

The school system will provide leadership to the community, assisting it to identify its educational needs.

Input Level

Safe, caring, and healthy educational community will attract environmentally safe industry to the area doubling our student population within three years.

More work will be done on the strategic plan development. First is to convert the missions from intentions to include criteria measurable on an interval or ratio scale. Next will be to take these mission objectives and identify needs — gaps between the current results and the ones which are now required. This will require some data collection and analysis. Then, the strategic planning committee, aided by representatives from each of the planning partner groups, will follow the strategic planning process.

The planning partners not only clearly understood the differences among planning levels — Mega, Macro, and Micro — they selected the Mega level. Any restructuring that the school system now does will be based upon rethinking the existing conventional (and less-than-completely-successful) purposes and bases for education. Revitalization and success will be the likely consequences.

Endnotes

1 While these are public domain materials, we appreciate Leon County School's permission in providing these materials here.

2 Members included: Bill Wooley, Jim Croteau, Freda Wynn, Ellen Darden, Charles Macon, Dawn Crum, Bob Reiser, Linda Recio, Chuck Lombardo, Roger Kaufman, Pat Kiper, and Emily Millett.

3 Zaheerah Shakir, Jenny Brock, Bart Marsh, Larry Sapp, and Fern Sloan.

4 These are still missing performance indicators which are measurable on an interval or ratio scale. These will be derived during the next strategic planning step. They also will provide data points for identifying needs.

5 Note that these are a mixture of levels. This is frequently found in initial activities where non-planners tend to mix both levels with interventions and resources. In subsequent planning, such statements will be refined.

6 These are not basically results-oriented, but again are typical of statements generated by first-time strategic planners.

References and Related Readings

1 Abell, D. F., & Hammond, J. S. (1979). *Strategic market planning: Problems and analytical approaches*. Englewood Cliffs, NJ: Prentice-Hall, Inc.

2 Ansoff, H. (1984). *Implementing strategic management*. Englewood Cliffs, NJ: Prentice Hall.

3 Banghart, F., & Trull, A. (1973). *Educational planning*. New York: Macmillan Company.

4 Below, J., Morrisey, G., & Acomb, B. (1987). *The executive guide to strategic planning*. San Francisco: Jossey-Bass, Inc.

5 Benjamin, S. (1989, October). "A closer look at needs analysis and needs assessment: Whatever happened to the systems approach?" *Performance & Instruction*.

6 Bennis, W., & Nannus, B. (1985). *Leaders: The strategies for taking charge*. New York: Harper & Row.

7 Blanchard, K., & Peale, N. V. (1988). *The power of ethical management*. New York: William Morrow & Co., Inc.

8 Blumer, H. (1969). *Symbolic interactionism: Perspective and method*. Englewood Cliffs, NJ: Prentice-Hall.

9 Bok, D. (1986). *Higher education*. Cambridge, MA: Harvard University Press.

10 Bryson, J. M. (1988). *Strategic planning for public and nonprofit organizations: A guide to strengthening and sustaining organizational achievement*. San Francisco: Jossey-Bass.

11 Buckley, W. (Ed.). *Modern systems research for the behavioral scientist*. Chicago, IL: Aldine Publishing Company (1968).

12 Bunning, R. (1979). "The delphi technique: A projection tool for serious inquiry." *The 1979 Annual Handbook for Group Facilitators*, pp. 174-181.

13 Burton, J., & McBride, B. (1988). *Total business planning*. New York: John Wiley & Sons.

14 Byars, L. (1987). *Strategic management: Planning and implementation concepts and cases*. New York: Harper and Row.

15 "Can corporate America cope?" (1986, November 17). Quotation of H. Ross Perot. *Newsweek*.

16 Carter, R. K. (1983). *The accountable agency* (Human Service Guide No. 34). Beverly Hills, CA: Sage.

17 Cawelti, G. (1987). "Strategic planning for curricular reform." *Phi Kappa Phi Journal*, *67*, 29-31.

18 Chaffee, E. (1984). "Successful strategic management in small private colleges." *Journal of Higher Education*, *55*, 212-241.

19 Cleland, D., & King, W. (1968). *Systems analysis and project management*. New York: McGraw-Hill Book Company.

317

20 Cook, W. (1988). A series of four videotapes in association with *Strategic planning for America's schools*. Arlington, VA: National Academy of School Executives and American Association of School Administrators.

21 Cooley, W., & Bickel, W. (1986). *Decision-oriented educational research*. Boston: Kiluwer-Nijhoff Publishing.

22 Deal, T., & Kennedy, A. (1982). *Corporate cultures: The rites and rituals of corporate life*. Reading, MA: Addison-Wesley Publishing Co., Inc.

23 Drucker, P. (1973). *Management: Tasks, responsibilities, practices*. New York: Harper & Row.

24 Drucker, P. (1985). *Innovation and entrepreneurship*. London: William Heinemann, Ltd.

25 Drucker, P. (1988, September-October). "Management and the world's work." *Harvard business review*.

26 Elam, S. (1990, January). Editorial. *Phi Delta Kappan*.

27 Fullerton Joint Union High School District (1990). District Goals and Objectives Annual Report 1988-89. Fullerton, CA.

28 Gough, P. B. (1990, January). "Farewell to the Eighties" (Editorial). *Phi Delta Kappan*.

29 Greenwald, H. (1973). *Decision therapy*. New York: Peter H. Wyden, Inc. Publishers. (Also available from EDITS, San Diego, CA)

30 Greenwald, H., & Rich, E. (1984). *The happy person*. New York: Stein & Day Publishers.

31 Harless, J. H. (1975). *An ounce of analysis is worth a pound of cure*. Newnan, GA: Harless Performance Guild.

32 Herman, J. (1988, October). "Map the trip to your district's future." *The School Administrator*. pp. 45, 16, 18, 23.

33 Herman, J. (1989). "School district strategic planning (part I)." *School Business Affairs*, *55*, pp. 10-14.

34 Herman, J. (1989). "School business officials' roles in the strategic planning process (part II)." *School Business Affairs*, *55*, pp. 20, 22-24.

35 Herman, J. (in process). "Action plans: A necessity to make your vision into reality." *NASSP Bulletin*.

36 Herman, J. (in process). "Creating a vision and mission statement." *NASSP Bulletin*.

37 Herman, J. (in process). "Conducting a S.W.O.T. (strengths, weaknesses, opportunities and threats) analysis for your school." *NASSP Bulletin*.

38 Hodgkinson, H. (1985). *All one system: Demographics of education, Kindergarten through graduate school*. Washington, DC: Institute for Educational Leadership, Inc.

39 Johnson, N. (1985). "The planner's role in strategic management." *Management Planning*, *33*, 16.

40 Kagan, S. (1989). "Early child care and education: Tackling the tough issues." *Phi Delta Kappan*, *70*, 433-4.

41 Kanter, R. M. (1983). *The change masters: Innovation for productivity in the American corporation*. New York: Simon & Schuster.

42 Kanter, R. M. (1989). *When giants learn to dance: Mastering the challenge of strategy, management, and careers in the 1990s*. New York: Simon & Schuster.

43 Kaufman, R. (1972). *Educational system planning*. Englewood Cliffs, NJ: Prentice-Hall.

44 Kaufman, R. (1986). "Assessing needs." In M. Smith (Ed.), *Introduction to performance technology, Part 1*. Washington, DC: National Society for Performance & Instruction.

45 Kaufman, R. (1987, May). "On Ethics." *Educational Technology*.

46 Kaufman, R. (1987, October). "A needs assessment primer." *Training & Development Journal*.

47 Kaufman, R. (1988a). *Identifying and solving problems: A management approach* (4th Ed.). Social Impacts: Edgecliff, NSW, Australia.

48 Kaufman, R. (1988b). *Planning educational systems: A results-based approach*. Lancaster, PA: Technomic Publishing Co.

49 Kaufman, R. (1988c). *Planning for organizational success: A practical guide* (rev. ed.). Social Impacts: Edgecliff, NSW, Australia.

50 Kaufman, R. (1988, July). "Needs assessment: A menu." *Educational Technology*.

51 Kaufman, R. (1988, September). "Preparing useful performance indicators." *Training & Development Journal*.

52 Kaufman, R. (1989, February). "Selecting a planning mode: Who is the client? Who benefits?" *Performance & Instruction Journal*.

53 Kaufman, R. (1989, February). "Warning: Proactive planning might be hazardous to your being-loved health." *Educational Technology*.

54 Kaufman, R. (1989, September). "Needs assessment: More than questionnaires." *Training & Development Journal*.

55 Kaufman, R. (in press). *Strategic planning plus: An organizational guide*. Glenview, IL: Scott Foresman.

56 Kaufman, R., & English, F. W. (1979). *Needs assessment: Concept and application*. Englewood Cliffs, NJ: Educational Technology Publishers.

57 Kaufman, R., & Harrell, L. W. (1989, February). "Types of functional educational planning modes." *Performance Improvement Quarterly*.

58 Kaufman, R., & Herman, J. (1983, October). "Organizational success and the planning role(s) and perspectives of a superintendent." *Performance & Instruction Journal*, 22(8).

59 Kaufman, R., & Herman, J. (1989, September). "Planning that fits any district." *The School Administrator*.

60 Kaufman, R., & Jones, M. (1990, February). "The industrial survival of the nation: Union/management cooperation." *Human Resource Development Quarterly*.

61 Kaufman, R., & Thiagarajan, S. (1987). "Identifying and specifying requirements for instruction." In R. M. Gagne (Ed.), *Instructional technology: Foundations*. Hillsdale, NJ: Lawrence Erlbaum Associates, Publishers.

62 Kaufman, R., & Valentine, G. (1989, November/December). "Relating needs assessment and needs analysis." *Performance & Instruction Journal*.

63 Langley, P. (1989). "Evaluating the economic and social impact of vocational rehabilitation programs in Victoria (Australia)." *Performance Improvement Quarterly*, 2(2).

64 Lenz, R. (1987). "Managing the evaluation of the strategic planning process." *Business Horizons*, 30, 34-39.

65 Lenz, R., & Lyles, M. (1986). "Managing human problems in strategic planning systems." *Journal of Business Strategy, 6*, 57-66.

66 Lessinger, L. M. (1970). *Every kid a winner.* New York: Simon & Schuster.

67 Levin, H. M. (1983). *Cost-effectiveness: A primer.* (New Perspectives in Evaluation.) Beverly Hills, CA: Sage Publications.

68 Lewis, J. (1983). *Long range and short range planning for educational administrators.* Newton, MA: Allyn and Bacon, Inc.

69 MacGillis, P., Hintzen, N., & Kaufman, R. (1989). "Problems and prospects of implementing a holistic planning framework in vocational education: Applications of the organizational elements model (OEM)." *Performance Improvement Quarterly, 2*(1).

70 Mager, R. F. (1972). *Goal analysis.* Belmont, CA: Fearon-Pitman Publishers, Inc.

71 Mager, R. F. (1975). *Preparing instructional objectives* (2nd ed.). Belmont, CA: Pitman Learning, Inc.

72 Mager, R. F. (1988). *Making instruction work: Or skillbloomers.* Belmont, CA: David S. Lake Publishers.

73 Mager, R. F., & Pipe, P. (1984). *Analyzing performance problems* (2nd ed.). Belmont, CA: Pitman.

74 Mahmood, S., & Moon, M. (1984). "Competitive analysis from a strategic planning perspective." *Management Planning, 33*, 37-42.

75 Majchrzak, A. (1984). *Methods for policy research.* Applied Social Science Research Methods Series, Vol. 3. Beverly Hills, CA: Sage Publications.

76 March, J. & Simon, H. (1958). *Organizations.* New York: John Wiley.

77 Marsh, S. (1984). "Strategic planning information outline: A step by step guide through major checkpoints: What database to use, when." *Database, 7*, 20-24.

78 Martino, J. (1983). *Technological forecasting for decision-making* (2nd ed.). New York: North-Holland.

79 McLagan, A. et al. (1983). *Models for excellence: The conclusions and recommendations of the ASTD training and development competency study.* Washington, DC: American Society for Training and Development.

80 Meising, P. (1984). "Integrating planning with management." *Long range planning, 17*, 118-124.

81 Morrisey, G., Below, P., & Acomb, B. (1988). *The executive guide to operational planning.* San Francisco, Jossey-Bass, Inc.

82 Myers, M. (1984). *An atlas of planet management.* New York: Anchor.

83 Naisbitt, J. (1982). *Megatrends: Ten new directions transforming our lives.* New York: Warner Books.

84 Naisbitt, J., & Aburdene, T. (1990). *Megatrends 2000: Ten new directions for the 1990's.* New York: William Morrow and Co.

85 Ohmae, K. (1982). *The mind of the strategist: Business planning for competitive advantage.* New York: Penguin Books.

86 Pascale, R. T., & Athos, A. G. (1981). *The art of Japanese management: Applications for American executives.* New York: Warner.

87 Peters, T. (1987). *Thriving on chaos: Handbook for a management revolution.* New York: Alfred A. Knopf.

88 Peters, T., & Waterman, R. H. Jr. (1982). *In search of excellence: Lessons learned from America's best run companies.* New York: Harper & Row.

89 Peters, T. J., & Austin, N. (1985). *The passion for excellence: The leadership difference*. New York: Random House.

90 Pfeiffer, J. W., Goodstein, L. D., & Nolan, T. M. (1989). *Shaping strategic planning: Frogs, bees, and turkey tails*. Glenview, IL: Scott, Foresman & Co.

91 Phi Delta Kappan. (1984). *Handbook for conducting future studies in education*. Bloomington, IN: Phi Delta Kappan.

92 Reagan, L. (1988, May-June). "An engineering approach to quality (Taguchi Methods Implementation in DSEG)." *TI Technical Journal*.

93 Ricoeur, P. (1986). *Lectures on ideology and utopia*. G. H. Taylor (Ed.). New York: Columbia University Press.

94 Reiser, R. A., & Gagne, R. M. (1982). "Characteristics of media selection models." *Review of Educational Research, 52*, 499-512.

95 Roberts, W. (1987). *Leadership secrets of Attila the Hun*. New York: Warner Books.

96 Rossett, A. (1987). *Training needs assessment*. Englewood Cliffs, NJ: Educational Technology Publishers.

97 Rummler, G. A. (1986). "Organizational Redesign." In M. Smith (Ed.), *Introduction to performance technology, Part 1*. Washington, DC: National Society for Performance and Instruction.

98 Ryans, J., & Shanklin, W. (1985). *Strategic planning: concepts and implementation*. New York: Random House.

99 Schaaf, M. "Wants: Whether We Need Them or Not," *Los Angeles Times*, Part V, p. 3 (October 24, 1986).

100 Shanker, A. (1990, January). "The End of the Traditional Model of Schooling—and a Proposal for Using Incentives to Restructure Our Public Schools." *Phi Delta Kappan*.

101 Sibley, W. (1986). "Strategic planning and management for change." *Canadian Journal of Higher Education, 16*, 81-102.

102 Sobel, I., & Kaufman, R. (1989). "Toward a 'hard' metric for educational utility." *Performance Improvement Quarterly, 2*(1).

103 *Strategic management and United Way: Organizational assessment*. (1985). Alexandria, VA: United Way of America.

104 Stufflebeam, D. L., McCormick, C. H., Brinerhoff, R. O., and Nelson, C. O. (1985). *Conducting educational needs assessment*. Hingham, MA: Klewer Academic Publishers.

105 Taguchi, G. & Phadke, M.S. (1984). Quality engineering through design optimization. *Proceedings of Globecome 84 Meeting*. IEEE Communication Society.

106 Timar, T. (1989, December). "The Politics of School Restructuring." *Phi Delta Kappan*.

107 Toffler, A. (1970). *Future shock*. New York: Random House.

108 Toffler, A. (1980). *The third wave*. New York: Morrow.

109 Tosti, D. T. (1986). Feedback Systems. In M. Smith, (Ed.), *Introduction to performance technology, Part 1*. Washington, DC: National Society for Performance and Instruction.

110 Watts, D. R., & Kaufman, R. (1989, May). "Strategic planning at a new Australian university: A technology application." *Educational Technology*.

111 *What lies ahead: Looking toward the '90s*. (1987). Alexandria, VA: United Way of America.

112 Wheeler, T., & Hunger, J. (1984). *Strategic management*. Reading, MA: Addison-Wesley Publishing Co.

113 Wilkinson, D. (1989). "Outputs and outcomes of vocational education programs: Measures in Australia." *Performance Improvement Quarterly*, 2(1).

114 Windham, D. (1975). "The Macro-planning of education: Why it fails, Why it survives, And the alternatives." *Comparative Education Review*.

115 Windham, D. M. (1988). *Indicators of educational effectiveness and efficiency*. IESS Educational Efficiency Clearinghouse, Learning Systems Institute, Florida State University for the U.S. Agency for International Development, Bureau of Science and Technology, Office of Education.

116 Zemke, R., & Kramlinger, T. (1982). *Figuring things out: A trainers guide to needs and task analysis*. Reading, MA: Addison-Wesley.

Index

About the Authors

Roger Kaufman

Roger Kaufman is Professor and Director of the Center for Needs Assessment and Planning at The Florida State University. He also is a faculty member in the Department of Industrial Engineering at the University of Central Florida. He holds a Ph.D. from New York University, and completed undergraduate and graduate work in psychology, education, and industrial engineering at Purdue, George Washington, Johns Hopkins, and University of California at Berkeley. He is a Fellow of the American Psychological Association, and a Diplomate of the American Board of Professional Psychology. He was the 1983 Haydn Williams Fellow at the Curtin University of Technology in Perth, Australia. He has served as president, and has been elected to the honor of Member-for-Life, of the National Society for Performance and Instruction (NSPI).

His interests in business, government, education, psychology, communication, and system planning have led to his development of a practical and useful needs assessment approach. This has been widely adapted throughout the world and is used by both public and private agencies to improve both organizational and individual effectiveness, efficiency, and productivity. He has over 110 journal articles and 20 books.

His work with the Center for Needs Assessment and Planning has provided a broad range of research and development services to state and national agencies, public and private sector organizations, and public institutions ranging from the Florida Department of Education and its Division of Vocational, Adult, & Community Education; the National Institute of Education, the Far West Laboratory for Educational Research and Development; Florida Departments of Health & Rehabilitative Services, Transportation, Administration, and Governor's Office of Planning and Budgeting.

Kaufman continues to serve as an international consultant to many educational, industrial, and military organizations in the United States,

Mexico, Australia, Latin America, and Europe. Among some of these clients are Texas Instruments, the Los Alamos National Laboratory, Australian Public Service Commission, Curtin University of Technology (Perth, Australia), Universidad De Tarapaca (Arica, Chile), the Technical University in Mexico City, University of Twente (the Netherlands), UNISYS, and MIM Holdings. He has assisted these and many other agencies by developing needs assessment, strategic planning, and evaluation frameworks.

Jerry Herman

Jerry Herman is Professor and Area Head for Administration and Educational Leadership at The University of Alabama-Tuscaloosa. He holds a Ph.D. from the University of Michigan in Educational Administration. He has received numerous national awards in the areas of staff development and educational administration including: North American's 100 Top School Executives (*Executive Educator*), Boss of the Year (Agape Chapter of American Business Women's Association), and Distinguished Alumni Award (Northern Michigan University).

Dr. Herman has served on the editorial board of the *Clearinghouse Journal* for sixteen years and been a consulting editor to *National Staff Development Journal* and *School Business Affairs*. Scores of presentations have been made by Dr. Herman on strategic planning and leadership. He has authored more than 100 articles on management, evaluation, administration, and strategic and operational planning. He has also produced several books on educational administration and planning.